MINISTERS AND PARLIAMENT

MINISTERS AND PARLIAMENT

Accountability in Theory and Practice

DIANA WOODHOUSE

CLARENDON PRESS · OXFORD
1994

Oxford University Press, Walton Street, Oxford OX2 6DP
Oxford New York Toronto
Delhi Bombay Calcutta Madras Karachi
Kuala Lumpur Singapore Hong Kong Tokyo
Nairobi Dar es Salaam Cape Town
Melbourne Auckland Madrid
and associated companies in
Berlin Ibadan

Oxford is a trade mark of Oxford University Press

Published in the United States
by Oxford University Press Inc., New York

© Diana Woodhouse 1994

British Library Cataloguing in Publication Data
Data available

Library of Congress Cataloging in Publication Data
Woodhouse, Diana.
Ministers and parliament : accountability in theory and practice /
Diana Woodhouse.
Revision of thesis (doctoral).
Includes bibliographical references and index.
1. Ministerial responsibility—Great Britain. 2. Cabinet system—
Great Britain. I. Title.
JN406.W66 1994 354.4104—dc20 93-30851
ISBN 0-19-827892-6

1 3 5 7 9 10 8 6 4 2

Typeset by Graphicraft Typesetters Ltd., Hong Kong

Printed in Great Britain
on acid-free paper by
Bookcraft (Bath) Ltd.
Midsomer Norton, Avon

PREFACE

THIS book is concerned with the accountability of ministers during the 1980s, and the institutional changes within Parliament and the government which have affected, or are likely to affect, its operation. It is based upon the premiss that British government is accountable government and that the mechanisms for achieving accountability are derived from the convention of individual ministerial responsibility. Hence ministers have a constitutional duty to account to Parliament, or more accurately the House of Commons; conversely, Members of Parliament have a constitutional duty to ensure that ministers comply with this obligation. However, in practice the dominance of Parliament by the executive means that accountability works unevenly, and in many respects, despite the reform of the select committee system, does not meet the objectives of the constitutional doctrine. The effectiveness of the traditional model of accountability is also tested by the complexity of modern government and the establishment of Next Steps agencies to improve the delivery of public services. These have raised questions about the practicality of a convention which requires the minister to be the vehicle for public accountability.

The failure of the practice to match the constitutional theory is evident in the examination undertaken in Part One of the development and content of the convention of individual ministerial responsibility. The effect upon accountability of this divergence is then pursued, first in Part Two with reference to ministerial resignations, which, it is argued, have a constitutional basis, but do not always fulfil the constitutional requirement of accountability, in the sense of 'giving an account'. Indeed, at times the resignation of a minister seems to be a means of evading such accountability. Secondly, it is demonstrated in Part Three with reference to institutional changes of the 1980s—that is, the reform of the select committee system and the establishment of Next Steps agencies. In the case of select committees, it is shown that ministerial responsibility may be used to prevent accountability rather than provide it, whilst the examination of executive agencies indicates the tension that exists between the insistence of government that the convention of ministerial responsibility requires no modification and the formalization of responsibilities attached to named civil servants.

In response to the problems of imperfect accountability, Part Four outlines some of the recent constitutional reforms which have taken place in Australia and New Zealand and makes a case for their adoption in Britain. It further proposes amendments to the convention of individual ministerial responsibility. Finally, it argues that Parliament needs to recognize more fully its responsibility within the accepted doctrine of the constitution for ensuring accountable government.

This work is an amended version of a doctoral thesis and as such owes much to the tutorial guidance and intellectual stimulation given to me by my supervisors, Peter Madgwick and Geoffrey Marshall, to whom I express my gratitude. Thanks are also due to Vernon Bogdanor for his encouragement and helpful comments on amendments. I would also like to acknowledge the help given to me by the Next Steps Project Team, Andrew Smith MP, Peat Marwick McKlintock, and the Bodleian Library, particularly the Official Publications section. However, I remain solely responsible for the content of the book.

D.P.W.

Oxford
1993

CONTENTS

PART FOUR.
CONCLUSION

ABBREVIATIONS

AAO	Agency Accounting Officer
AAT	Administrative Appeals Tribunal
AO	Accounting Officer
CAG	Comptroller and Auditor General
CPRS	Central Policy Review Staff
DES	Department of Education and Science
DOC1	Directorate of Custody 1
DTI	Department of Trade and Industry
FMI	Financial Management Initiative
HC Deb.	House of Commons Debates
HL Deb.	House of Lords Debates
ITC	International Tin Council
HMSO	Her Majesty's Stationery Office
MINIS	Management Information System for Ministers
MMC	Monopoly and Mergers Commission
NFU	National Farmers' Union
PAC	Public Accounts Committee
PPR	power to send for persons, papers, and records
SIB	Security Investments Board
TCSC	Treasury and Civil Service Committee
UGC	University Grants Council

PART ONE

The Convention of
Individual Ministerial Responsibility

The Accountability of Ministers to Parliament

1.1. INTRODUCTION

A fundamental principle of the British Constitution is that the government is accountable through its ministers to Parliament. The constitutional requirement and the political need for accountability are most obvious when mistakes have been made and the government is under pressure, but there is also the expectation of routine accountability by ministers for the actions of their departments. Such accountability is central to the concept of responsible government, and may be regarded as essential in a system with a dominant executive and without the legal checks provided by a constitutional court.

There are, of course, broader perspectives of accountability and different means by which it may be achieved. The government is held accountable through its responsibility to the party and through the electoral process and by the critical scrutiny of the mass media. It is also accountable to the courts for the legality of its actions. These are all important locations of accountability, but, in a constitution which centres upon the supremacy of Parliament, accountability to the legislature is constitutionally of most significance. However, despite its significance within the constitution, there is an elusiveness about the concept of accountability which is reflected in the conventions which provide for it, and which makes it difficult to define and perhaps impossible to refine.

Traditionally accountability is seen as operating through the conventions of both collective and individual ministerial responsibility. Collective responsibility provides Parliament with the means of holding the government as a body accountable, and individual ministerial responsibility enables the House to focus on a particular minister and his responsibilities without the need to censure the whole government. However, the inclusion of collective responsibility as a mechanism for accountability may be questioned. Its origins and development suggest that its primary function is to protect ministers and to ensure the continuance of the government. Today it is only in extreme circumstances, when the government fails to achieve a majority on a specified vote of confidence, that collective responsibility provides public accountability through the resignation of the government (or more usually a dissolution of Parliament and a general election). At other times, it is more appropriate to see the convention as laying down the ministerial ground rules which ensure solidarity and confidentiality and hence serve the interests of the government, rather than the cause of accountability.

The focus of the following chapters will therefore be on individual ministerial responsibility, which has a much wider constitutional significance. It underpins the British Constitution and affects the operation of Parliament and the executive. It is the constitutional mechanism by which Parliament claims to fulfil its function of controlling and scrutinizing the executive, and it therefore permeates the procedures and language of the legislature. Indeed, much of the business both on the Floor of the House and in select committees centres on individual ministers and their departmental responsibilities. This, in turn, has ensured that the structure and mode of operation of departments serve the constitutional requirement for ministerial accountability and the political need to avoid embarrassing challenges to the minister and consequent damage to his standing.

The convention of individual ministerial responsibility has also influenced the framing of legislation, especially the location of executive power in ministers, and the attitude of the courts towards such discretionary powers. Parliament has frequently been held by judges to provide a more appropriate check than the courts on the exercise of ministerial discretion, a view which upholds the sovereignty of Parliament, enables the judiciary to remain detached from the political arena, and emphasizes the constitutional importance of political, rather than legal, checks upon the system.

Individual ministerial responsibility is, therefore, more than a constitutional convention which prescribes the varying relationships between ministers and Parliament, ministers and their departments, and ministers and the courts. It is an integral part of the system of government and has imposed itself upon the administrative and parliamentary structure. As a result, any fundamental change to the convention may need to be reflected in practical changes across the institutions of government. Conversely, changes within Parliament or the departments are likely to have an important effect upon ministerial accountability.

1.2. THE DEVELOPMENT OF THE CONVENTIONS OF ACCOUNTABILITY

The mid-nineteenth century is traditionally seen as the high point for ministerial accountability to Parliament. This view owes much to constitutional writers of the time,[1] who needed to demonstrate a workable theory of political accountability to accommodate a constitution in which Parliament was supreme, both as legislator and as a check on the executive. A theory which focused on conventions as the means of providing this accountability also reassured the ruling élite that the government of the country would remain in its hands, despite the rapid extension of the franchise up to 1867, for the essence of conventions is that they are developed by those who operate the system and are not imposed from outside.

Some of this constitutional writing was prescriptive rather than descriptive. Nevertheless, during the mid-nineteenth century, Parliament, or more accurately the House of Commons, demonstrated its determination and ability to hold ministers to account and to 'exercise a constant supervision of all governmental affairs'.[2] Such scrutiny and control of ministers was essential to the doctrine of parliamentary government, as stressed by Earl Grey, writing in 1858:

It is the distinguishing characteristic of Parliamentary Government that it requires the powers belonging to the Crown to be exercised through Ministers, who are held responsible for the manner in which they are used, who are expected to be members of the Houses of Parliament . . . and who are considered entitled to hold their offices only while they possess the confidence of Parliament, and more especially the House of Commons. . . .

[1] e.g. Bagehot, Dicey, Freeman, Maitland.
[2] F. W. Maitland, *The Constitutional History of England* (Cambridge: Cambridge University Press, 1908), 380.

The exercise of their high authority is . . . placed under the check of a strict responsibility and control, and its possession is made to depend on the confidence placed by the Representatives of the People in the Minister to whom it is committed . . .[3]

It was expected that ministers had to work to retain the confidence of the House. Submission to parliamentary examination, either by answering questions in the full House or before a specially convened committee, was part of the process, and successive governments accepted the right of Parliament to hold ministers to account and, if appropriate, to express its displeasure through votes of censure.

The development of the conventions of collective and individual ministerial responsibility was necessary to fulfil the needs of accountability, providing both the principle and the mechanism for its operation. However, as is usual in the British system, changes took place incrementally, and principles emerged as a result of the developing practice, rather than practical adjustments being made to accommodate constitutional theory. Thus, although the conventions were heralded during the latter half of the century as established and essential features of parliamentary government, it is difficult to state with certainty when practice acquired an element of moral obligation.

Collective Responsibility and Party Allegiances

Cabinet solidarity would seem to have become a rule by 1815 and the collective or common responsibility of the Cabinet to Parliament was established within the next few decades.[4] During the period 1832–67 ten governments were brought to an end because they failed to sustain the support of the House of Commons,[5] and from the 1860s a regular definition of collective responsibility, as the doctrine which required the resignation of all ministers if the government lost the confidence of the House, was appearing in authoritative expositions of the constitution.[6]

The development of collective responsibility was concurrent with

---

[3] The Third Earl Grey, 'Parliamentary Government, 1858', in H. J. Hanham, *The Nineteenth Century Constitution: Documents and Commentary* (Cambridge: Cambridge University Press, 1969).

[4] See A. H. Birch, *Representative and Responsible Government* (London: Unwin Hyman, 1964), Ch. 10.

[5] Ibid.   [6] e.g. Bagehot, Dicey, Freeman, Maitland.

the growth in the importance of political parties and the changing position of ministers from representatives of the Sovereign to representatives of such parties. Maitland, writing in the 1880s, noted the connection between parliamentary accountability and party:

> We must remember in . . . [the] context [of collective responsibility] that the presence of ministers in the House of Commons was long disliked by the House. So far from wishing to have ministers there to answer for their doings, the House struggled to exclude them. But the ideal changed; the House wished to have the ministers before it—became accustomed to have them before it—to support them, to attack them, to regard them not merely as the representatives of the King, but also as the representatives of a party, so that a defeat of a minister would be a defeat of a party.[7]

Collective responsibility was, therefore, in part a response to party politics, but the development of the convention also in its turn heightened the need for party organization, both for supporters of the government and for the Opposition. This point was recognized by Walter Bagehot: 'The only mode by which a cohesive majority and a lasting administration can be upheld in a Parliamentary government, is party organization. . . . Parliamentary government is, in its essence, a sectarian government, and is possible only when sects are cohesive.'[8]

The effect of the growth of party machinery on the ability of a government to remain in office resulted in the development of collective responsibility tied to party organization in the House of Commons as the focus of accountability. But collective responsibility was not the only means by which Parliament held the government to account. Individual ministers were also accountable to Parliament, and the development of the convention of individual ministerial responsibility during this period has had far-reaching consequences.

The Responsibility of Individual Ministers

Individual ministerial responsibility had its origins in the need for Parliament to act as a check on ministers, without having to resort to their impeachment, and in the recognition by ministers that they must ultimately rely on the support of the Commons for their

[7] Maitland, *The Constitutional History of England*, 396.
[8] W. Bagehot, *The English Constitution* (London: Fontana, 1963).

policies. The principle that ministers were responsible to Parliament for their departments was thus firmly established prior to the nineteenth century, but the extent of this responsibility and its consequences were not settled. Ministers were certainly required to answer for the departments they controlled, and, according to Lord Palmerston, this meant they needed to be involved themselves in the detail of the department:

In England the Ministers who are at the head of the several departments of the State, are liable any day and every day to defend themselves in Parliament; in order to do this, they must be minutely acquainted with all the details of the business of their offices, and the only way of being constantly armed with such information is to conduct and direct those details themselves.[9]

It is possible that Lord Palmerston's account of ministerial involvement, which goes on to contrast the virtues of the British system of ministerial accountability with what he considered to be the shortcomings of the continental system, was exaggerated. However, at the early part of the century the scale of government business may have made this detailed involvement by ministers possible. A study of the operation of the Colonial Office at this time supports the view. 'The most striking feature of British administration in the first quarter of the nineteenth century was the extent to which the work of government departments was performed by the ministers themselves'.[10] A minister could also be individually censured by the House of Commons and thus forced to resign without affecting the standing of his colleagues. 'We may find one minister resigning because he cannot get on with parliament, while his colleagues retain office; quarrelling with him is not quarrelling with them, nor are they honour bound to support his cause'.[11]

Collegial Support and Individual Responsibility

The development of collective responsibility increasingly gave ministers collegial support when the 'cause' was a matter of policy.

[9] Lord Palmerston in a letter to Queen Victoria, 25 Feb. 1838, in Hanham, *The Nineteenth Century Constitution*, 322.

[10] D. M. Young, *The Colonial Office in the Early Nineteenth Century*, quoted in H. Parris, *Constitutional Bureaucracy* (London: Allen & Unwin, 1969), 1.

[11] Maitland, *The Constitutional History of England*, 396.

Moreover, as Bagehot suggested, collective cover could be effective in preventing a parliamentary motion for an inquiry into departmental business.[12] This was particularly so as the century progressed and the organization of party allegiances within the House of Commons became more effective. However, until the second part of the nineteenth century there remained some uncertainty about the situations in which support, either from colleagues or party, would be forthcoming. It was, therefore, prudent for ministers to continue individually to seek to retain the support of Parliament, to 'look as much to Parliament as the Cabinet'.[13]

This was especially true in the middle decades of the century, for this was a time of uncertain majorities, and there was sufficient independence within the House to make forced resignations common enough to be 'a real threat to errant ministers'.[14] Finer lists five resignations during the period 1855–67, those of Lord Russell, Lord Ellenborough, Robert Lowe, Lord Westbury, and Hugh Walpole,[15] which he attributes to there being no absolute majority within the House. The lack of a majority meant that the Cabinet could not give its support, assuming that it wanted to, as this would have resulted in the downfall of the government.

Indeed, the precarious nature of administrations at this time may have led some ministers to feel an obligation to resign office in the face of a censure motion without waiting for the vote, in case the government was endangered or embarrassed. Thus in 1855 Lord John Russell resigned his office as Colonial Secretary before the taking of the vote on a censure motion, criticizing his conduct in negotiations in Vienna, which had 'shaken the confidence of this country in those to whom its affairs are entrusted'.[16] Similarly, in 1858 Lord Ellenborough resigned when faced with a parliamentary vote of censure for having published a confidential dispatch to the Viceroy of India. This enabled the government to accept the subsequent motion of condemnation without the need to defend the minister's actions.

The actions of Robert Lowe, Vice-President of the Committee of the Council on Education, also averted the need for government involvement, although his motive would seem to have been the

---

[12] Bagehot, *The English Constitution*, 191.
[13] Hanham, *The Nineteenth Century Constitution*, 78.   [14] Ibid.
[15] S. E. Finer, 'The Individual Responsibility of Ministers', *Public Administration*, 34 (1956), 377–96.   [16] *Annual Register* (1855), pt. 1, p. 154.

protection of his honour. He resigned in 1864, after the Education Department was censured for the practice of amending the reports of HM Inspectors. Lowe, who claimed that he was unware that amendments were being made and that he had forbidden the practice, was offered Cabinet support but considered his honour had been impugned and thus that his resignation was appropriate.

The above resignations may suggest what Sir Ivor Jennings called a 'rather high sense of obligation in the ministers concerned'.[17] The ministers accepted that they should take personal responsibility, even if, as in Lowe's case, there was no personal involvement and the issue could have been made a collective one.[18]

Apart from the group of resignations in the middle decades, there would seem to be only one other in the nineteenth century which could be categorized as individual ministerial responsibility. This was the resignation in 1894 of A. J. Mundella, President of the Board of Trade, because of his involvement in a company he was meant to be investigating. The comparative lack of resignations by individual ministers supports the view that the convention of collective responsibility had become dominant by the latter part of the century[19] and that ministers were protected by the convention and the party majority in Parliament. Thus, only when a minister's conduct upset his own party could his resignation be forced.

If resignation is taken as a benchmark of the operation of individual ministerial responsibility, it could be argued that from the mid-nineteenth century the convention declined in importance. During the earlier part of the century, when ministers still acted as individuals, it was central to accountability, for it was the only means by which a check could be kept on the conduct of the executive. However, as collective responsibility developed, so the importance of individual responsibility diminished as a means of censure. This did not necessarily mean that a minister could feel secure in his position. The principles of solidarity and shared

---

[17] Sir I. Jennings, *Cabinet Government* (3rd edn., Cambridge: Cambridge University Press, 1961), 498.

[18] But after a parliamentary inquiry into the matter, which exonerated Lowe, the House of Commons was told that his resignation had not been necessary (see Finer, 'The Individual Responsibility of Ministers').

[19] This view was put forward by S. Low (*The Governance of England* (London: T. Fisher Unwin, 1904; rev. edn., 1914), 138) and by A. L. Lowell (*The Government of England* (New York: Macmillan, 1919), 73).

responsibility meant that the individual minister had to act in a way which retained the support of colleagues, or risk either exposure in Parliament or removal from office by the prime minister. To an extent, therefore, collective responsibility acted as a compensating check. A minister might be less frequently forced from office by the House but might find himself replaced or moved to a different department by the prime minister instead.

The Development of Departmental Government

However, resignation is only one aspect of the convention. The requirement that individual ministers account to the House for their areas of responsibility did not diminish. Indeed, the convention became more complex as ministers were increasingly seen as the preferred vehicles through which accountability to the House should be effected.

As the state's role as regulator grew, so did the need for an effective mechanism to ensure accountability for its expanding functions and the bureaucracy that accompanied them. It was the practice up to the 1850s to establish independent boards to regulate industrial and social activities. But the work of the new offices, particularly the Poor Law Commission, was often controversial, and Members of Parliament became increasingly dissatisfied with the arrangements for accountability. Members of the Boards or Commissions were rarely Members of Parliament and thus responsibility had to be exercised through a parliamentary spokesman who had no direct authority. In addition, no one member of the Board had overall responsibility for the Board's actions, so no person could be held ultimately accountable.

It was, therefore, practically convenient for responsibility and control to pass to ministers who would be the final authority and fully answerable to Parliament. Thus in 1847 a new type of Poor Law Board was established which was headed by a minister, who usually sat in Cabinet. Shortly afterwards in 1850 the Select Committee on Official Salaries noted: '[the] increasing necessity to have for the control even of the details in all the public departments, persons acquainted with the views and practice of the House of Commons.'[20]

[20] *Report from the Select Committee on Official Salaries* (1850), HC611, HMSO.

So while on the Continent administrative courts were being established to police the administrative functions of the state, and in the United States the foundations of a regulatory system centring on agencies were being laid, in Britain ministerial departments were established and began to absorb the responsibility for most regulatory functions. Such a development had apparent benefit for both Parliament and the administrators. It ensured answerability to the House by the responsible minister whilst at the same time providing protection for the administration against the 'incessant tyranny' of Parliament, which, according to Bagehot, made the functioning of 'an independent unsheltered authority' impossible.[21] The minister was therefore a 'protecting machine',[22] in the sense that he prevented parliamentary interference, as well as a vehicle for accountability. Moreover, his power and areas of influence were increased, since control was a prerequisite for responsibility. The relationship between control and responsibility was subsequently demonstrated in 1912 when the Speaker refused an adjournment motion to consider alleged failures by the Port of London Authority because, although the minister, through the Board of Trade, was represented on the Authority, he had no control over its decisions and actions.[23]

Civil Service Accountability

The focus on the individual minister and his responsibility for the workings of his department was aided by parallel administrative reforms and developments. The rising importance of political parties and the increase in administrative functions required a more obvious split between politicians and officials and the establishment of a permanent non-political administrative body. In addition, the effectiveness of the mechanisms for the accountability of officials was called into question. There was a marked tendency towards centralization, evident in the establishment of the Local Government Board and later the Board of Agriculture and the Board of Education, and the widening scope of official work, especially within the Local Government Board, the Home Office, and the Board of Trade. These developments meant an increase in the

---

[21] Bagehot, *The English Constitution*, 191.
[22] Ibid.   [23] Jennings, *Cabinet Government*, 94.

numbers of officials whose responsibility was to the centre, rather than at local level.

As the number of officials and the range of functions grew, direct responsibility to Parliament became impossible. Responsibility therefore shifted. Officials became responsible to ministers, and ministers became responsible to Parliament for the actions of their officials, as well as for their own actions. This did not happen overnight. For some time the principle was uncertain and controversial, its operation thwarted by both sides. First, those Whitehall officials who had entered service before 1870, when public competitive examinations became the normal means of securing a position, often felt a strong personal responsibility. Such officials had been public officers; for them, anonymity and the requirement that they distance themselves from the political arena were unfamiliar and unwelcome.

It was difficult for them to accept the idea that the minister should be the sole channel between themselves and those to whom they felt an obligation. They wished also to report direct to parliament, to publicize their views in the press, to work through Select Committees and interest groups.[24]

Secondly, in 1864 Parliament was still insisting that civil servants were directly responsible to the House. The matter concerned a report from HM Inspectors of Schools which had been amended prior to its receipt by Parliament. The incident culminated in Lowe's resignation (noted above). During the parliamentary debate the House of Commons accepted the argument of Lord Robert Cecil that the report was intended for use by the House and therefore should be provided to the House directly. It rejected Lowe's contention that this direct responsibility was incompatible with ministerial responsibility.[25]

However, within a decade the House seemed to reject the notion of such direct responsibility to Parliament. In 1873 it indicated that an individual official was answerable to the minister not Parliament. This suggests that the convention was established by then, although this latter incident concerned administrative malpractice by a civil servant and did not affect what Parliament saw as its unqualified right to information, which was its concern in the Lowe case. Thus the House of Commons could hold: '[The

---

[24] Parris, *Constitutional Bureaucracy*, 99.   [25] Ibid., 104.

civil servant concerned] is not responsible to us. We ought to look to the heads of Departments . . .'[26]

The division between politicians and officials therefore became established. However, it was necessary for the close relationship between policy and administration to remain, so that Parliament could continue to scrutinize all aspects of departmental business. 'This feat . . . [was] achieved through ministerial responsibility. . . . The minister being responsible for everything done in his department, everything that is done may be the subject of Parliamentary scrutiny.'[27]

A Complex but Untried Convention for the Twentieth Century

Individual ministerial responsibility therefore became the political rationale and the procedural logic around which an expanding system of government was structured. However, the sophisticated version of the late nineteenth century was largely untried and untested. The convention had been transformed since the beginning of the century. In its original form the principle laid down that a minister was answerable to Parliament for his department, over which he had very close control, and from which he was required to resign if he lost the support of Parliament. This simple doctrine gave way to a complex set of arrangements governing the relationships between ministers, officials, and the House of Commons.

The development of these arrangements owed much to the mid-century success of Parliament in its role of scrutineer and controller. This fostered the belief that accountability through ministers to Parliament was practically and constitutionally superior to other forms of accountability. However, by the time the mechanisms necessary for the extended accountability of ministers were consistently accepted, the balance between Parliament and the executive had changed, and Parliament's power was declining. The recognition of the upgraded version of individual ministerial responsibility would therefore seem to have post-dated the period during which it would have been most effective. As a result, even at the very beginning of the twentieth century, the effectiveness of the convention was being questioned. Sidney Low commented: 'It is very

---

[26] Ibid.   [27] Jennings, *Cabinet Government*, 133.

difficult to bring a government to account for anything done in its ministerial work.'[28]

Despite such concern, in 1918 the Haldane Committee supported the principle that the minister should have sole responsibility for the administration of his department.[29] Yet by this time there were already developments which made such a convention a questionable means for securing government accountability: first, the increasingly pervasive nature of the domination of the House of Commons by party and the corresponding decline in parliamentary power; and, secondly, the rapid expansion in the size and complexity of the government.

1.3. LIMITATIONS ON THE EFFECTIVENESS OF INDIVIDUAL MINISTERIAL RESPONSIBILITY

The Decline of Parliamentary Power

A Dominant Executive

The decline of parliamentary power was directly linked to the increasing importance of the electorate, as the prime source of government power, and the development of party politics. After the passing of the 1867 Reform Act, the role of the House of Commons began to change. Its main purpose became to support the elected government and to pass its legislation. Acting as a check on the executive became a function of the Opposition, and thus of limited effectiveness, as the party machine, operated by the Whips' Office, imposed ever tighter party discipline. The priorities of the House therefore changed. It acted first as a legislative machine and only second as a check upon the executive.

By the 1900s the House of Commons was dominated by the executive. This dominance was confirmed by changes in the rules of procedure. These were necessary to ensure the passage of increasing amounts of legislation. However, as well as minimizing obstructions to the government programme, the procedural changes curtailed the opportunities for extensive debate or scrutiny. The

[28] Low, *The Governance of England*, 139.
[29] *Report from the Machinery of Government Committee* (Chairman, Lord Haldane) (1918), Cmnd 9230, HMSO.

final alterations in 1902 gave the government the ability to arrange practically all the business of the House. The Opposition had a formalized role, but only Friday afternoons were made available for private Members. The power of the government was thereby increased and the nature of the House of Commons altered.

The new Standing Orders marked the end of a process which had definitely changed the functions of the Commons. In earlier years, the House had been able, on occasion, to take a different view from that of the Cabinet and to act as a positive check on its actions. Now the Commons became an instrument in the hands of the Ministry, with the Opposition and private Members retaining facilities for making their views known rather than any actual power.[30]

Thus by the 1920s there was a recognized decline in the ability of the House of Commons to act 'as an agency for effective criticism and containment of the executive'.[31] Attacks were still launched on the government and individual ministers, but they lacked the weight of earlier times when there was always the possibility of formal censure.

The Diminishing Reputation of Parliament

Along with the practical changes occurring in the House of Commons went a change in the public's perception of Parliament. In the nineteenth century there was public belief and confidence in the power of Parliament and support for its role of protecting the nation from the possible excesses of an over-enthusiastic executive. It was the forum of the nation and exemplified democracy in action. Moreover, those who sat within it were seen as custodians of the nation's good, gentlemen, whose words could be trusted and whose actions would be motivated not by personal advancement but by national benefit.[32] Parliament therefore represented

---

[30] J. P. Mackintosh, *The British Cabinet* (London: Stevens, 1962), 191.

[31] Ibid.

[32] This trust in Members of Parliament is demonstrated by the reassurance offered by Dicey about Parliament's ability to pass any law it likes. Members of Parliament, he claimed, would not pass a morally repugnant law (see A. V. Dicey, *Introduction to the Study of the Law of the Constitution* (10th edn., London: Macmillan, 1959), 42).

the morality of the nation, or at least the values held by the ruling and middle classes.

By the early years of the twentieth century Parliament's high reputation was declining, as was interest in it. Debates and speeches no longer featured in the newspapers. It was losing its position as the hub of political life and the social conscience of the nation. This decline has continued through the century as attention has focused on personalities, particularly the leaders of the political parties, rather than institutions, while Downing Street, the television studios, and party conferences have become alternative arenas for politics. The decline of Parliament has further been hastened by changes within the House of Commons, which has been increasingly operated, often quite crudely, by the party whips, and in Members themselves, who are now professional politicians looking for career advancement rather than men of independent means with an interest in politics. Any sense of Parliament as the conscience of the nation has long gone.

The House of Commons has, therefore, been transformed since the last century from an assembly of parliamentarians with changeable alliances to inflexible party groupings under the discipline of the whipping system. The effect on ministerial responsibility has been fundamental, for, as the discipline has increased, so has the protection that beleagured ministers can expect. Except in extreme cases, they are able to rely on the unconditional support of their back-benchers, who are reluctant to damage the government and are aware that their ministerial aspirations, and even their chances of reselection, depend on their loyalty to the government, and more particularly the prime minister.

The Control of Information by the Executive

A further restriction upon the effectiveness of ministerial responsibility lies in the government's control of information. Not only can the government ensure that its back-benchers protect ministers from the hostile attacks of the Opposition; it can also reduce the possibility, or sustainability, of such attacks by providing Parliament with the minimum of information. During the nineteenth century private Members had been able to call for papers from the departments; and even in the latter years of the century, when the government could largely control the information made available, there was 'no positive intention to deceive the House and when questions were asked, the explanations were usually full and frank'.[33] 'Parliament had no conscious feeling that it was being starved of information or opportunities.'[34]

This was to change during the twentieth century, in regard both to the opportunities to seek or demand information and to the information made available. The reform of the procedures in the House removed the opportunity for a private Member to call for papers, and other practices have developed which 'frustrate any depth of scrutiny'.[35] In addition, as government has become more complex and technical, it has become more difficult for Members to ask penetrating questions. Yet there has been little incentive for specialization. Members of Parliament generally make their reputations through demonstrating their ability to cover any matter with the appropriate party line rather than to present an expert opinion on a particular subject. In any case, Members seldom have the necessary research and advisory resources and thus the minister, with the weight of the civil service behind him, always has the advantage.

The tendency by successive governments towards secrecy has been perhaps of most significance. This has resulted in 'dwindling sources of information'[36] being available to Members of Parliament and a reluctance of ministers to provide the full and frank answers necessary for effective accountability. The moral obligation of a minister to submit to the scrutiny of the House for all the decisions and actions taken within his area of responsibility therefore seems in practice to have become an obligation to submit to scrutiny only if the minister sees fit and has been unable to avoid the House securing sufficiently detailed information to pursue him. This could be viewed as demonstrating the capacity of conventions to adjust to the mores of the time, except that, of course, ministers acknowledge no such adjustment. More appropriately, the failure of ministers to fulfil their obligations can be seen as an indication of the weakness of the House of Commons. Members may go through the motions but in the end they seldom use their inherent power to insist on the information and answers required.

---

[33] Mackintosh, *The British Cabinet*, 192.   [34] Ibid.
[35] P. Bennett and S. Pullinger, *Making the Commons Work* (London: Institute of Public Policy Research, 1992).   [36] Mackintosh, *The British Cabinet*, 500.

The Growth of Quasi-Government and Indirect Control

Just as the start of Parliament's decline can be dated from the nineteenth century, so the acceptance that the state should have an extended role can be attributed to this time. The growth in the size and diversity of departments was already making it impossible for a minister to be personally aware of all that was happening in his name, and this trend continued apace. Yet despite this, the principle that all the functions of government should be under democratic control, which in the case of central government meant that they should be contained within departments, was firmly supported by the Haldane Committee. It noted:

attempts had been made to distribute the burden of responsibility by other means. In some cases recourse had been to a system of administrative Boards. We draw attention to the findings of the Royal Commission on the Civil Service that this system is less effective in securing responsibility for official action and advice than the system followed in Departments where full responsibility is definitely laid upon the Minister.[37]

However, by the end of the first quarter of the twentieth century the principle of direct responsibility 'seemed rapidly to lose its vitality'.[38] The enlarged social and economic activities made the retention by ministers of direct control and responsibility in some instances impractical and even undesirable, and increasingly agencies, operating outside departments and at arm's length from the minister, were established.[39] These quasi-governmental bodies, or non-departmental public bodies as they have more recently been called, were, and continue to be, constitutionally awkward. They require the reconciliation of the arm's length approach with ministerial responsibility.

There are a number of reasons why such bodies developed. There was a need to offload detailed managerial and technical work from departments, which were already becoming overburdened, to

[37] Haldane Report (1918), s31.

[38] D. L. Keir, *The Constitutional History of Modern Britain* (9th edn., London: A. C. Black, 1969), 522.

[39] The number of such agencies has always been difficult to calculate. In 1980 Pliatzky estimated that there were 489 executive bodies (these included operational and regulatory agencies) and 1,561 advisory bodies (*Report on Non-Departmental Public Bodies* (1980), Cmnd 7797, HMSO, paras. 20–33).

provide a degree of specialization, usually difficult to achieve internally, and to enable a greater flexibility than had come to be associated with the Whitehall machine. Further, it was particularly important, at least with regard to regulatory bodies, for such functions to seem to be independent from government and outside the political arena.[40] Hence the whole ethos of non-departmental public bodies rests on there being minimal departmental control, and to this end statutory frameworks provide varying degrees of independence and discretion. However, this absence of control conflicts with the concept of ministerial responsibility, where control is inextricably connected to accountability. Indeed, the very reason that regulatory and operational functions were transferred from independent boards to departments in the nineteenth century was as a response to this connection.

Control is maintained over broad policy matters, and usually the minister has the power of appointment and dismissal of board members. He may also have some control over expenditure. For such matters he has direct responsibility to Parliament. However, in other matters accountability is indirect. The minister acts merely as an instrument for referring questions asked in Parliament back to the responsible body or reporting to Parliament what he has been told by the Board. This may be seen as a necessary adaption of the convention of individual ministeral responsibility by which it allows for both direct and indirect responsibility, or it may be viewed as 'an attenuated and tardily applied version of ministerial responsibility'.[41] Either way it may generally be seen as unsatisfactory, raising the same problems of accountability that were recognized in the previous century.

Nationalized Industries and Blurred Lines of Responsibility

Nowhere were these problems more acute, and more debated, than in relation to the nationalized industries, which until they were dismantled raised a serious problem of accountability. Although nationalized industries were not strictly categorized as non-departmental public bodies,[42] their constitutional position was very

---

[40] This has been particularly evident in the 1980s with regard to the regulatory bodies established to police the newly privatized industries (e.g. Ofwat, Ofgas, Oftel).   [41] Keir, *The Constitutional History of Modern Britain*, 524.
[42] Pliatzky excluded the nationalized industries from his classification of non-departmental public bodies on the basis that they were different and should be

similar. They operated outside departments, at arm's length from the minister. They were characterized by a clear split in responsibility. The Board had statutory responsibility for day-to-day administration, and the minister had responsibility for overall policy, the appointment of board members, the approval of capital development, including borrowing and investment, and for 'general directions' issued in the national interest.

Despite the apparent clarity of the division between ministerial and Board responsibilities, in practice the lines of responsibility were blurred. Ministers rarely resorted to the formality of giving 'general directions', preferring an informal approach, and the way in which legislation was drafted enabled a minister to be 'anything from a cypher to an absolute autocrat'.[43] The covertness of ministerial intervention meant that the degree of interference within an industry was uncertain, as was the extent to which the minister should take responsibility before the House.

The minister only answered directly for his own responsibilities. The blueprint for ministers answering questions on the nationalized industries was laid down by Herbert Morrison in 1947:

A Minister is responsible to Parliament for actions which he may take in relation to a board, or action coming within his statutory powers which he has not taken. This is the principle that determines generally the matters on which a question may be put down for answer by a Minister in the House of Commons. Thus the Minister would be answerable for any directions he gave in the national interest, and for the action which he took on proposals which a board was required by Statute to lay before him.

It would be contrary to this principle, and to the clearly expressed intention of Parliament, in the governing legislation, if Ministers were to give, in replies in Parliament or in letters, information about day-to-day matters.[44]

Morrison's statement was less clear than he seems to have thought; ministers, it was true, answered on policy, not on day-to-day administration. However, the categorization of 'policy' and 'day-to-day administration' was uncertain and provided ministers with

---

looked at as industrial or commercial enterprises and not as 'adjuncts to government' (Cmnd 7797 (1980)).

[43] F. Milligan, 'The Limits of Ministerial Action', in A. H. Hanson (ed.), *A Book of Readings* (London: Allen & Unwin, 1963), 282.

[44] HC Deb., 4 Dec. 1947, col. 566.

considerable scope for evasion, particularly as decisions relating to the appropriateness of questions were largely left to ministers.

if a Minister has previously shown himself willing to answer questions of a certain type, i.e. to accept responsibility, then further Questions of that type will be in order; if a Minister denied responsibility in a certain area and refused to answer, then further Questions in that area would appear to be out of order.[45]

Ministers, therefore, had considerable discretion regarding the answering of questions and they varied in the extent to which they would be forthcoming, both by answering directly and by answering on behalf of the Board. Only on rare occasions, when the matter was of public concern, might a minister be pressed to answer. Thus Parliamentary Questions, at best a poor mechanism for obtaining information from the government, became even more ineffectual when the nationalized industries were involved.

The accountability debate over the nationalized industries illustrated the changed balance between Parliament and the executive. In the middle of the nineteenth century the House of Commons had laid down the rules for accountability. A hundred years later, the government controlled the playing field and therefore the rules which applied.[46] The problem of accountability posed by the nationalized industries was removed with their privatization. However, it was replaced by concern over how to achieve the effective accountability of the regulatory bodies, which were established to police the private industries (see above). In addition the nationalized industries have left a legacy of the policy–administration divide, which has come to be used by ministers as a limitation to direct departmental responsibility.[47]

An Enlarged Bureaucracy

The increase in the size and complexity of government has of necessity been accompanied by the enlargement of the bureaucracy to administer it.[48] Since the mid-nineteenth century this has

---

[45] *Report from the Select Committee on Nationalized Industries* (1967–8), HC371, para. 850.

[46] However, Parliament did set up a Select Committee on Nationalized Industries which lasted until the reform of the select committee system in 1979.

[47] The policy–administrative divide was first raised in this way by James Prior (see Ch. 7.2), and subsequently by Kenneth Baker (see Ch. 8.3).

[48] In 1870 there were just over 50,000 civil servants. The number rose to 80,000 in the early 1890s and to 282,420 by the time of the First World War. The number

developed into 'an immensely powerful and intricate organization of power'.[49] The civil service is an organization whose individual members have no public accountability, for in law and by convention power is exercised on behalf of the minister, who is therefore accountable for it. The traditional nineteenth-century departmental model, upon which both law and convention rest, works on the premiss that the minister has direct control over the actions of his civil servants. It is on this basis that Parliament passes statutes that delegate power to departments, albeit in the name of the minister, so that they can make the necessary rules or regulations to implement the policy. Such delegation has become increasingly necessary as the sphere of government power has extended and the subject-matter has become more technical. However, these very factors have also meant that it has become difficult for ministers always to exert the required control over their departments. The power of officials may have increased, while control decreases.

The effectiveness of ministerial responsibility may therefore be questioned as a mechanism for controlling officials. Indeed, some critics suggest that ministers, if not controlled, are certainly captured by their departments, and thus come to act in departmental rather than governmental interests. In addition, both the left and right of the political spectrum have accused civil servants of frustrating ministerial policies.[50]

1.4. INDIVIDUAL MINISTERIAL RESPONSIBILITY IN THE FINAL QUARTER OF THE TWENTIETH CENTURY

Since the Second World War and the development of the welfare state, the responsibility of ministers to Parliament has become extensive, diverse, and confused. Moreover, the convention through which it operates has been criticized both for its ineffectiveness in providing accountability to Parliament and for its inability to control the civil service. However, the individual responsibility of ministers is still a key feature of responsible government. Indeed,

---

peaked in 1975 at 747,000 and in 1984, after Mrs Thatcher's cull, had declined to 630,000 (figures from P. Hennessy, *Whitehall* (London: Fontana Press, 1990), 26, 51, 59, 261, 600).

[49] Keir, *The Constitutional History of Modern Britain*, 524.

[50] In 1977 the Expenditure Committee reported that civil servants frequently acted to frustrate ministerial policies (*Report from the Expenditure Committee* (1977), HC535, HMSO).

as the century has progressed it would seem that the focus has frequently been more upon the individual minister than the collectivity of government.

There are a number of reasons why this should be the case. First, as government has become more complex, and the practice and myth of collective decision-making has diminished, the individual minister has more frequently been identified with departmental policies. He is seen as having the backing of Cabinet, although unattributable sources may suggest reservations, but the policy belongs to him. The advantage for government is that, if the policy should become unsustainable, collective cover can be removed and the policy failure will be seen as a failure not of the government but of the minister alone.[51]

Secondly, the dominance by the executive of the House of Commons, together with the strictness of party discipline, ensures that, unless there is a minority government or a government with a very small majority, there is no possibility of the Opposition ever forcing the resignation of the government, or even getting close in a vote of no confidence. Indeed, it can be argued that the function of checking the executive has transferred to the government back-benches. The drama as well as the effectiveness has therefore gone out of collective responsibility as a means of enforcing accountability.

Thirdly, there has been a 'significant change in the style of the House',[52] which is demonstrated by the decline in the occurrence and importance of debates. The focus of parliamentary attention has shifted to Question Time. However, this is frequently used as an opportunity for scoring party points and for launching personal attacks rather than for seeking and providing information and justification. Roy Jenkins comments:

Except on rare occasions debate had ceased to be central to the parliamentary process. It had been replaced by the quick exchange of Prime

[51] e.g. the apparent failure of economic policy by the end of the 1980s came to be attributed to Nigel Lawson, the Chancellor of the Exchequer, not the government; Kenneth Clarke was personally associated with the reforms in the Health Service; Kenneth Baker, and subsequently John Patten, with education reform. (In contrast, in 1992, when Britain left the ERM, the Prime Minister, John Major, insisted that economic policy was the policy of the whole government. However, this did not prevent the replacement of Norman Lamont as Chancellor in a Cabinet reshuffle in 1993.

[52] R. Jenkins, *A Life at the Centre* (London: Macmillan, 1991), 565.

Ministerial question time and similar responses to statements by major ministers. . . . there developed a parliamentary style with a rhythm like that of a game of snap.[53]

Jenkins suggests that the change in the House was in part brought about by Mrs Thatcher's personal style. This point is supported by research which indicates that Mrs Thatcher during her time in office took little part in the proceedings of the House and certainly less than her predecessors. '[She was] far and away the least active prime minister in the Commons for the last hundred and twenty years. Her abandonment of debating interventions, and her very infrequent speeches set her strongly apart.'[54]

The infrequency of major debates in the House, and the failure of the Prime Minister to participate in those that there were, would seem to have acted to reduce the effectiveness of attacks on the government as a whole. These need to be addressed to the prime minister, who as leader is the personification of the government, or at least be made in his or her presence with the expectation of a prime ministerial response.

Fourthly, the tightness of the party machinery has made it unwise for a government back-bencher seeking advancement not to support the government. However, back-bench frustrations grow and revolts may threaten, particularly if the government is losing its popularity. If criticism becomes unavoidable, then the whips prefer it to be directed towards the individual minister rather than at the collectivity of the government. In an extreme case the individual can then be persuaded to relinquish office. This, it is hoped, will leave his colleagues untouched, back-benchers satisfied, and the government's standing with the electorate undiminished.

A Revived Interest in Individual Ministerial Responsibility

Thus, partly through choice and partly because there has been no satisfactory alternative, accountability has focused again on the individual minister. The convention of individual responsibility with all its inherent problems is therefore still at the forefront of British government and its relationship with Parliament.

[53] Ibid.

[54] P. Dunleavy, *et al.*, 'Prime Ministers and the Commons: Patterns of Behaviour', *Public Administration*, 68 (1990), 137.

Moreover, since the early 1980s it has featured prominently. First, a spate of resignations, attributable to the convention, has revived interest in its application and the requirement of resignation. Secondly, institutional reforms in Parliament and within government have heightened debate about the extent of the convention and its effectiveness.

The reform of the select committee system in 1979 was an attempt by the House of Commons to redress the balance between Parliament and the executive. The balance that is achieved is clearly fundamental to the accountability of ministers and is likely to affect the workings of the convention of individual ministerial responsibility. Similarly, the establishment of Next Steps executive agencies, which alters the structure of departments and the relationship of ministers with their officials, must in the long term affect the convention of individual ministerial responsibility. This is true even if in the initial stages the government lists among the virtues of its reform the unchanged nature and functioning of the convention.

Such a claim in itself raises important questions, for neither the content nor the application of individual ministerial responsibility is sufficiently firmly grounded for there necessarily to be agreement as to what constitutes change. The following chapter will, therefore, address the question of the content of the convention and examine the variability of its application. The analysis will then provide a framework for the examination of ministerial resignations and parliamentary and government reforms.

2

The Content of the Convention

2.1. RESPONSIBILITY AND CONTROL

The description of individual ministerial responsibility as a single convention is convenient, but perhaps misleading. More appropriate is an understanding of individual ministerial responsibility as a group of conventions which gives effect to the constitutional requirement that ministers alone are responsible to Parliament for their departments.

The constitutional position of ministers has provoked considerable debate, particularly concerning the meaning of responsibility,[1] a meaning that has become more complex as ministers have acquired responsibilities outside their departments and those within departments have become more diverse. Responsibility does not, however, stand alone but in direct relation to control. The nineteenth-century development of the convention of individual ministerial responsibility was based on this relationship. The accountability constitutionally required, therefore, varies depending on the degree of control exercised by the minister. Today it is unlikely that ministers exert detailed control over the activities of their departments. Rather, they maintain a supervisory authority and thus the power to direct or intervene should they wish to do so. However, 'control' is still a useful term, because of its relevance to the distinction between direct and indirect forms of accountability.

Where the minister has no control or supervisory authority, no accountability is expected of him.[2] Thereafter the requirements

---

[1] See e.g. G. Marshall and G. Moodie, *Some Problems of the Constitution* (London: Hutchinson, 1959), N. Johnson, *In Search of the Constitution* (London: Methuen, 1977).

[2] As held by the Speaker of the House in 1912 regarding the Port of London Authority (see Jennings, *Cabinet Government*, 94).

of accountability stretch through a range from mere redirection of responsibility to the absolute response of resignation. Attention has tended to focus upon ministerial resignations, the infrequency of which is often cited as an indication, even a cause, of the inadequacy of ministerial accountability. This emphasis on resignation as the main form of accountability deflects consideration from other less dramatic means by which the minister may be accountable to Parliament. Resignation lies at the top of the scale of constitutional accountability, but the other levels at which accountability operates should not be neglected. In the day-to-day routine of accountability, they are far more significant.

2.2. LEVELS OF OPERATION

Redirectory Responsibility

Redirectory responsibility is the starting-point for accountability; the requirement is simply for the minister to 'redirect' questions from Members of Parliament as appropriate. Such redirection applies to questions related to the day-to-day running of the nationalized industries, where the minister's responsibility is indirect, and to other areas of government from which the minister is deliberately distanced—for example, decisions involving individual taxation or immigration appeals. Increasingly important within this category are matters which fall within the responsibility of the Chief Executives of Next Steps agencies.[3] However, here the minister retains a direct responsibility, and thus a Member can still insist upon a ministerial answer.

A disadvantage of redirectory responsibility for Members of Parliament has been that, unlike written responses from ministers, the answers to redirected questions are not published. They are addressed only to the individual Member concerned. However, the concern of the House over this, with regard to questions redirected to agencies, has resulted in new mechanisms being established for the publication of answers from Chief Executives.[4] Redirection concerns mostly written questions or oral questions

[3] A full analysis of these responsibilities will be found in Ch. 11.
[4] See Ch. 12.

requiring routine information or explanation. It is not meant to be a mechanism for the redirection of politically sensitive issues away from the parliamentary arena. Such questions still demand a ministerial answer.

Reporting or Informatory Responsibility

The second level of ministerial responsibility requires the minister simply to report to Parliament what has happened in one of the areas of his responsibility. This type of responsibility has been described as 'explanatory' by Geoffrey Marshall,[5] but this suggests a more reasoned account than is often proffered. Any requirement for an 'explanation' from the minister is, of course, ambiguous, and responses can range from a simple informatory statement to a detailed account. The latter, however, would seem more appropriate for the third level of accountability considered below.

More applicable here would be to refer to 'reporting' or 'informatory' responsibility.[6] Again this particularly concerns the operational matters of nationalized industries or non-departmental bodies, where the minister frequently prefaces his statement with 'the Chairman has told me . . .', or 'I have been advised by the Chairman . . .'. Such remarks indicate that the minister's responsibility is confined to acting as a mechanism for the indirect accountability to Parliament for the day-to-day administration of an organization.

Informatory responsibility is improper when the advising agent is a departmental civil servant. However, ministers at times utilize the associated phraseology in an attempt to distance themselves from an incident concerning their department. The use by the Home Secretary of the preface, 'I was advised by the director-general of the prison service . . .',[7] when he was accounting to the House for the escape from Brixton Prison, should be seen as such a strategy. The director-general of the prison service is in fact a

[5] G. Marshall, 'Police Accountability Revisited', in D. Butler and A. H. Halsey (eds.), *Policy and Politics: Essays in Honour of Norman Chester* (London: Macmillan, 1978), 61–2.

[6] Geoffrey Marshall has more recently suggested 'non-executive' or 'indirect' accountability as a convenient label (see G. Marshall, 'Parliamentary Accountability', *Parliamentary Affairs*, 44/4 (1991)), 463.

[7] HC Deb., 8 July 1991, col. 653 (see Ch. 8.3 for an analysis of responsibility for the Brixton escape).

departmental civil servant and thus the minister bears a direct, not indirect, responsibility to the House. This requires more than reporting or informatory responsibility. It requires explanation, possibly amendatory action, and even resignation.

Explanatory Responsibility

The third level at which responsibility operates involves far more from the minister. It requires him to explain or account for his own and his department's actions. The extent to which a minister is constitutionally required to explain to Parliament is not clear, although politically it will be the minimum the House will accept. Gladstone asserted that there was no requirement for him to give information to Parliament and that the accountability of ministers lay in their recognition of the right of Parliament to vote them out of office. This has not stopped Parliament seeking information and explanation from ministers, and it would certainly seem in the modern context that 'explanatory' accountability is a parliamentary and public expectation, if not always a reality. The Select Committee on Defence made it clear in its report on Westland that it was unacceptable for a minister to accept responsibility but to refuse to explain what had happened.[8]

The production of financial statements, and the more recent introduction of reports indicating achievements in terms of performance criteria and budgetary targets, are a worthwhile development in the accountability process, but the concept of accountability requires more. It is necessary for those to whom accountability is owed to have opportunities to question and probe beyond the limits set by departments through these reports. They, and not ministers and civil servants, need to set the agenda for accountability.

Explanatory responsibility is at the centre of a minister's accountability to Parliament. Moreover, since the reform of the select committee system in 1979, it is increasingly important, and involves civil servants as well as ministers in the accounting process. Despite its central importance, explanatory responsibility has often been found wanting. This is particularly the case in matters

---

[8] *The Fourth Report from the Defence Committee: Westland plc: The Government's Decision-Making* (1985–6), HC519, HMSO, para. 235.

of political controversy or government embarrassment, such as the Westland affair (1986), the salmonella in eggs scare (1988), and the sale of Rover (1989), when ministers have conspicuously failed to account adequately either on the Floor of the House or before select committees.[9]

Amendatory Responsibility

At the fourth level, the minister is required to provide more than an explanation of what has happened. He is required to make amends for his own or his department's shortcomings.[10] At its simplest, an apology to the House may suffice, particularly if coupled with the announcement that corrective action has been taken. This may be the installation of new procedures to prevent a repeat of the incident, the holding of an internal inquiry, or the disciplining of the official responsible. When the incident has had serious consequences, then some kind of financial compensation may be appropriate, as with the collapse of Barlow Clowes and the scare over salmonella in eggs.[11] An external inquiry may be necessary as an initial step. After both the Maze (1983) and Brixton Prison (1991) escapes, the announcement by the minister responsible of an external inquiry can be seen as such an amendatory measure.[12]

The announcement of an inquiry suggests full fact-finding and public accountability, but accountability may be limited by the terms of reference of the inquiry and the timing and extent of the publication of its report. It can in practice be a useful device for the minister, delaying full disclosure of the facts until public interest has subsided and, if carefully timed, the House is in recess. Thus the extent to which the announcement of an inquiry can be seen as the minister seeking to make amends for what has happened needs to be modified by consideration of the limitations upon the inquiry and its usefulness to the minister in evading amendatory action.[13] An inquiry is in any case only the initial step in the amendatory process. Much depends on how the minister acts upon the findings of the report.

[9] See Chs. 6.2, 4.2, 8.2 for an analysis of these incidents.
[10] The phrase 'amendatory accountability' was coined by Colin Turpin (see C. Turpin, *British Government and the Constitution* (London: Weidenfeld and Nicolson, 1985; 2nd edn., 1990), 346).
[11] See Chs. 8.2, 4.2.   [12] See Chs. 7.2, 8.3.
[13] See Ch. 9 for discussion of limitations on inquiries.

The public disciplining of officials as an amendatory measure is infrequent. It is a constitutional requirement that the minister protects his officials from public scrutiny. This means their anonymity should be preserved and any public accountability of officials must be either through the minister—for instance, when the minister answers for his department on the Floor of the House —or on behalf of the minister, as when a civil servant answers a letter or gives evidence before a select committee. Thus, even with a fully published report, the minister may face accusations of shifting responsibility downwards to someone unknown to the public, who is unable publicly to defend himself.

There have, however, been important cases of 'naming and blaming'. After the Crichel Down inquiry, five officials were named and one transferred to other duties.[14] The inquiry into the collapse of Vehicle and General in 1972 named an under-secretary and two assistant secretaries as culpable.[15] More recently, after receiving the report on the Brixton Prison break-out, the Home Secretary announced the transfer to another section of a named civil servant, and in both the Maze and Brixton incidents the prison governors took early retirement.[16]

Such publication of disciplinary measures and naming of officials took place after external inquiries. The internal unpublished inquiry is more controversial. This was demonstrated by the Westland affair. Five officials figured in the report by Sir Robert Armstrong into the leaking of the Solicitor-General's letter. The report was never published and the civil servants were never officially named or disciplined, although one of them, Miss Colette Bowe, subsequently left her position. However, the extent of her culpability and that of the other officials remained unestablished.[17]

The situations in which an official may be publicly blamed would seem likely to increase with the establishment of Next Steps agencies. These provide for the greater public accountability of named civil servants, and, in cases of mismanagement or maladministration within the agency, the appropriate amendatory action may be the public disciplining of those civil servants in charge.

---

[14] Report from the Public Inquiry into the Disposal of Land at Crichel Down (1954), Cmnd 9176, HMSO.
[15] Report of the Tribunal of Inquiry on the Vehicle and General Insurance Company (1971–2), HC133, HMSO.
[16] See Chs. 7.2, 8.3.　　[17] See Ch. 6.2.

Indeed, there is some support for such amendatory measures extending to senior departmental civil servants. After a series of incidents involving the Home Office, which included the Brixton Prison escape, prison riots, the ruling that the Home Secretary had been in contempt of court, and responses to joy-riding and the problem of dangerous dogs, *The Times* declared: 'Civil servants . . . should more often be disciplined or sacked both as a punishment and a deterrent. Starting with the permanent under-secretary . . . where down the line did responsibility lie?'[18]

Such 'naming and blaming' of civil servants, except in extreme circumstances, does not accord with the traditional constitutional doctrine that ministers should protect the anonymity of their officials. However, the extent of the protection given would seem to be decreasing.[19] Whilst examples of 'naming and blaming' are infrequent occurrences, both the reform of the select committee system, which provides for constant public scrutiny of officials, and the establishment of Next Steps agencies may suggest an erosion of this principle. Amendatory action may increasingly involve the public disciplining of named officials.

Sacrificial Responsibility

The fifth and highest level of responsibility is sacrificial responsibility.[20] This requires the minister to resign. Ministerial resignations are the most obvious and the most dramatic form of accountability. However, there has frequently been debate about the constitutional requirements for resignation—that is, under what circumstances is a minister obliged, or does he feel himself obliged, to resign. There is little dispute that a personal error by the minister, whether categorized as a private indiscretion or political misjudgement, may require resignation. Whether or not it is necessary for a minister to relinquish office depends on the extent to

[18] *The Times*, Editorial, 30 Nov. 1991.

[19] In 1968 the Select Committee on the Parliamentary Commissioner reported that the convention of ministerial responsibility could no longer be expected to provide complete anonymity. The investigative powers given to the Commissioner made such an expectation impossible (*Report from the Select Committee on the Parliamentary Commissioner* (1967–8), HC350, HMSO).

[20] This term was suggested by Geoffrey Marshall (see G. Marshall (ed.) *Ministerial Responsibility* (Oxford: Oxford University Press, 1989)), 10.

which he offends the public face of morality or embarrasses his colleagues and the party.

There has, however, been uncertainty over whether a minister is required to resign for departmental fault in which he was not involved and of which he was unaware. The most absolute version of individual ministerial responsibility requires ministers to be vicariously accountable for the errors of their civil servants, even to the extent of resignation for these errors if they are sufficiently serious. Thus Turpin writes:

the convention of individual ministerial responsibility is traditionally supposed to fix the blame on the minister for every failure of departmental policy or administration, whether it is the minister himself who was at fault, or a civil servant, or if the failure resulted from a defect of departmental organization. The minister must submit to the judgement of Parliament, and if the failure is a serious one, should resign from office without waiting for a vote of censure.[21]

The responsibility is similarly expressed by Munro:

the principle is said to be that a minister takes the praise for the successes of his department and the blame for its failures. The sanction for misconduct of government is that a minister is exposed to criticism and censure in the House, and, if the misconduct is serious, may be expected to resign.[22]

The requirement of ministerial resignation for errors within departments would seem to have arisen partly as a response to the inability of Parliament to remove an errant official from office because of his permanent status. Parris states: 'The difficulty was eventually resolved by an extension of the doctrine of ministerial responsibility. In extreme cases, ministers resigned while officials stayed on.'[23]

Yet the circumstances in which a minister is required to resign, while the officials involved remained in office, have never been clarified. It is generally recognized that, when the convention developed in the mid-nineteenth century, ministers believed resignation was required for all serious errors within their departments. However, the requirement for resignation would seem to have

---

[21] Turpin, *British Government and the Constitution*, 353.
[22] C. Munro, *Studies in Constitutional Law* (London: Butterworths, 1987), 37.
[23] Parris, *Constitutional Bureaucracy*, 105.

been based on the assumption that ministers controlled, or should control, their departments personally. Ministers were therefore not expected to accept vicarious responsibility, in the sense that they should resign for mistakes or misjudgements in which they had no part, for it was assumed that they would have been involved in, or at least aware of, departmental mistakes or misjudgements. The expectation was that ministers accepted personal responsibility through resignation.

Doubt has therefore been expressed as to whether the most absolute version of individual ministerial responsibility has ever been the constitutional requirement. Marshall suggests a confusion between the legal requirement of vicarious responsibility, in which the minister takes full responsibility for all acts and decisions of his department, and the conventional requirement.[24] Certainly the assumption that ministers should accept vicarious responsibility would seem to be unsupported by precedents. These indicate the need for a direct connection between ministerial awareness or involvement and the requirement for resignation.

When in 1864 Lowe resigned, after a report from a school inspector had been altered by his department, his resignation was not an acceptance of vicarious responsibility for the actions of his officials, but a relinquishing of office by a minister who considered his honour had been impugned by the accusations made in the House. Moreover, after a select committee investigation had found that Lowe, as he had always insisted, had been unaware of the alterations, and in fact had given instructions that such alterations should not be made, the House was told that Lowe's resignation had been unnecessary.[25] The incident suggests that a minister is not required to resign if he has acted properly and had no involvement in the errors or misjudgements made.

This precedent was reinforced by the resignation of the Irish Secretary, George Wyndham, in 1904. He resigned after his permanent under-secretary's scheme for the devolution of power in Ireland met with a hostile public and political response. However, again Wyndham's resignation was not an acceptance of vicarious responsibility. It was an acceptance of his own responsibility, for he had failed to read correspondence about the scheme, which his official had sent him, and thus had not moved to stop it going

[24] Marshall, *Ministerial Responsibility*, 8.   [25] See Ch. 1.

ahead. It seems, however, that, if his ignorance of the scheme had been because of a failing on the part of his department, rather than through his own negligence, he would have felt it constitutionally acceptable to repudiate the actions of his official.[26]

Resignations attributable to departmental fault rather than personal indiscretion or political misjudgement have been very infrequent. Indeed, prior to the 1980s the only other case which could be cited with certainty was Crichel Down in 1954.[27] This case has been frequently quoted as the classic example of a minister, Sir Thomas Dugdale, accepting vicarious responsibility for the administrative failings of his officials. However, more recently this idea has been questioned, and Dugdale's resignation has been attributed largely to his own error in continuing a departmental policy which was known to be unpopular with party back-benchers and powerful interests. Any maladministration by officials is seen as being secondary to this main error.[28]

Such a revision does not affect the categorization of the resignation as being on the grounds of departmental fault. Nor does it diminish the value of Crichel Down as a precedent for a minister honourably refusing to hide behind the faults of his civil servants. It does, however, serve as confirmation that ministers do not

---

[26] See Finer, 'The Individual Responsibility of Ministers', for his interpretation of this resignation.

[27] Resignations attributed to individual ministerial responsibility 1900–79: 1905 Lord Westbury, 1914 Col. Seely, 1916 A. Birrell, 1917 A. Chamberlain, N. Chamberlain, 1918 Lord Rothermere, 1922 E. S. Montagu, 1935 Sir S. Hoare, 1936 J. H. Thomas, 1938 Viscount Swinton/Earl Winterton, 1947 H. Dalton, 1948 J. Belcher, 1954 Sir T. Dugdale, 1958 I. Hardy, 1962 T. Galbraith, 1963 J. Profumo, 1972 R. Maudling, 1973 Lords Lambton and Jellicoe, 1974 Lord Brayley. Of these resignations only Sir Thomas Dugdale's can with certainty be described as 'departmental fault'. (Sources: D. Butler and G. Butler, *British Political Facts 1900–1985* (London: Macmillan, 1986); Finer, 'The Individual Responsibility of Ministers'.)

[28] See I. F. Nicolson, *The Mystery of Crichel Down* (Oxford: Oxford University Press, 1986), a commentary by Prof. J. A. G. Griffith in *Contemporary Record*, 1/ 1 (1987), 35–40; and Lord Boyle of Handsworth, 'Address to the Royal Institute of Public Administration', *Public Administration*, 58 (1980), 1–12. Lord Boyle stated that Crichel Down had frequently been 'misunderstood':

> Sir Thomas Dugdale . . . did not resign because he accepted responsibility for an act of maladministration; he resigned because he was not prepared to abandon . . . the decision that his Department should retain and equip Crichel Down as a single farm unit—which was unacceptable to an influential section of his own party in Parliament, as well as individuals and interests outside. And he rightly and honourably refused to explain away his decision by pleading that he had been misled by incompetent officials. (p. 10)

resign unless they are personally involved in departmental errors, and as a reminder that the rhetoric surrounding a resignation can be misleading.

The reinterpretation of Crichel Down has not ended its appeal as a high point of constitutional morality against which ministers under pressure for departmental fault can be measured.[29] Nor has it yet extinguished the belief, which seemed at the time to be given substance in Crichel Down, that ministers should accept vicarious responsibility. This is illustrated by an editorial in the *Independent* in 1991 which claimed: 'until recent decades constitutional convention had it that it was for a minister whose civil servants made a grave error to shoulder the responsibility and resign.'[30]

The adherence to this standard is questionable, because of the uncertainty of its validity. Probably the safest statement on the question of whether ministerial resignations are constitutionally required for civil service fault in which the minister is not personally implicated is that offered by Geoffrey Marshall: 'No post-war case has involved such an assumption and it can be said with confidence that the convention of ministerial responsibility contains no requirement of any such vicarious accountability.'[31]

This supports Maxwell-Fyfe's statement made after Crichel Down, which contained no explicit reference to the obligation of the minister to resign for error or misconduct which is attributable to an official.[32] In addition, this constitutional position has been confirmed by Sir Robin Butler, Head of the Civil Service, who told the First Division Association of Civil Servants: '[Ministers] cannot and should not be expected to shoulder the blame for decisions of which they know nothing or could be expected to know nothing.'[33]

Thus, even if there was in the past vicarious accountability, it seems no longer to exist. This may mean that the use of the term

---

[29] Hence the asking of questions such as that put by Mr David Winnock after the Home Secretary, Kenneth Baker, had made a statement to the House on the escape of two prisoners from Brixton Prison: 'What does he [the Home Secretary] feel that Sir Thomas Dugdale would have done if he had been Home Secretary?' (HC Deb., July 8 1991, col. 657).

[30] *Independent*, editorial, 2 Dec. 1991, after the Court of Appeal's ruling that Kenneth Baker, Home Secretary, was in contempt of court.

[31] G. Marshall, *Constitutional Conventions* (Oxford: Clarendon Press, 1986), 65. [32] HC Deb., 20 July 1954, vol. 530, cols. 1285–7.

[33] P. Hennessy, 'Whitehall Watch', *Independent*, 14 Nov. 1990.

'sacrificial' is more appropriately applied in the political context.[34] The resignation of a minister may well be a sacrifice of the minister or by the minister for the sake of the government, or more particularly the prime minister. It is not, however, an acceptance of responsibility for the errors of civil servants in which the minister had no part.

The convention of individual ministerial responsibility can therefore most accurately be defined as requiring resignation for personal fault or private indiscretion on the part of the minister, or for departmental fault in which the minister was involved or of which he knew, or should have known. Where there is maladministration within a department of which the minister was unaware and which cannot be attributed to his negligence, he is still responsible, but this responsibility is limited to explanatory or amendatory accountability. There is no requirement for his resignation.

2.3. A MULTI-LAYERED CONVENTION

The responsibility of the minister to Parliament can therefore be seen as multi-layered, requiring the minister to provide a range of responses from redirection through to resignation, according to the degree of control or supervisory authority he exercises. Indirect control may allow the minister to limit accountability to redirecting or providing information. Direct control, on the other hand, requires explanation, possibly amendatory action, and, in extreme circumstances, resignation.

However, recent changes within government and Parliament have affected the operation and level of accountability required. The establishment of Next Steps agencies has produced a considerable expansion in redirectory responsibility, although agencies are still held to be under direct ministerial control. This has important implications for the convention of individual ministerial responsibility as government services are increasingly delivered in this way. The select committee system may act as a counter to this move towards the lighter end of the accountability scale. Select committees

---

[34] Marshall has suggested the term 'abscessive' as an alternative (see Marshall, 'Parliamentary Accountability').

have concentrated the focus upon explanatory responsibility, and at times have moved to extract amendatory accountability. In addition, the public scrutiny of officials, albeit appearing on behalf of the minister, has acted to reduce civil service expectations of anonymity. Next Steps agencies have continued the process, opening the way to greater public civil service accountability. Altogether these changes suggest that revisions to the convention of individual ministerial responsibility are necessary.

PART TWO

Resignations and Non-Resignations
The Operation of
Individual Ministerial Responsibility
in the 1980s and 1990s

3

The Requirement for Resignation

Ministerial resignations are frequently called for, most often by the Opposition as part of a standard demand for ministerial accountability, but seldom proffered. Indeed, in the period from the Second World War to 1979 there were only eleven resignations which could be attributed to the convention of individual ministerial responsibility.[1] However, despite the lack of resignations, the language used, both inside the House and in the media, has continued to assume that there is a constitutional requirement for resignation. The House of Commons has still been seen as having 'punitive authority . . . as distinct from a mere right to information'.[2]

The 1980s and early 1990s produced a number of resignations (those of Fairbairn, Carrington in conjunction with Luce and Atkins, Parkinson, Brittan, Currie, Nicholls, Ridley, and Mellor) which indicated that this punitive authority existed, although, not surprisingly, given the party and executive dominance of Parliament, its efficacy should more accurately be attributed to party and the prime minister rather than to the House of Commons. Assessments as to what these resignations indicate about the convention of individual ministerial responsibility and the requirements for resignation have produced varying conclusions, the variation to an extent dependent on the criteria used. Thus the resignation of Lord Carrington has been declared by both Pyper and Judge not to be a reassertion of individual ministerial responsibility,[3] but by

[1] Butler and Butler, *British Political Facts* (see Ch. 2 n. 27 for list).
[2] Marshall and Moodie, *Some Problems of the Constitution*, 81.
[3] R. Pyper, 'The F.O. Resignations: Individual Ministerial Responsibility Revived?', in L. Robins (ed.), *Updating British Politics* (London: Politics Association, 1984), 47–57; D. Judge, *Ministerial Responsibility: Life in the Strawman yet?* (Strathclyde Papers in Government and Politics, 37; Glasgow: Unit for the Study of the Government of Scotland, 1984).

Geoffrey Marshall to be a 'further precedent for the existence of a rule requiring a minister who is personally culpable of misjudgment or negligence to offer his resignation'.[4]

The way in which a resignation is interpreted also depends upon the scheme of analysis used. A study based upon the purported, or actual, motivation of the resigner or upon the cause of the resignation is likely to produce the conclusion that the resignation was induced not by constitutional considerations but by political pragmatism. However, the interpretation may be different if the analysis also includes an examination of whether the resignation was constitutionally required. The relationship between political and constitutional requirements is, therefore, fundamental in determining the nature of a resignation and the precedent it establishes.

The temptation when examining individual ministerial responsibility is to look back to its development in the mid-nineteenth century and to assign no political reasons to resignations. This, however, is a false perspective and fails to recognize that the convention grew out of the political practice. It was Parliament's ability to force resignation that gave substance to the belief that ministers were required to resign for serious departmental fault. Indeed, it was the existence of this political power that gave rise to the theory initially, as noted by Mackintosh: 'there would have been no need to acknowledge errors in this way [through resignation] but for the power of the House of Commons to move and carry a motion censuring the individual in question without necessarily dislodging the government.'[5]

What would seem to have been peculiar to the mid-nineteenth century was that, for a short period of perhaps thirty years, the constitutional and political requirements coincided. The critical and the positive morality of the constitution were in harmony and pulled in the same direction.[6] Subsequently this has not always have been the case. The change in the power relationship between

---

[4] Marshall, *Constitutional Conventions*, 65.

[5] Mackintosh, *The British Cabinet*, 443.

[6] The terms 'critical' and 'positive' morality are here used in a limited sense to distinguish between the different motivations behind constitutional obligations and political reality. Geoffrey Marshall describes the positive morality of the constitution as 'the beliefs that the major participants in the political process as a matter of fact have about what is required of them', and the critical morality as 'the rules that the political actors ought to feel obliged by, if they have considered the precedents and reasons correctly' (Marshall, *Constitutional Conventions*, 11–12).

the executive and the legislature has meant that the House of Commons is no longer able to force the resignation of a minister unless the governing party requires it and the prime minister fails to provide collective cover. Indeed ministers, whilst still constitutionally accountable to Parliament, are politically accountable to their party and to the government, particularly the prime minister. This may produce a divergence between what a minister believes he 'ought' to do in constitutional terms and what he knows is politically required of him.

Nevertheless, it would be inappropriate to conclude that the constitutional values no longer have significance. Judge suggests:

No minister would deny his individual and collective responsibility for executive actions. In this sense ministers subscribe to the theory of constitutional conventions. Correspondingly, no minister believes his responsibility to be absolute. Responsibility is therefore tempered by practicalities and positive morality.[7]

This view of ministerial responsibility as a compromise of moral principle by political pragmatism may suggest an undermining of constitutional morality. However, it would be a mistake necessarily to see this as a modern contraction of responsibility. This balance has always been made; it is a rare minister who would resign whilst still having sufficient political support to remain in office. The difference lies in the fact that, whilst in the mid-nineteenth century support within the House was seldom assured, today the dominance of the legislature by the executive means that it usually is.

A resignation seldom occurs unless there is both a constitutional and a political requirement for it. This suggests that at particular instances during the 1980s there was an unusual and perhaps surprising degree of coincidence between the requirements: unusual because only during the mid-nineteenth century and possibly in the period 1914–22 would there seem to have been a similar degree of coincidence necessary to produce a spate of resignations;[8] surprising because the 1980s was a time of stable governments with strong majorities and the continuity provided by one prime minister. This might lead to speculation that during the

---

[7] Judge, *Ministerial Responsibility*.

[8] During the period 1855–1967 there were five resignations (see Ch. 1); in 1914–22 there were six (see Ch. 2).

1980s there was a stricter interpretation of what constituted a serious mistake, or that serious ministerial misjudgements were more frequent than in previous decades.

The following chapters in Part Two will examine the resignations attributable to individual ministerial responsibility which occurred during the 1980s and early 1990s. They will also examine cases where ministers managed to retain their positions despite concerted calls for their resignation. These cases will be analysed to see whether resignation was constitutionally required, and whether responsibility was, using Judge's expression, 'tempered' by political considerations or whether the constitutional and political requirements coincided. To this end the background to the resignation situation will be considered and the part played by various groups in the production or otherwise of a resignation will be assessed. The political actors involved vary according to the situation but include the prime minister, the parliamentary party, the Opposition, the Press and sometimes television, the constituency party, and powerful interest groups.[9]

The analysis of resignations and non-resignations will be made on the basis that the convention of individual ministerial responsibility requires resignations in two different situations. First, it requires ministers to resign for personal fault. This may be either because of private indiscretion, as was the case with Cecil Parkinson, Patrick Nicholls, and David Mellor,[10] or because of a political error made when acting in a ministerial capacity but without departmental backing. The resignations of Nicholas Fairbairn, Edwina Currie, and Nicholas Ridley can be seen in this light. Secondly, the convention requires the resignation of a minister for serious departmental fault in which he was involved, or of which he knew or should have known. The resignations of Carrington and Brittan come within this category, as do the cases of non-resignation—that is, Nott, Whitelaw, Prior, Young, and Baker.

[9] Much of the material for the background of the resignation–non-resignation cases has been produced by cross-referencing accounts in the quality Press. *The Times, Independent, Daily Telegraph,* and *Guardian* have been used extensively. References to these sources are usually only given for a quotation, or if it is appropriate to attribute a point to one particular newspaper.

[10] The resignation of Patrick Nicholls is not individually analysed because he was a relatively obscure junior minister. Moreover, it was immediate and uncomplicated (see Ch. 5.1 for a brief outline).

4

Resignations for Personal Fault: Political Errors

4.1. NICHOLAS FAIRBAIRN: AN ERROR OF JUDGEMENT

Background

On 20 January 1982 Nicholas Fairbairn, Solicitor-General for Scotland, gave a statement to the Scottish Press about the decision not to prosecute three men arrested for a brutal attack and rape in Glasgow. The rape had increased public concern over the apparent rise in the incidence of the crime, at a time when many believed the existing law was inadequate in securing prosecutions. Complaints were also made about the lack of a consistent sentencing policy and the non-custodial nature of the punishments, the failure of the police to deal properly with women's allegations of rape and to pursue the crime with their normal vigour, and the seeming reluctance of the Crown at times to bring prosecutions.

The decision not to prosecute in the Glasgow rape case was taken, it would seem, by the Crown Office and the Crown Counsel without reference either to Lord Mackay, the Lord Advocate and senior law officer, or to Nicholas Fairbairn, the Solicitor-General. Initial reports stated that it had been abandoned because psychiatrists had advised that the woman would suffer permanent mental damage if she gave evidence. Indeed, at the time the decision was made, she was also physically unable to attend court. Subsequently, however, the victim stated that she was prepared to appear in court, but it was too late. Letters had already been sent to the suspects, stating that there would be no prosecution. Such letters closed the door to future action by the Crown.

The announcement that there would be no prosecution caused public outrage, and seemed to confirm all the complaints about the inadequacy of the law and the attitude of the police and the courts. Morever, it damaged the image of Scotland's independent prosecution service. As Jack Ashley commented:

The widespread outrage at the decision has shattered the cosy image of Scotland's independent prosecutors, the procurators-fiscal, nurtured by the actor, Iain Cuthbertson, in the popular television series Sutherland's Law and has brought obloquy on the head of the prosecuting system's chief law officer, the Lord Advocate.[1]

The decision was rightly laid at the door of the Lord Advocate, for he was the senior law officer and responsible to Parliament. If Fairbairn had stayed silent, or restricted himself to repeating statements by Lord Mackay, it is probable that he would not have become embroiled in the affair. However, the comments made by Fairbairn to the Press fanned the flames and served to direct attention to him rather than to the Lord Advocate. The *Glasgow Daily Record* reported Fairbairn as having said that there would be no prosecution because 'the prosecution did not have sufficient, competent or available evidence to stand any chance of a conviction'.[2] Fairbairn also stated, according to the *Record*, that the decision not to prosecute was a correct one, and that the victim's state of mind and her ability to give evidence in court had been irrelevant. This led to strong condemnation by Members of Parliament, who now had an individual upon whom to focus their attack. Fairbairn was criticized for the validity of the decision not to prosecute and for his failure to make a statement to the House before speaking to the Press. On 21 January he resigned.

Factors Influencing Fairbairn's Resignation

Parliament

The reaction of Members of Parliament forced Fairbairn to the dispatch box, where he had to satisfy the House on three counts. First, Members required reassurance about the ability and willingness of the law and the courts to deal with rape cases effectively and fairly. This, of course, was not Fairbairn's responsibility but that of the Home Secretary, William Whitelaw, who the day before

---

[1] *The Times*, 21 Jan. 1982.   [2] Ibid.

had agreed that all rapists should receive custodial sentences and had indicated that he would accept relevant back-bench amendments to the Criminal Justice Bill, then before Parliament. The concern over rape cases in general was not abated, however, and was reflected in the attitude of the House to Fairbairn.

Secondly, Members wished to be told the details behind the decision not to prosecute in the Glasgow rape case. There was a general feeling that the discretion available to the law officers had been misused. Thirdly, the House wanted an apology from Fairbairn for his behaviour in talking to the Press before informing Parliament, and an explanation of the comments he was reported to have made.

Fairbairn failed to satisfy the House. He did apologize, but Francis Pym, Leader of the House, had preceded him in making a statement on behalf of the government, and thus Fairbairn's apology lost any impact. Fairbairn read a statement from Lord Mackay which did little to explain the decision not to prosecute—details of such decisions are considered confidential—although it stated that in future all such decisions in rape cases would be referred to the Lord Advocate for approval. It was Fairbairn's task to convince Members of Parliament that the decision, which he had supported in the Press, was a reasonable one and that there had not been a miscarriage of justice. This he failed to do.

Moreover, probably more important from the point of view of his career, Fairbairn failed to give a satisfactory account of his reported remarks. He denied that he had said the victim's state of mind was 'irrelevant' to the decision not to prosecute, and told the House that her health had been a crucial factor. But the House was in no mood to accept that he had been misquoted by the Press. In addition, he did not, or could not, explain a fundamental difference between Lord Mackay's statement and his reported remarks. The Lord Advocate's statement said: '[the] view taken by Crown Counsel [was] that in the light of all circumstances, in the absence of the complainer, it would not have been proper to proceed . . .'[3] However, Fairbairn was reported as saying that there was insufficient evidence for a prosecution. There was an obvious and an important difference between the two statements.

[3] HC Deb., 21 Jan. 1982, col. 438.

The Opposition demanded Fairbairn's resignation, and neither the government nor Conservative back-benchers resisted the calls.

The Prime Minister and senior ministers

The 1922 Committee appeared to have no hand in Fairbairn's resignation. It seems that there was no need for the views of back-benchers to be transmitted officially. The decision was taken quickly at the highest level that Fairbairn should go. The Prime Minister, Leader of the House (Francis Pym), the Government Chief Whip (Michael Jopling), and the Secretary of State for Scotland (George Younger) were all reported to be displeased with Fairbairn's remarks to the Press.[4] It seems that the Prime Minister was particularly concerned that his comments demonstrated a lack of legal judgement, for Fairbairn had made public observations about the evidence in the Glasgow case while there was still a possibility of a private prosecution. According to *The Times*: 'Former colleagues at the Scottish bar and on the bench considered this most indiscreet, and Mrs Thatcher consulted the senior Scottish law officer, Lord Mackay, the Lord Advocate, before deciding that Mr Fairbairn should go.'[5]

The removal of cover so quickly by the Prime Minister and her clear desire that Fairbairn should leave office demonstrate the narrow line between resignation and dismissal. Presumably, if Fairbairn had hesitated, he would have been dismissed. He chose, however, to take the 'honourable' way out. It may be more accurate to see such cases as constructive dismissal rather than resignation, for, once a minister has lost the support of his prime minister, he has little option but to leave the government.

The Press

The Press was already running a campaign which featured the public concern about rape cases and their treatment in the courts. The decision in the Glasgow case was portrayed as another example of the seeming inadequacies of the system. Nicholas Fairbairn's statements, reported in the *Glasgow Daily Record*, were picked up and run as front-page news in the English papers. The case moved too swiftly, however, for the Press also to campaign for Fairbairn's resignation.

---

[4] *The Times*, 22 Jan. 1982.   [5] Ibid.

Fairbairn's Resignation Classified

Fairbairn resigned on 21 January after making his statement to the House. His letter of resignation read:

I have been considering my position following the apology which preceded the statement I made in the House this afternoon about the Glasgow rape case.

I wish to make it abundantly clear that I am entirely satisfied that the Crown Office and Crown Counsel handled the delicate decision in the Glasgow rape case with total propriety. However, I appreciate that in my dealings with the press I may have made errors of judgement. In the circumstances I have decided that I ought no longer to remain in office as Solicitor General for Scotland.[6]

The letter was a clear expression of support for his department. There was no suggestion of departmental error, nor was Fairbairn accepting vicarious responsibility for fault that the public and Members of Parliament perceived to exist. The reason he gave for his resignation was his personal misjudgement in talking to the Press.

It is difficult to assess whether there was departmental fault, for the full reasoning behind the decision not to prosecute was never known. Circumstantial evidence would suggest, however, that there had been misjudgement within the department, and Lord Mackay's assurance that in future all such decisions should be referred to him may confirm this. Moreover, even if the decision was a reasonable one in relation to the law, it was politically unacceptable and Lord Mackay was politically accountable for it. It is likely, therefore, that, had Fairbairn not spoken to the Press, the pressure would have been on Lord Mackay. Certainly there was no constitutional requirement for Fairbairn, a junior minister, to shoulder the blame.

However, there was a requirement for him to accept responsibility for his own remarks to the Press. Such behaviour was indiscreet. Moreover, Fairbairn was at fault, if, as it seems, his comments were inaccurate, and to this extent his resignation could be coupled with that of Edwina Currie.[7] Whether the fault was sufficiently serious by itself to warrant calls for his resignation is doubtful. There were, however, other factors which may have influenced the political actors in their judgement of seriousness,

[6] Ibid.   [7] See Ch. 4.2.

for this indiscretion occurred shortly after Fairbairn's personal life had come under Press scrutiny following an attempted suicide in which it had been his misfortune to be involved.[8]

Moreover, Fairbairn's statement to the Press before he had addressed the House or before Lord Mackay had given a statement in the Lords was seen by Parliament as behaviour unacceptable in a minister. A popular minister, or one with an unsullied record, would no doubt have been forgiven after an apology; the error he had made would not have been considered serious enough to warrant resignation. But Fairbairn appeared to have no body of support in the House.

There were also suggestions that senior Conservatives were already campaigning for his dismissal. Fairbairn's indiscretion in talking to the Press over the Glasgow rape case and the subsequent publicity which he again attracted helped to strengthen their case. Grant Jordan suggests that in fact there was a conspiracy.

This version of events then suggests that instead of Fairbairn being driven from Office by the massed concern of the House, Pym engineered 'a squeeze'. Through the 'usual channels' (i.e. the Whips machinery) he asked Michael Foot to request a statement. Pym's statement BEFORE Fairbairn spoke put Fairbairn in a very bad light; it was an episode designed to draw attention to Fairbairn.[9]

Fairbairn's resignation can therefore be seen to have three constitutional components. First, Fairbairn had been at fault as a minister in giving an inaccurate statement to the Press about departmental matters. Secondly, he had been at fault as a minister in failing to honour his obligations to Parliament; he had accounted to the newspapers and not to the House. Thirdly, this was the second incident within a month which had made him the focus of Press attention and which some saw as raising doubts about his suitability as a minister.

The three components produced a political judgement of 'compound' fault which was serious enough to warrant the request for Fairbairn's resignation, if it was not volunteered, and which could be used to political advantage by the government. It would serve

---

[8] See e.g. *The Times*, 23, 24, and 29 Dec. 1981.
[9] G. Jordan, 'Individual Ministerial Responsibility: Absolute or Obsolete?', in D. McCrone (ed.), *Scottish Yearbook* (Edinburgh: Unit for Study of Government of Scotland, 1983), 132.

to remove some of the pressure on the government over the Scottish rape case in particular, where Fairbairn's resignation would be seen by the public as an admission of responsibility, and it might also reduce some of the public anxiety over rape cases in general, with the government appearing to take firm action. Fairbairn may therefore be seen as a political scapegoat. This does not mean, however, that his resignation was not constitutionally required, but rather that constitutional requirements provided a platform for political opportunism.

4.2. EDWINA CURRIE: SALMONELLA IN EGGS

Background

On 3 December 1988 Mrs Edwina Currie, Under-Secretary of State for Health, stated, during an interview broadcast by ITN: 'We do warn people now that most of the egg production of this country, sadly, is now infected with salmonella.'[10]

Her statement was understood to mean that most eggs were contaminated, an interpretation that she did nothing to contradict. Indeed, on 6 December she confirmed the remark on BBC, despite an instruction from her senior minister to refrain from further comment, and despite the storm it had already caused both in the House and in the Press the previous day. The effect of her comments was a dramatic fall in egg sales. This was followed by two weeks of political controversy, which focused on the policy issue of food quality, and the constitutional issue of accountability.

For most of this time the requirements of individual ministerial responsibility were overridden by collective responsibility, which worked to protect both Mrs Currie and the government. Considerable damage had been done to the egg-producing industry, and any admission of culpability or acceptance of responsibility by the junior minister would strengthen the case for substantial compensation, the bill for which would have to be met by the taxpayer. This would harm not only the reputation of Edwina Currie but also that of the government. Under these circumstances the

---

[10] *First Report from the Agriculture Committee: Salmonella in Eggs* (1988–9), vol. i, HC108–I, HMSO, para. 96.

convention of individual ministerial responsibility, with its requirement for accountability, was an embarrassment. Hence the collective took over the responsibility from the individual, both to ensure the containment of information and, it was hoped, the loyalty of back-benchers.

The government's strategy was to deflect attention away from Mrs Currie's controversial remarks by focusing on the advice given by the Chief Medical Officer, Sir Donald Acheson, and thus to depoliticize and de-personalize the affair. Mrs Currie was instructed by her senior minister, Kenneth Clarke, not to speak on the matter, an instruction given after consultation by telephone with John MacGregor, the Minister for Agriculture, who was in Brussels.[11] This imposition of silence was later criticized by the Agriculture Committee, both for its naïvety and because it prevented explanation or correction by Mrs Currie of her comments. The Committee, however, recognized the collective nature of the decision, and thus saw it as 'a failure of government, and not just a single minister . . .'.[12]

By 16 December, however, the collective approach was unsustainable and the cover was withdrawn, leaving Mrs Currie exposed to the requirements of the convention of individual ministerial responsibility. Parliament, the 1922 Committee, and the Press all played a part in removing the cover, aided by the egg producers, who were backed by the National Farmers' Union.

Factors Influencing Edwina Currie's Resignation

Parliament

On 5 December the House expressed its concern about Mrs Currie's remarks. There were calls for clarification and indeed for her resignation. Mr Robin Cooke was quick to point out the inconsistency between previous guidance from the Ministry of Health, which stated that the risk of any individual egg being infected was likely to be very small, and Mrs Currie's comments. He asked:

Which of these statements reflects the Department's view? Is the right hon. and learned gentleman content to preside over a Department that

---

[11] *First Report from the Agriculture Committee: Salmonella in Eggs: Minutes of Evidence and Appendices* (1988–9), vol. ii, HC108–II, HMSO, Q575.
[12] HC108–I (1988–9), para. 100.

issues two totally and utterly contradictory views in the space of two weeks? . . . Surely it must be clear that the hon. Lady's embarrassment quotient exceeds her entertainment value? Is it not about time he removed such a major obstacle to our taking his Department seriously?[13]

Mr Clarke, however, insisted there was no inconsistency and defended Mrs Currie fully: 'My hon. Friend the Under-Secretary of State for Health is an extremely valuable member of the team in this Department and the Government. It may be that many hon. Members are a little envious of her natural gift for obtaining publicity.'[14] Moreover, when asked to declare his unequivocal support for Mrs Currie's comments, Kenneth Clarke answered: 'My hon. Friend was quite right to answer a question put to her on another occasion, stressing the concern that we feel about infection in eggs and drawing attention to the advice the Department had already been giving over the previous few months.'[15]

The collective cover was therefore quickly provided by Clarke; all criticisms of Edwina Currie were deflected, and the advice already given by the department emphasized. However, it was clear that members from both sides of the House were angry over Mrs Currie's statement, that was variously described as 'rash', 'unsustainable', and 'half-baked, half-boiled, irrational'.[16] Their concern was over apparent contradictions which confused the consumer, but more particularly over the effect on the egg-producing industry.

The concern for the egg producers was shown again the following day by Robin Maxwell-Hyslop, who spoke of the harm done to the poultry industry by 'a junior minister with an uncontrollable tongue and an insatiable desire for self-advertisement'.[17] He went on to ask the Prime Minister what action she intended to take over Mrs Currie, but Mrs Thatcher side-stepped the question, using the opportunity to refer to the advice of the Chief Medical Officer and indicating that she had eaten eggs for lunch. The government was clearly hoping that reassurance in general, coupled with advice for the young, old, and infirm, would lay the matter to rest.

The strategy proved to be unsuccessful, however, because of a

---

[13] HC Deb., 5 Dec. 1989, col. 20.   [14] Ibid.
[15] Ibid., col. 22.
[16] Ibid., col. 19 (Hal Miller), col. 20 (Peter Emery), col. 22 (Roy Beggs).
[17] Ibid., 6 Dec. 1989, col. 169.

continued attack both by the Opposition parties and by many Conservative back-benchers. The government's refusal to do more than repeat the advice of the Chief Medical Officer served to increase suspicions that the full truth was not being told; either Mrs Currie's comments had been wrong, in which case the egg producers should be compensated, or they were right, in which case the health of consumers was being put at risk to ensure the profits of the producers. Moreover, the issue was becoming wider, embracing the relationship between the Ministry of Agriculture and the Department of Health and the whole matter of food hygiene. The general concern of the House was heightened by the desire of the Opposition to embarrass the government, and the personal animosity that many Conservative back-benchers felt for Mrs Currie.

On Thursday, 15 December, David Steel stated that Members from all sides of the House were intending to vote against the Ministerial and Other Salaries Order the following Tuesday, if Mrs Currie were still in office. He drew the attention of the Leader of the House, John Wakeham, to early-day motion 200, which stated:

That this House does not approve the draft Ministerial and Other Salaries Order 1988, which was laid before this House on 8th December, on the grounds that the Order provides for an increase in the salary of the Parliamentary Under-Secretary at the Department of Health ... whose performance of her Ministerial duties, in general, and whose damaging remarks on the risks of contracting salmonella from the consumption of eggs in particular, have rendered her unfit to continue to hold ministerial office.[18]

Mr Steel stated that Mrs Currie's 'careless talk' had cost jobs, caused bankruptcies, and resulted in the slaughter of chickens. He added: 'On any basis of the doctrine of ministerial responsibility, the hon. Lady should, by now, have been relieved of her job.'[19]

There were many in the House who supported this appeal to the constitutional convention. However, Mr Steel was probably incorrect to speak of the applicability of the convention 'on any basis'. As a junior minister, Currie, like Fairbairn, did not bear responsibility for the department. She could not, therefore, be expected to account to Parliament for matters within the department, even if

---

[18] Ibid., 15 Dec. 1989, col. 1095.   [19] Ibid.

they were within her area of concern, unless directed to do so by her Secretary of State. This, however, did not absolve her of her personal responsibility when acting as a minister, as distinct from responsibility for the acts of officials, and here the doctrine of individual ministerial responsibility was applicable.

Personal animosity and the agriculture lobby aside, there was indignation within the House at the failure of Mrs Currie to account for her comments, and a feeling that she should pay the price for her misconceived statements and resign. The constitutional requirement of resignation for ministerial error coincided with the political requirement for Mrs Currie's resignation to appease both the farming lobby and Members of Parliament. The calls for resignation from the House of Commons were not in themselves responsible for Edwina Currie's departure from government, but the strength of feeling within the House, particularly from government back-benchers, contributed to the removal of the collective cover.

The 1922 Committee

On the evening of 15 December the eighteen members of the Executive of the 1922 Committee met in Commons Committee Room 14 to discuss whether they should call for Currie's resignation. It was by no means a unanimous decision, some members believing that they should rally round the minister, but the wishes of a 'vociferous minority' prevailed.[20] After the meeting of the Executive, the weekly meeting of the rank and file was held, but Mrs Currie was never mentioned, and some Members of Parliament thought she might have survived. However, Cranley Onslow, the Chairman of the Committee, later informed David Waddington, the Government Chief Whip, of the Committee's decision.

The 1922 Committee's decision can therefore be seen as sealing Mrs Currie's fate. It needs to be noted, however, that the decision was taken by the most senior members, not the rank and file, and thus belies the suggestion that government back-benchers have taken over the constitutional responsibility of the Opposition in bringing the government to account. Indeed, back-benchers with ministerial aspirations are well advised to be totally acquiescent and to act only in accord with the wishes of the whips, even, it

[20] *Sunday Times*, 18 Dec. 1989.

has been suggested, to the extent of supporting them in the removal of more independently minded back-benchers from official positions on the 1922 Executive Committee.[21]

This may suggest that the Leader of the House and the Chief Whip orchestrated the Executive Committee action against Currie in order to remove pressure from the government, some of which was coming from its own back-benches. Alternatively, the decision to call for her resignation may have been taken because of personal animosity towards Mrs Currie and because of the self-interest of senior back-benchers, some of whom had farming constituencies. They were no doubt under pressure from their constituents to restore confidence in the egg industry, and pragmatic considerations—the need to get re-elected—thus prevailed.

The Prime Minister

The Prime Minister, it seems, did not wish Edwina Currie to resign. This was not just because resignations reflect badly upon governments (and on the personal management skills of the prime minister), but because of a personal liking, or at least admiration, for the junior minister. This was demonstrated by the half-hour interview granted to Mrs Currie when she handed in her resignation, and by the Prime Minister's expression of 'great personal sadness' upon the resignation.

However, events suggest that the collective line was about to be redrawn. Indeed, shortly after Mrs Currie's resignation on 16 December, John MacGregor, Minister for Agriculture, made an interim statement in the House about plans for financial help to the egg producers. Such a scheme, which envisaged the expenditure of up to £19 million, was an admission of serious fault consequent on Mrs Currie's remarks. Her resignation was therefore necessary before MacGregor's announcement. He could then state that 'it was not the case that most eggs are infected',[22] although it was not until 19 December that MacGregor categorically stated,

---

[21] Hugo Young (*Guardian*, 22 Dec. 1988) stated that there was not 'the slightest doubt' that Wakeham, as Leader of the House, and Waddington, government Chief Whip, were responsible for the removal of Michael Mates and Dame Jill Knight from office in the 1922 Committee. Dame Jill had campaigned unsuccessfully against the imposition of dental and eye test charges. Michael Mates had campaigned, again unsuccessfully, for an amendment to poll tax legislation.

[22] HC Deb., 16 Dec. 1989, col. 1280.

'it is not the case that most egg production is infected'.[23] Mrs Thatcher must have been aware of the implications of both the compensation scheme and MacGregor's statement.

Mrs Thatcher may have regretted the resignation of Edwina Currie. She may have regretted even more the appearance of having given in to the farming lobby and to the Opposition in Parliament, but she was unable to keep a collective line which would protect the junior minister without inflicting further damage upon the government.

The Press

Mrs Currie's statement about eggs became the media event of December 1988. Indeed, during the select committee inquiry into salmonella, it was suggested that Mrs Currie's resignation was a direct result of the continued media attention to this remark:

It was not history that elevated that sentence, it was the media the day after. Attention was focused upon that sentence. The refusal of Mrs Currie to clarify that sentence . . . led directly to her subsequent resignation because of the continued media attention . . .[24]

This may be an exaggeration of the power of the media. It is probably more accurate to see Mrs Currie's resignation as an indirect result of media attention, rather than seeing the media as extracting accountability. Nevertheless, both Press and television gave extensive coverage to Mrs Currie and to salmonella. They also started to delve deeper, examining the relationship of the National Farmers' Union (NFU) with the Ministry of Agriculture, the power of the agriculture lobby, cutbacks in research, and food hygiene in general.[25] The requirement of the media was for information with 'news value', and when the government refused to provide it, both Press and television sought what they could, from whatever sources would provide it. By so doing, they kept the topic fresh in the public's mind and ensured that Members of Parliament would not let it slip from the agenda.

Attitudes towards Mrs Currie in the Press were mixed. The *Guardian* considered she had acted irresponsibly. Others—for

[23] Ibid., 19 Dec. 1989, col. 31.
[24] HC108–II (1988–9), Q578 (Mr Calum MacDonald).
[25] See e.g. *Independent*, 17 Dec. 1989.

example, the *Observer* and the *Sunday Times*—believed her comments had some foundation but were strongly critical of her failure to explain them, as was the *Daily Telegraph*, which stated that her exaggerations made her unsuitable for office. The *Independent*, however, firmly supported Mrs Currie as the champion of the consumer. It reserved its criticisms for the government's handling of the affair.

The agricultural lobby

Much was made in the Press of the strength of the agricultural lobby and its part in Mrs Currie's downfall. The egg producers, supported by the NFU, certainly campaigned for Mrs Currie's resignation, believing that it would be seen by the public as an admission of fault, and would therefore help to restore confidence in eggs.

The campaign was run in the Press but also at Westminster. The NFU does not officially sponsor Conservative Members of Parliament, but it has a close relationship with perhaps fifty members from rural constituencies.[26] However, what is expected from these members is unknown and indeed disputed.[27] It is known, however, that the NFU regional offices and the egg producers put pressure on their local MPs, and that some two hundred Members received letters from the NFU and many were given telephone briefings. David Waddington, the Government Chief Whip, was individually lobbied in his constituency in the Ribble Valley by producers, supported by the NFU, while Simon Gourlay, the NFU president, wrote to Mrs Thatcher and met John MacGregor in Brussels. He made clear to both of them that the NFU would encourage the egg producers to sue the government for damages.

On 16 December, the day of her resignation, Mrs Currie received the first writ from Thames Valley Eggs, which read:

The plaintiff's claim is for damages for slander of goods and/or malicious falsehood and/or negligent misstatement in an interview broadcast by

---

[26] The increase in suburbia suggests a decrease in the number of constituencies where the NFU has a major influence.

[27] The *Independent* reported Bernard Hobeche, the NFU's parliamentary adviser, as saying that selected MPs were being kept closely informed of all developments. One of these MPs was named as Sir Hal Miller. However, Sir Hal subsequently made a statement in the House repudiating this claim (HC Deb., 19 Dec. 1989, col. 167).

ITN on Saturday, 3rd December 1988 and repeated in an interview during the one o'clock news programme broadcast by the BBC on 6th December 1988.[28]

In all there were twelve writs served on the junior minister. She, of course, did not have to assume responsibility herself for defending the actions. Even after resignation, the principle of collective responsibility provides for the government to defend such actions, unless comments have been made in a private capacity, rather than as a government minister, or unless they are party political.[29]

The campaign by the egg producers and the NFU seemed to have the desired effect—Mrs Currie resigned and substantial compensation, in the form of an intervention package, was paid. However, this may have owed less to the public campaign (which to an extent backfired by raising questions about the farmers' lack of concern for the health of the consumer) than to the closeness of the relationship between the Ministry of Agriculture and the NFU and the egg producers, many of whom had directors with considerable influence within the Ministry.[30]

Edwina Currie's Resignation Classified

Mrs Currie resigned on Friday, 16 December. In her letter of resignation she neither explained her remarks nor apologized for them. She resigned because she considered that 'in all the circumstances this is the best course'.[31] There was no mention of her responsibility as a minister, nor recognition that others, if not herself, believed she had been at fault. Mrs Currie gave no indication that she saw her resignation as a requirement of the convention of individual ministerial responsibility.

---

[28] *Independent*, 17 Dec. 1989.

[29] The Treasury Solicitor, *Independent*, 17 Dec. 1989.

[30] The egg industry, with its £1 billion turnover, had directors with considerable influence in the Ministry. The Chairman of Dalgety, which owns Dean Farm Eggs, was Sir Peter Carey, who was permanent secretary at the DTI, 1976–83, while John Biffen was a non-executive director of J. Bibby & Sons. Moreover, the poultry-feed industry, which was also affected by the drop in egg sales, was also well endowed with directors who were likely to have inside connections. For example, Unilever, which owns BOCM Silcock, feed suppliers, listed Lord Hunt of Tamworth as an advisory director. It was, therefore, little wonder that the lobbying appeared so effective and little wonder that subsequently there was disquiet about the influence of the producers. (Information from *Sunday Times*, *Observer*, and *Independent*.)

[31] *Independent*, 17 Dec. 1989.

However, the convention would appear to require resignation when a minister has made a serious misjudgement, and this is what Mrs Currie had done. She was right to bring to the attention of the public the dangers of salmonella, but the way in which she did this caused alarm, even panic, and unnecessary (although exaggerated) financial damage to egg producers. In her defence it can be said that her remarks were misinterpreted. She did not say that most eggs were infected, but that most egg production was infected. However, she did nothing to correct the interpretation, and in any case 'most' was imprecise and misleading, and the difference between 'egg production' and 'eggs' seems slight, and likely to lead to the conclusion that, if the production process were contaminated, then so were the eggs.

The first time Mrs Currie clarified her remarks was in a letter, dated 25 January 1989, to the Agriculture Committee which was inquiring into salmonella in eggs. She stated:

> I did NOT mean and did not say, as was incorrectly reported in the Press, that most of the EGGS in this country are infected. I intended to explain that a significant number of the egg-laying hens in many of the egg-laying flocks in this country are infected with salmonella.[32]

This is not only a statement of what she meant to say and a comment on the misinterpretation of her remarks, but also a retreat from what she actually said—a move away from 'most' egg production to 'a significant number' or 'many'.

It is not clear if Mrs Currie had any evidence for her statement or whether it was unsubstantiated. She told the Committee: 'I have always based everything that I have said in public as a Minister on published information.'[33]

However, she did not disclose the published information from which she had drawn the conclusion that 'most egg production' was infected. The Committee reported: 'Her refusal to retract the key word "most" has led people to suppose that she was privy to a body of information not generally available. We are satisfied, both from her own assurances and from other evidence, that this was not the case.'[34]

It would seem, therefore, that Mrs Currie had no firm foundation for her statements. No information publicly available at the

---

[32] HC108-II (1988–9), p. 183.
[33] Ibid., Q593.   [34] HC108-I (1988–9) para. 98.

time indicated that salmonella was so extensive as to justify the use of 'most'. The Agriculture Committee concluded that Mrs Currie 'inadvertently mis-stated the position', adding, 'she could, and should, have made this clear'.[35]

The consequences of her remarks were immediate and, with the drop in egg sales, measurable. This put Mrs Currie in a special category. Frequently the mistakes or misjudgements of ministers are only realized after they have left government or have been moved to another position—as, for instance, with Lord Young and the sale of Rover.[36] It is also rare for a mistake to be quantifiable and to have financial consequences for an identifiable group of people, rather than being less specifically damaging to taxpayers generally. Furthermore, most injudicious statements are made to the Press on a non-attributable basis and can be denied, if necessary, to avoid the minister's being held responsible.[37]

However, Mrs Currie might have saved herself had she explained her comments and corrected the misinterpretation of them. She did speak once, two days later, but, instead of rectifying the misunderstandings, she confirmed her statement. Thereafter she was silent, acting on instructions from her senior minister, Kenneth Clarke. As a junior minister, Mrs Currie's constitutional position was different from that of her Secretary of State. She was accountable, not directly to Parliament, but to the Secretary of State. He was constitutionally accountable to Parliament for all the affairs of the department, although he could, and did, expect Mrs Currie to represent the department in matters of public health. Because Mrs Currie always spoke on such matters, and was clearly identified with them, her failure now to account to the House for her comments was seen as a political ploy rather than constitutional correctness. Moreover, regardless of the constitutional position concerning departmental accountability, junior ministers are

---

[35] HC108–I (1988–9), para. 98.   [36] See Ch. 8.2.

[37] Such an instance involved Nigel Lawson, then Chancellor of the Exchequer, who on 5 November 1988 gave a non-attributable briefing at which the possibility of means testing some pension benefits was raised. This created a storm of protest when it was printed in the Sunday papers, and Lawson felt obliged to bring forward plans to help poorer pensioners, which may not have been intended without the reduction of benefits of others. He was able, however, to deny that the idea of means testing had originated from him, and, although it was widely believed that he was the source of the story, there was no direct link between the damage and Mr Lawson. The situation was very different with Mrs Currie.

accountable for their personal behaviour, and Members of Parliament and the public could therefore reasonably expect that she should account for her own actions or statements. It is not known whether Mrs Currie agreed with the imposition of silence, although she was subsequently to say: 'I'm sad that I didn't have an opportunity to put them [the words] right.'[38]

This suggests she would have preferred to speak out and admit her mistake, but the evidence, particularly her appearance before the select committee, when she was uncooperative, indicates that a retraction, apology, or even an explanation was not at the forefront of her mind. Moreover, she did have the chance to put the record straight, two days after her original statement, but this she failed to do. Silence, however, did not serve her cause, nor was it in the interests of accountability.

The decision by the government not to correct misinterpretations or issue denials seems to have been intended as damage limitation, perhaps in the hope that the comments would be seen as another example of Mrs Currie overstepping the mark, and that, after an initial reaction by the public, all would return to normal. (After all, fish and chip shops had not gone bankrupt in Newcastle after Mrs Currie had told Northerners to cut down on their intake of fat.) It may have been believed that a denial that most eggs were infected would lead to a requirement for the government officially to quantify the risk of salmonella in eggs. Even though this would be lower than 'most', the fact that it was official rather than from the Minister for Health, known for her provocative statements, might cause even greater concern.

In the event this question and many others were asked in any case, and the government's attempt to prevent accountability failed. This was clearly an instance of the government acting with doubtful constitutional propriety by imposing the solidarity and confidentiality of collective responsibility in order to hide inefficiencies and mistakes that might be revealed if the requirements of individual ministerial responsibility were met.

Nevertheless the resignation is still an example of individual ministerial responsibility, even if it was forced for political reasons. In the end Mrs Currie had to take responsibility for her mistake as a minister and resign. Moreover, even though she did

---

[38] *Independent*, 14 June 1990.

not consider herself to be acting in deference to constitutional principles, her resignation accorded with constitutional practice. There were also indications in Parliament of undertones of constitutional obligation. These reinforced the political requirements. However, on Mrs Currie's part there was no pretence of a voluntary sacrifice in the cause of public accountability. If Lord Carrington's resignation can be seen as a constitutional resignation that suited the political circumstances,[39] Mrs Currie's resignation can be seen as a political resignation which fitted the constitutional requirements.

4.3. NICHOLAS RIDLEY: INDIVIDUAL OR COLLECTIVE RESPONSIBILITY?

Background

On 12 July 1990 the *Spectator* magazine published an interview with Nicholas Ridley, Secretary of State for Trade and Industry, in which he stated his views about the reunification of Germany, European monetary union, and the dominance of the European Community by Germany. It was not, however, Ridley's concern about German domination which caused the ensuing uproar, but the way in which this concern was expressed and the anti-German sentiments it conveyed. Nicholas Ridley spoke of monetary union as 'a German racket designed to take over the whole of Europe' and of the strength of the German economy resulting from the 'habits' of the Germans, who, he maintained, were 'already running most of the Community'.[40]

His comments concerning the institutions of the European Community were also less than flattering. He dismissed the Commission as 'seventeen unelected reject politicians' and accused the 'supine' European Parliament of 'pandering' to the Commission. He even included the French in his vitriolic attack, accusing them of 'behaving like poodles to the Germans'. However, most offensive was his comment that giving up sovereignty to the EC was akin to giving it to Adolf Hitler, and his suggestion that he would

---

[39] See Ch. 6.1.
[40] D. Lawson, 'Saying the Unsayable About the Germans: An Interview with Nicholas Ridley', *Spectator*, 14 July 1990.

perhaps 'prefer shelters and the chance to fight back' to being taken over by economics.

The reaction to the Ridley interview in Westminster was one of outrage, and the statements of condemnation were not confined to British politicians. There was understandable concern expressed in Bonn and by British Euro MPs. Even the Governor of the Bank of England, Sir Robin Leigh-Pemberton, who usually remains outside the political arena, felt moved to comment that the sentiments expressed were 'intemperate' and 'misplaced'.[41] There were also signs of concern in the City, which was worried about continued divisions within the government over entry to the European Exchange Rate Mechanism.

Ridley himself was in Hungary and therefore not available for comment. However, during the morning a statement was issued on his behalf which stated: 'On reflection, I very much regret the remarks reported in the *Spectator* and unreservedly withdraw them.'[42] It seems that, in Ridley's absence, the statement was drawn up by Charles Powell, the Prime Minister's private secretary, and then passed through the Department of Trade and Industry (DTI) to the Secretary of State.

The retraction enabled the Prime Minister to disassociate herself from the remarks, when she appeared in the House for Prime Minister's Question Time, without completely isolating herself from Ridley.[43] It was not, however, effective in saving Ridley's ministerial career. During the next two days pressure mounted from the party in Westminster for his resignation, and when Nicholas Ridley returned to England late on the Friday evening, it was to find that the question being asked was not whether he would resign, but when.

In the event Ridley surprised most people by delaying his resignation until late on Saturday afternoon. It would seem that a small group within the Conservative Party tried to persuade him to stay and that he was bolstered by the support the tabloids suggested existed at constituency level. Moreover, he needed to be convinced that the Prime Minister herself wanted him to resign. It seems that this wish was conveyed to him during the fifteen-minute telephone conversation he had with Mrs Thatcher, and his resignation was announced from Number Ten soon after 5.30.[44]

---

[41] *The Times*, 13 July 1990.   [42] Ibid.
[43] HC Deb., 12 July 1990, col. 449.   [44] *Observer*, 15 July 1990.

Factors Influencing Ridley's Resignation

Parliament

It was the Prime Minister and not Nicholas Ridley who faced questions from the Opposition over the interview in the *Spectator*. She disassociated herself and the government from Ridley's remarks, but then came under pressure from Neil Kinnock to dismiss her Secretary of State. Mr Kinnock argued that, if the views expressed by Mr Ridley were not those of the government, then, 'Under the terms of collective responsibility as everybody understands it, a secretary of state who expresses views strongly and graphically that are contrary to the views of the government, that secretary of state is sacked.'[45]

This statement (despite its grammatical awkwardness) indicates the overlap between individual and collective responsibility, for Kinnock could alternatively have argued that, under the terms of individual ministerial responsibility, a minister who commits a serious error of political judgement may be required by Parliament to resign. The emphasis here is on personal fault, which few could deny had occurred, rather than on a collective view held by the government. Kinnock's chosen ground of collective rather than individual ministerial responsibility was no doubt intended to heighten the debate over whether in fact there was a collective line concerning the British government's attitude to Germany and the European Community or whether divisions remained within the Cabinet.

This was a point taken up by Mr Paddy Ashdown, who suggested that Nicholas Ridley's remarks revealed a 'deep and irreconcilable split' on Europe in the Cabinet. Moreover, he contended that the failure of the Prime Minister to sack Ridley was tantamount to condoning his comments.[46]

Mrs Thatcher's response to attacks upon Ridley, and indeed upon herself, was to counter with her own understanding of the constitution as it applied to the House rather than to government practices.

The Secretary of State has expressed his very great regret and unreservedly withdrawn his remarks. They do not represent the Government's view or indeed my view. I have always understood that it is the custom

---

[45] HC Deb., 12 July 1990, col. 449.   [46] Ibid., col. 450.

of the House when remarks have been apologised for and unreservedly withdrawn, as they have in this case, that withdrawal is gracefully accepted.[47]

Mrs Thatcher's understanding of the position was correct in certain circumstances. When ministers or Members have misled the House or have committed a breach of privilege by using unparliamentary language or by abusing the privilege of free speech, Parliament may well 'gracefully' accept an apology or withdrawal of the remarks. However, Ridley had neither misled the House nor abused any of its privileges. He had made comments which Parliament considered were incompatible with his position as a minister. Moreover, his apology and retraction were not made in a personal statement to the House, but in a general release from the department.

The 1922 Committee

The strength and influence of the 1922 Committee, or more significantly its Executive, was again evident in Ridley's resignation. At the weekly meeting on the Thursday evening the main concern was that Ridley's remarks had reopened the division within the Conservative Party about Europe. To prevent this division becoming more apparent, discussion of the Secretary of State's remarks was limited to ten minutes, and Members were told to inform the whips about their views.[48]

However, it would seem that for the sake of party unity the Executive of the Committee had already decided that Ridley should go. Indeed, Cranley Onslow, the Chairman of the Committee, had earlier indicated as much to the Prime Minister,[49] and when the Executive met prior to the full meeting, only two of its eighteen members were prepared to support Ridley.[50] Thus, as with Currie, it was not government back-benchers as a body that decided Ridley's fate, but the senior representatives.

The Prime Minister

The Prime Minister gave Nicholas Ridley no personal support either in the House or unattributably. It seems that she hoped that the retraction by Ridley of his remarks would be suffcient for his

---

[47] Ibid., col. 449.   [48] *Observer*, 15 July 1990.
[49] Ibid.   [50] *Sunday Times*, 15 July 1990.

survival and that her disassociation from them would prevent her from being implicated in the sentiments he expressed. However, for many in her own party her failure to dismiss Mr Ridley was seen as weakness and as suggesting that her disassociation was incomplete. She was known to share many of his concerns about Europe in general and Germany in particular, and to consider him an ally against the stronger European line taken by Major, Hurd, and other Cabinet colleagues.

Mrs Thatcher clearly did not want to be the one who pushed Ridley from office. However, her attitude towards the Secretary of State comes close to constructive dismissal, particularly when compared with the support she had given to other beleaguered ministers. She offered no collective cover, in effect washing her hands of him and leaving his fate to others. Moreover, she must have known what that fate would be.

However, Ridley was not prepared to resign unless he was sure that was what the Prime Minister wished. On Saturday morning he spoke to officials at Number Ten and it is suggested that he was told that the Prime Minister believed that his continuation in office would further damage her and the government. At 12.45 p.m. he spoke to Mrs Thatcher herself, and it would seem that, during the fifteen-minute conversation, the Prime Minister convinced him that he should resign. During what official sources called 'a period of further contemplation'[51] Ridley composed his resignation letter. In the end, therefore, Mrs Thatcher would seem to have played a more direct role, albeit reluctantly, in this minister's resignation than was her usual practice.

The Press

The campaign waged by the quality Press for Ridley's resignation was countered by some of the tabloids, who indicated support for the minister and his comments. The *Independent*, *The Times*, the *Daily Telegraph*, and the *Guardian* all expressed the opinion that the language used by Nicholas Ridley in his interview was unacceptable for a minister and that he should resign. These papers also addressed the division within the Conservative Party over Europe and the dangers that this posed for the party. In contrast, the *Sun* demonstrated its support for Ridley with the headline 'Hans off Nick!', and the *Daily Star* insisted that its phone-in

[51] *Observer*, 15 July 1990.

survey indicated that 94 per cent supported Ridley's comments. It was headlines such as these that would seem to have been in part responsible for Ridley's delay in resigning. For a while he thought that support from the constituencies might be enough. Whether the quality Press can be seen as a factor in bringing about Ridley's resignation is therefore doubtful, although it clearly reinforced the line taken by the party at Westminster.

Ridley's Resignation Classified

Nicholas Ridley's resignation demonstrates the lack of definition that exists between the conventions of responsibility. On the one hand, resignation can be seen, as Mr Kinnock saw it, as the penalty paid for failing to follow the collective line and thus breaching the convention of collective responsibility. The area that Mr Ridley's comments addressed certainly went beyond the boundaries of his departmental responsibilities and infringed those of the Chancellor of the Exchequer and the Foreign Secretary. However, Ridley's rather rambling interview did not amount to putting forward an alternative policy to that of the government, partly because of its lack of cohesion and partly because there was some doubt regarding government policy on Europe. Hurd and Major seemed to have been engaged in a strategy of pulling Britain towards greater European integration, and Ridley's interview appeared to contravene their line. The government's increased commitment to the European Community was still somewhat ambiguous; nevertheless, Ridley's comments were out of tune with the image that the British government was trying to create for itself as a full partner in Europe.

Ridley himself did not believe he had contravened the convention of collectivity. In his resignation letter he outlined his opposition to 'the straitjacket of a single currency, with economic policy decided by people who are not accountable to the electors and taxpayers'. He then continued:

I believe that the views I have expressed in this letter are very much in line with those of the Government. But I recognise the difficulties which my failure to use more measured words have caused and, in the circumstances, I think it would be best if I now left the Government.[52]

[52] *Sunday Times*, 15 July 1990.

From Ridley's letter, therefore, it would seem more appropriate to see his resignation as an acceptance of personal fault in line with the convention of individual ministerial responsibility and this too would seem to be the view held by Mrs Thatcher and senior ministers. In his capacity as a minister he had made a political misjudgement which was considered sufficiently serious by the leading political actors to require his resignation. It was serious not just because it was offensive to the Germans, the French, and the European Commissioners, but because it stepped beyond his own departmental responsibilities (in this it differed from the errors made by Fairbairn and Currie), and, most important of all, because it brought to the surface yet again the split within the Conservative Party over Europe. Mr Ridley's continuation in office might perpetuate the division by providing a focus around which like minds could gather. His resignation was therefore essential to both the party and the government.

5

Resignations for Personal Fault: Private Indiscretion

5.1. CECIL PARKINSON: AN ILL-TIMED REVELATION

Background

On 6 October 1983 Cecil Parkinson, Secretary of State for Trade and Industry, issued a public statement concerning his long-standing relationship with Miss Sara Keays. He announced that she was expecting his child in January, but, although he had at one time indicated his intention of marrying her, he now planned to stay with his wife. He would, he said, be making financial arrangements for the baby. He also stated that neither he nor Miss Keays would be making any further statements or answering questions.

Parkinson was immediately supported by a statement from Number Ten Downing Street which declared this to be a private matter and one over which the Prime Minister saw no reason for a resignation. The timing of the announcement by Mr Parkinson was not of his, nor presumably the Prime Minister's choosing, for the Conservative Party Conference was to begin the following week. However, *Private Eye* had printed a story which drew attention to Miss Keays's pregnancy and linked her name with that of another Member of Parliament. Miss Keays, it seems, had insisted on a statement by Parkinson to protect her reputation and prevent further speculation.[1]

There was strong condemnation of Parkinson from sections of the Conservative Party, both at Westminster and in the country. His affair was seen by some as damaging the party's image. The

---

[1] S. Keays, *A Question of Judgement* (London: Quintessential Press, 1985), 104.

Conservative Party prided itself on being the party of the family, and Mrs Thatcher had made much of 'Victorian values', using the phrase to depict morality, duty, and discipline. Mr Parkinson's position as a minister, therefore, seemed somewhat inappropriate, although interestingly it appeared to be Mr Parkinson's failure to divorce his wife and marry Miss Keays, rather than his adulterous relationship, which caused the greater concern. A government minister was quoted as saying: 'Why doesn't he get divorced and do the decent thing? Other people have. The government is full of them.'[2] The adoption of such a strategy, it was implied, would have made Mr Parkinson better equipped to be a minister, or at least would have enabled him to be on equal terms with his colleagues.

One senior member of Parliament, interviewed by the *Sunday Times*, managed to roll all the complaints against Parkinson into one:

He's let the party down.... If his private life becomes public, he must take the consequences. In his statement he said he promised to marry the girl and changed his mind. I can't see how he can possibly hold his head up. How can we give a standing ovation to an admitted adulterer?[3]

Whatever the particular complaint, there was dissatisfaction among many senior back-benchers, who indicated that they intended to inform John Wakeham, Government Chief Whip, and Edward Du Cann, Chairman of the 1922 Committee, of their desire for Parkinson's resignation. However, despite the criticisms and concern in some quarters, Parkinson had important support. The Prime Minister saw no reason for his resignation and (the *Sunday Times* suggested) was committed to retaining Parkinson in his Cabinet post 'unless he decides that his position has become untenable'.[4] He also had support from many Cabinet colleagues and at the opening of the Conservative Party Conference key party members rallied around him. Mr John Selwyn Gummer, who had succeeded Parkinson as Party Chairman only a month previously, praised his predecessor's work and endorsed the belief that Parkinson should remain as Secretary of State for Trade and Industry. The Chairman of the Executive Committee, Sir Russell Sanderson, also offered his support.

[2] *Sunday Times*, 9 Oct. 1983.   [3] Ibid.   [4] Ibid.

Indeed, it looked as if Parkinson might survive. His fate appeared to depend upon the reception he received at the Party Conference on 13 October, when he wound up the debate on free enterprise and industry. This proved to be mostly favourable. Moreover, he was strongly supported on the platform by the Prime Minister and ministerial colleagues who led the applause that followed his speech. Overnight events, however, changed the situation and made Parkinson's position untenable. Miss Keays had given a statement to *The Times*[5] which, because of its timing, distracted attention from the achievements of the party and the government. Miss Keays maintained that Mr Parkinson had broken his side of the bargain by talking about their affair during the *Panorama* programme on Monday evening,[6] and she challenged his suggestion that his statement to the Press had contained all the facts.

She alleged that Parkinson had originally proposed marriage to her in 1979, and not after she became pregnant, as some papers had implied. Indeed, she stated that it was after Parkinson found she was pregnant that he changed his mind and decided to stay with his wife, only to change it back again on election night, 9 June, before he spoke with the Prime Minister. Miss Keays stated that Mr Parkinson had told the Prime Minister that he would be getting a divorce and marrying Miss Keays, and he had spoken in the same terms to members of Miss Keays's family. He asked for time to sort out his affairs. On 1 September, however, after returning from a holiday with his family, he told Miss Keays finally that he would not be marrying her.

Miss Keays's statement appeared on the front page of *The Times* on 14 October. It was the lead story, occupying three columns, while Parkinson's reception at the Conservative Party Conference was given only one column. Before its impact had been felt at the Conference, however, Cecil Parkinson had resigned.

Factors Influencing Parkinson's Resignation

The constituency party

The role of the Conservative Party in bringing about Parkinson's resignation was unusual. In normal circumstances involvement in

---

[5] *The Times*, 14 Oct. 1983.　　　[6] *Panorama*, BBC TV, 10 Oct. 1983.

such matters is confined to the 1922 Committee at Westminister, although it no doubt takes account of the reaction in the constituencies. However, because of the timing of Parkinson's initial statement and of the subsequent one by Sara Keays, the Conservative Party in the country, or at least its representatives at the Conservative Party Conference, for once played a visible part in a ministerial resignation. The Conservative Party Conference was the venue for another resignation in 1990, that of Patrick Nicholls, a junior Environment minister. He was arrested for drink-driving the day after the Home Secretary had promised the Conference new measures against drinking in public places. Nicholls resigned immediately. It would have been inconceivable for him to return to the Conference, and in that sense the constituency party exacted its punishment for ministerial indiscretion. Nicholls was not publicly well known, and the incident was quickly forgotten. However, it was unusual in that the minister's indiscretion was related to his ministerial duties. More frequently any link is at best tenuous, although, as Parkinson discovered, this may be sufficient. There would seem to have been the feeling at constituency level that Parkinson had 'done wrong' and should be punished. Resignation was seen as the appropriate punishment.

The Press

The resignation was also unusual, again because of the timing, in that Parliament had no role, not even as a vehicle for information. The Press, however, ensured that the public was fully informed and kept the issue alive. Indeed, it was 'mildly rebuked' at the opening of the Conference for being more interested in Parkinson than in Conservative policies.[7]

The Prime Minister

The Prime Minister was supportive of her minister in public, and according to Parkinson in private as well, and made it known initially that she did not consider that resignation was required. It was suggested that she may in fact already have effected a punishment by denying him the coveted post of Foreign Secretary, giving him Trade and Industry instead.[8] However, this has been denied

---

[7] *The Times*, 11 Oct. 1983.   [8] Ibid.

by Cecil Parkinson, who has stated that it was at his request that he was placed in a less exposed position. The Prime Minister would still have made him Foreign Secretary.[9]

Parkinson's decision to resign was regretted by the Prime Minister. Parkinson, it seems, saw her at Blackpool, as soon as he became aware of Miss Keays's statement to *The Times*. He told her that he considered himself to be a liability to the government and therefore intended to resign. According to Parkinson, Mrs Thatcher asked him to 'sleep on it' but recognized that it was a matter for him to decide.[10] It was clear, however, that she was determined that Parkinson should return to the Cabinet as soon as possible.

Parkinson's Resignation Classified

Cecil Parkinson's resignation presents little problem of classification. It is an example of ministerial resignation for personal fault, in this case the personal fault of a minister in his private life not in his official capacity as a minister.

There is not a constitutional requirement for a minister to resign for committing adultery, or for fathering a child out of wedlock, and there may not always be a political requirement for resignation either. Much depends on the attendant publicity and the political situation at the time. Publicity about the private misdemeanours of a senior minister, who until recently was the Chairman of the Party, was particularly damaging during the Party Conference. However, Parkinson might have survived but for allegations which suggested that he was indecisive and unreliable and which emphasized the imprudent nature of his affair. These resulted in further moral judgements about his private life and in a questioning of his suitability as a minister.

Constitutionally, resignations are described in terms of duty or obligation rather than punishment. A minister has the duty to resign if he makes a mistake or misjudgement that Parliament or, more appropriately today, the party, considers sufficiently serious. The duty of a minister in these circumstances is therefore to punish himself by relinquishing office. The phraseology may be different and so may the perception—'doing one's duty' sounds more

---

[9] *The Cecil Parkinson Story*, BBC2, 26 Sept. 1992.   [10] Ibid.

honourable than 'being punished'—but the outcome is the same. Cecil Parkinson spoke in terms of duty and example, during the *Panorama* interview, when he stated: 'If I became a liability . . . I would leave immediately.'[11]

It seems that Parkinson became a liability both to the party and to the government, and that this was recognized by himself and his supporters. His greatest crime was that he had been found out, and as a result his private affairs were interfering with his ability to function as a minister and the maintenance of public confidence in him. Resignation therefore became a constitutional requirement and a political necessity, as John Selwyn Gummer explained: 'It was a private matter but when a private matter interferes in the public affairs of a minister's job then he has a duty to resign.'[12]

Parkinson's resignation would seem to have been unavoidable after Sara Keays had issued her statement and can perhaps be viewed as an example of the hypocrisy of the British public, which demands that its leaders should be seen to conform to a sexual morality which society no longer practises. Cecil Parkinson's resignation was seen by most to be a punishment, but it was sufficiently honourable to enable him to be brought back into office after he had served his sentence.

5.2. DAVID MELLOR: THE VICTIM OF A PRESS CAMPAIGN

Background

On Sunday, 19 July 1992, the *People* newspaper reported that David Mellor, Secretary of State for National Heritage (popularly referred to as the 'Minister for Fun'), had been having an affair with an actress, Antonia de Sancha, for the previous three months. The following day David Mellor offered his resignation to the Prime Minister. The offer was rejected and John Major indicated, and subsequently reaffirmed, his support for his minister.[13]

During the next ten days Mr Mellor was constantly in the headlines. The continual coverage was partly due to Press activity,

---

[11] *The Times*, 11 Oct. 1983. [12] Ibid., 15 Oct. 1983.
[13] Downing Street press statements carried in all papers, 21 and 23 July 1992.

which kept the story running with pictures of 'Mellor's Love Nest'[14] and revelations that Ms de Sancha had appeared in a 'soft porn' video.[15] However, continued Press attention was also due to Mellor's actions and reactions. His initial statement on the revelation of the affair showed little regret but raised the spectre of Press invasion of privacy and the matter of his children. The statement did little to engender sympathy for the minister. Many considered Mellor had himself shown a disregard for his children by embarking on the affair with Ms de Sancha. This feeling was reinforced when the *Daily Mirror*'s interview with Mellor's in-laws alleged that Mellor had phoned his wife's parents and told them to stop talking to the media or 'you'll never see your grandchildren again'.[16]

Mellor's references to 'privacy' also turned out to be ill-advised. His ministerial portfolio included responsibility for the media and the possible steering of controversial legislation on privacy through Parliament.[17] The effect of Mellor's statement was to raise doubts about his credibility regarding any such legislation. These doubts were heightened after the Press Council, to whom he complained about the activities of the Press, ruled that the newspapers were justified in revealing his affair with Ms de Sancha.[18]

Later that week Mellor, acting, it would seem, on the advice of Sir Tim Bell (Mrs Thatcher's ex-image-maker),[19] made a well-publicized visit to his in-laws. However, if the visit was intended to provide good publicity, Mr Mellor was to be disappointed. Headlines such as 'The Mellors Play at Happy Families . . . or is it Charades?'[20] suggested a public-relations exercise that had gone wrong.

During August there was a lull in Press interest in Mr Mellor, but on Monday, 7 September, the *Sun* began a three-day account of the Mellor–de Sancha affair. The intimate details that were revealed, whether true or not, succeeded in turning the minister into a figure of ridicule, and his position within government was

[14] *Daily Mirror*, 20 July 1992.   [15] *Sun*, 22 July 1992.
[16] *Daily Mirror*, 22 July 1992.
[17] The government was at this time awaiting the Report of the Calcutt Committee, which was considering whether new legislation was necessary.
[18] Mellor had complained about the revelations made in the *People* and the fact that the information had been obtained by recording a telephone conversation between himself and Ms de Sancha (*Daily Mail*, 22 July 1992).
[19] *Daily Mail*, 25 Sept. 1992; *Daily Telegraph*, 29 Sept. 1992.
[20] *Daily Mail*, 25 July 1992.

once more questioned. However, Downing Street again insisted that Mellor had the Prime Minister's support.[21]

On 10 September the *Daily Mail* revealed that the chauffeur-driven Mercedes, in which Mellor had visited his wife's in-laws in July, had been lent to him by Elliot Bernard, a property developer, who had at times also lent Mellor his luxury Mayfair flat. There was no suggestion that there was anything improper in the relationship between Mellor and Bernard, but rather that the acceptance of Bernard's hospitality showed a lack of judgement on the part of the minister.

However, Mellor, with the Prime Minister's support, continued in office. Yet he must have been aware that more details of his private life were about to be revealed in a forthcoming libel action, which was being brought against the *People* by a close friend of the Mellors, Mrs Mona Bauwens. Mrs Bauwens's action concerned an article in the newspaper two years previously which had revealed that the Mellors had holidayed with Mrs Bauwens in Marbella for a month at the time of the outbreak of the Gulf crisis. Mr Mellor was at this time Arts Minister. The article suggested that Mrs Bauwens was not a suitable companion for the Mellors, because her father was an executive member of the Palestinian Liberation Organization. Mrs Bauwens considered the article damaging to her reputation.

The hearing of the case started on Monday, 14 September, and ended on 22 September with the jury failing to reach a verdict. During the trial it emerged that Mrs Bauwens had paid for the air tickets to Spain for Mr and Mrs Mellor and their children, and for the villa as well. Indeed the case, which could not have come before the courts at a worse time for Mellor, 'centred on his action and political judgement'[22] in accepting such hospitality and gifts from Mrs Bauwens. When linked with the Bernard revelations, this suggested a pattern of behaviour which might be considered inappropriate in a minister.

Bryan Gould, the Shadow Heritage Minister, suggested that the matter could be referred to the Select Committee on Members' Interests,[23] and he also wrote to the Prime Minister concerning the

[21] Downing Street press statement carried by all papers, 9 Sept. 1992.
[22] *Daily Telegraph*, 24 Sept. 1992.
[23] BBC, *The Six O'clock News*, 22 Sept. 1992.

propriety of Mellor's actions in relation to the Cabinet document, *Questions of Procedure for Ministers*. The document, which, amongst other things, lays down rules about accepting gifts and hospitality, states:

It is a well established and recognised rule that no Minister or public servant should accept gifts, hospitality or services from anyone which would, or might appear to, place him or her under an obligation. The same principle applies if gifts etc. are offered to a member of their family.

This is primarily a matter which must be left to the good sense of Ministers. But any minister in doubt or difficulty over this should seek the Prime Minister's guidance.[24]

Lord Blake, interviewed for *The Times* Diary,[25] was of the opinion that, if Mellor had breached the guide-lines on ministerial gifts, he had no option but to resign. The questions that required answers were whether Mr Mellor had exercised his 'good sense' in accepting gifts and hospitality which 'might appear to place him under an obligation' and whether he had sought the advice of the prime minister, at that time Mrs Thatcher.

In his reply to Bryan Gould, John Major indicated that, in his view, Mr Mellor had complied with the guide-lines in the document:

David Mellor took the view that the holiday which he and his family took with Mrs Bauwens at her expense was a purely personal matter and did not touch on his ministerial responsibilities or place him under any obligation in respect of his ministerial duties. His decision not to refer the matter to the then Prime Minister was entirely consistent with the guidelines.[26]

David Mellor was at pains to point out when interviewed on BBC2 *Newsnight*[27] that the Prime Minister's response had been made in consultation with Sir Robin Butler, the Cabinet Secretary, and that their adjudication put an end to the matter. However, it was not an end to Mellor's problems. Another factor had come into play. Following Britain's withdrawal from the Exchange Rate Mechanism, Parliament had been recalled for an emergency debate on the economy and a meeting of the 1922 Committee had

[24] *Questions of Procedure for Ministers* (London: Cabinet office, 1992).
[25] *The Times*, 24 Sept. 1992.   [26] *Daily Telegraph*, 24 Sept. 1992.
[27] *Newsnight*, BBC2, 23 Sept. 1992.

been arranged. Senior members of the Committee were already indicating that Mr Mellor should go, and his chances of survival were reported to be slight.[28] In addition, the broadsheet papers were now also calling for Mr Mellor to resign.[29]

In an attempt to pre-empt the meeting of the 1992 Committee, Sir Tim Bell arranged for Mellor to give interviews on *Newsnight* and *ITN News*.[30] Mellor used the opportunity to launch a full attack upon the tabloid Press. He admitted that he had behaved 'foolishly' with regard to his relationship with Ms de Sancha, but continued: 'I think that for a lot of people in this day and age that was not a resigning matter. The trouble is, one or two tabloid editors nailed themselves on the hook that I had to go and now everything else is turned and distorted.'[31] He contended that the matter had become a battle between the Prime Minister and the tabloids, with the Prime Minister wishing him to stay in office and the editors of some tabloids determined that he should go. It was, Mellor insisted, a matter of 'who decides who is to be a member of the British Cabinet, the Prime Minister or the *Daily Mail*?'[32] On both programmes Mellor stated that he would resign if his colleagues considered that he had become an embarrassment, but he added that, if he did resign, it would be out of a 'sense of duty and not of shame'.

The following day, 24 September, Mellor did indeed resign. It seems that he received a phone call from Sir Marcus Fox, Chairman of the 1922 Committee, early in the morning. Sir Marcus indicated Mellor had little support from members of the Executive.[33] After speaking to the Prime Minister several times during the day, Mellor's resignation was officially announced at 5.36 p.m. His letter of resignation and his subsequent statement to the House gave no apology for the embarrassment he had caused the government but made clear that he believed he was a victim of Press persecution:

I have concluded that it is too much to expect my colleagues in Government and in Parliament to have to put up with a constant barrage of stories about me in certain tabloid newspapers. Rather than have this turn

---

[28] *Independent*, 24 Sept. 1992.
[29] *Guardian, Daily Telegraph, Independent.*
[30] *Daily Telegraph, Daily Mail*, 24 Sept. 1992.
[31] *ITN News*, 23 Sept. 1992.   [32] *Newsnight*, BBC2, 23 Sept. 1992.
[33] *Daily Mail*, 25 Sept. 1992.

into a trial of strength between the Government and some sections of the Press about my future, I have decided to resolve it by resigning.[34]

Even Mellor's resignation was controversial, both because of his accusations against the Press and because of its timing. This acted to take attention away from the government's performance in the emergency debate in the Commons that afternoon. The resignation took the headlines in news reports during the evening and featured prominently on all the front pages of the Press the following day.[35] Some Labour supporters considered that the timing was deliberate. Bryan Gould commented: 'In the timing of his resignation David Mellor has done his Prime Minister one last favour, by deflecting attention from John Major's difficulties in the Commons.'[36]

Factors Influencing Mellor's Resignation

The 1922 Committee

The series of incidents involving David Mellor occurred while the House of Commons was in recess. Indeed, it may be considered a misfortune for Mellor that Parliament was recalled for an emergency session just after the revelations from the Bauwens libel action. The recall meant that, as well as the scheduled sittings of the House of Commons, the Executive of the 1922 Committee would also meet.

It was this core group of eighteen members, who are 'effectively the keepers of the party soul',[37] that sealed the fate of David Mellor. The Executive was due to meet in the evening of 24 September. However, its chairman, Sir Marcus Fox, did not wait for the scheduled meeting to make the decision on Mellor's future. Instead it would seem he polled individual members of the Executive as they returned to Westminster. The outcome was unfavourable for Mellor. Many members disliked the way in which the minister had handled the situation. However, two concerns seem to have been particularly evident. First, Mellor was seen as weakening Mr Major's efforts to restore the government's authority in the wake of the sterling crisis.[38] Secondly, back-benchers were asking

---

[34] *Independent*, 25 Sept. 1992.
[35] Only front-page feature of *Daily Mirror*, *Today* newspapers.
[36] *Today*, 25 Sept. 1992.   [37] *Daily Mail*, 25 Sept. 1992.
[38] *Daily Telegraph*, 24 Sept. 1992.

whether it was 'conceivable' for David Mellor to address the Conservative Party Conference the following month.[39] No doubt there were memories of Cecil Parkinson's conference disaster in 1983.

Early in the morning Sir Marcus Fox informed David Mellor that he had little support from the party,[40] thereby allowing Mellor the opportunity of resigning before the Committee officially required him to do so. The Executive of the 1922 Committee had again demonstrated its strength. It was responsible for Edwina Currie's resignation and it should also be seen as the instrument behind Mellor's departure from office. As the *Daily Mail* commented: 'from the 1922 Committee, it had been another show of awesome power. Executive Members are not called the Knights of the Long Knives for nothing.'[41]

The Prime Minister

The Prime Minister would seem to have played no part in bringing about the resignation of David Mellor, who was his personal friend. Mr Major offered his support throughout, despite suggestions after the Bauwens revelations that this showed a lack of judgement, the *Independent* at one point asking, 'What must a minister do to be fired?'[42]

Mr Major was, of course, unable to provide collective cover for David Mellor, as the misjudgements concerned were of a personal and not a political nature, but he indicated his regret at the departure of Mellor from the Cabinet.[43] It is not known whether Mellor discussed with the Prime Minister the timing of his resignation, although they spoke together on four occasions on 24 September.[44]

The Press

David Mellor was insistent that his resignation had been caused by the tabloid Press. He further charged that this had challenged the right of the Prime Minister to choose who was in his Cabinet. The tabloids were at pains to demonstrate that they were not responsible for the minister's resignation, fearing perhaps retaliatory privacy legislation from the government. They pointed out

---

[39] *Guardian*, 11 Sept. 1992.   [40] *The Times*, 24 Sept. 1992.
[41] Ibid.   [42] *Independent*, 24 Sept. 1992.
[43] See Prime Minister's letter in response to Mellor's resignation letter, *Independent* and others, 25 Sept. 1992.   [44] *Daily Mail*, 25 Sept. 1992.

that the broadsheets too had been critical of Mr Mellor and had questioned his position in the government[45] and insisted that Mr Mellor's colleagues not the Press had decided the minister's fate. Alastair Campbell, the *Daily Mirror*'s political editor, wrote, 'the truth is that the Heritage Secretary was rejected by his peers',[46] while the editorial in *Today* stated: 'Mr Mellor is a servant of the public. He is accountable to the Prime Minister but more importantly, he is accountable to the people for his actions. These actions—not their reporting—are what have cost Mr Mellor his job.'[47] Similar sentiments were echoed by Paul Johnson in the *Daily Mail*. He accepted that 'the initial intrusion by *The People* newspaper into Mr Mellor's privacy was unwarranted and the way it was done was reprehensible'. However, he continued:

But this is not why Mellor has lost office. What rightly caused his downfall was the information—which emerged quite accidently in the course of a libel action and the media had totally failed to discover—that the holiday he and his family shared with Mona Bauwens had been subsidised by her.[48]

The broadsheets, too, expressed the opinion that it had been the revelations during the libel action that had lost Mr Mellor the support of his colleagues and resulted in his resignation.[49] This would seem to be correct, and Mellor's resignation cannot be attributed directly to the Press. It was the Executive of the 1922 Committee that made the crucial decision. However, the newspapers undoubtedly played a part in producing the resignation. The tabloids, by exposing Mellor's affair and keeping it as a front-page story, acted to mobilize popular hypocrisy, which requires ministers to lead blameless lives, and made Mellor vulnerable to other more serious revelations. The broadsheets acted at least to confirm political opinion about the future of Mr Mellor.

The extent and nature of the coverage of Mellor's indiscretion seems to have broken new ground. This was partly because of the availability of material about it, but it also suggests a confirmation

---

[45] *Daily Mail* surveyed the coverage by the broadsheets in the two days prior to Mellor's resignation. It noted the column inches to be as follows: *Independent*—Wed. 61″, Thurs. 86″; *Guardian*—Wed. 83″, Thurs. 78″, *Daily Telegraph*—Wed. 55″, Thurs. 166″; *The Times*—Wed. 90″, Thurs. 84″.

[46] *Daily Mirror*, 25 Sept. 1992.   [47] *Today*, 25 Sept. 1992.

[48] *People*, 25 Sept. 1992.

[49] See *Independent, The Times, Daily Telegraph*, 25 Sept. 1992.

of the position of the tabloid Press as outside the establishment 'club'. In the early part of the century newspapers would seem to have seen their interests best served by maintaining an uneasy alliance with public figures, and thus they did not seek out or dwell upon the sexual misdemeanours of ministers. In contrast today, some elements of the Press see their interests served by sensationalizing sexual scandals, and thereby boosting their circulation figures. The political consequences for ministers who are found out are therefore potentially more serious.

Mellor's Resignation Classified

Mr Mellor's resignation can be classified as personal fault. He was considered to have made a series of misjudgements which on their own may not have been sufficiently serious to require resignation, but cumulatively suggested he should no longer remain in office. It would be a mistake to see Mellor's resignation as being forced because of sexual indiscretion. Despite Sir Tom Bell's aim to make David Mellor 'the first Tory minister in history to survive a sex scandal',[50] modern precedents suggest that another element is required to produce a resignation. In the case of Profumo it was that he lied to the House;[51] in the case of Cecil Parkinson that he seemed indecisive and broke his promise.[52] Mellor provided two further elements, his acceptance of gifts and hospitality and his handling of the Press.

Mellor's acceptance of gifts and hospitality suggested that he was not fully aware of the standards expected of a minister and brought into question the effectiveness of the document *Questions of Procedure for Ministers*, causing Lord Blake to suggest that 'there is no point having guidelines if that means they can simply be ignored'.[53]

Mellor's handling of the Press made his position as the responsible Secretary of State untenable. The point was reached when there could be no public confidence in the presentation by Mellor of any policies which related to the media. This distinguishes Mellor from Parkinson. Parkinson's misjudgements did not have a direct effect on his ministerial position; Mellor's did. This suggests that

---

[50] *Daily Mail*, 25 Sept. 1992.   [51] Resigned in 1963.
[52] See Ch. 5.1.   [53] *The Times Diary*, 24 Sept. 1992.

it may be less easy for Mellor to make a return to the front-benches than it was for Parkinson. A further factor which may hinder such a return was Mellor's manner of resignation. The minister went before he was pushed, but, despite the embarrassment he had caused the government and the party, 'there remained about Mellor a damning aura of unrepentance'.[54] This is not a characteristic that senior back-benchers find endearing.

[54] *Daily Telegraph*, 24 Sept. 1992.

6

Resignations for Departmental Fault

6.1. LORD CARRINGTON: THE INVASION OF THE FALKLAND ISLANDS

Background

On Friday, 2 April 1982, Argentina invaded the Falkland Islands in a dramatic, and as it turned out abortive, attempt to resolve the long-running dispute between Britain and Argentina over the sovereignty of the Islands. The invasion resulted directly in the resignations of the Foreign Secretary, Lord Carrington, and two junior Foreign Office ministers, Richard Luce and Humphrey Atkins, and indirectly in an examination of Foreign Office policy and management during the years preceding the invasion, particularly while Lord Carrington had been Foreign Secretary.[1]

Lord Carrington believed that the only solution to the dispute over sovereignty was the negotiation of a leaseback arrangement. However, he would not contemplate such an arrangement without the agreement of the Falkland Islanders, which would in any case be necessary before the approval of the British Parliament could be obtained.

The degree of emotion aroused in Parliament by the issue was evident when, in December 1980, Nicholas Ridley, then Minister of State in the Foreign Office, was 'savaged' by the House after making a statement which referred to leaseback as a possible option.[2] The idea of leaseback was received no better in the Islands. Indeed, in January 1981 the Falkland Islands Joint Council issued a statement which demanded that any negotiations with

[1] *Report by a Committee of Privy Councillors: The Falkland Islands Review* (Chairman Lord Franks) (1983), Cmnd 8787, HMSO.
[2] P. Cosgrave, *Carrington: A Life and a Policy* (London: J. M. Dent, 1985), 17.

Argentina must contain 'an agreement to freeze the dispute over sovereignty for a specified period of time'.[3]

The 'freezing' of the issue of sovereignty would clearly be unacceptable to Argentina, and it was recognized by the Foreign Office and Carrington that talks must be held with Argentina which at least appeared to offer some hope of a settlement in the future; otherwise Argentina might try to achieve its ends by economic or even military means. Carrington pursued these talks in the hope that the Islanders would change their minds, although this must have been recognized at best as unlikely.

The British government was in fact in an impossible position. It had to contain the situation so that Argentina remained at the negotiating table, although the constraints imposed by Parliament and the need to secure the agreement of the Falkland Islanders meant there was nothing to negotiate. In recognition of the situation that this produced, officials in the Foreign Office suggested that a public education campaign should be run on the advantages of leaseback. The idea was rejected by Lord Carrington, who later told the Franks Committee that such a plan would not have been approved by his colleagues because it appeared to put pressure on the Islanders to change their minds, and might have been taken as an indication that, if sufficient public support was obtained, the Islanders would have been overruled.[4] However, the rejection of the campaign meant that there could be no move towards a solution which met Argentinian expectations.

Even so, Argentina believed that it had received a political signal from the British government. In June John Nott, Secretary of State for Defence, announced in Parliament that HMS *Endeavour* was to be withdrawn from service in the South Atlantic.[5] This decision was opposed by Carrington, who considered that the withdrawal would be seen as a lack of British commitment to the area. He made further attempts in early 1982 to get the policy changed, but the decision remained and was supported by the Prime Minister in the House.

Throughout 1981 positions hardened. The Argentinians became more determined in their claim to sovereignty over the Falklands, and the Islanders became more determined in their resistance. The

---

[3] *Falkland Islands Review*, para. 83.   [4] Ibid.
[5] HC Deb., 25 June 1981, col. 387.

Foreign Office continued to be conciliatory, reassuring both sides of the British government's good intentions, although Carrington recognized that there was little room for manœuvre and he was not optimistic about the outcome of the next round of talks. These took place at the end of February 1982, and, despite the joint communiqué, which reaffirmed the commitment of both sides to find a solution to the issue of sovereignty, there was from then on a rapid deterioration in diplomatic relations.[6]

The Foreign Office recognized the possibility of confrontation and of Argentina's taking military action, but did not see the threat as immediate. Its concern was to avoid inflaming the situation and to keep working towards a diplomatic solution. Even when there were distinct signs that President Galtieri was planning an invasion, the Foreign Office still maintained a conciliatory attitude. On 30 March, despite the uncertain situation in the South Atlantic, and, it seems, against the advice of some of his officials,[7] Carrington left for a planned visit to Israel. He was subsequently to be criticized in the House for his absence at this time.[8]

Carrington, however, believed the trip was too important to postpone. Moreover, he considered that Argentina was posturing, as it had done before. In that case, he reasoned, it was best to adopt a 'business as usual' approach. His decision was based on the view that there would be no invasion. 'He found it hard . . . to imagine that a civilised and pro-Western country such as Argentina would take up arms against another Western country with which she had long established ties over a trifling argument about who owned some islands in the South Atlantic.'[9]

Carrington's absence meant that Richard Luce, now Minister of State, had to reassure both the House of Commons and the 1922 Committee that appropriately stern measures were being taken to prevent Argentina from acting aggressively. However, at the same time he had to continue to use reassuring and persuasive tactics with Argentina to prevent the complete collapse of the diplomatic process.

On Thursday, 1 April, Carrington returned to London, by which time all the evidence pointed to an Argentinian attack upon the

---

[6] *Falkland Islands Review*, para. 84.
[7] Cosgrave, *Carrington: A Life and a Policy*, 19.
[8] HC Deb., 3 Apr. 1982, col. 654.
[9] Cosgrave, *Carrington: A Life and a Policy*, 19.

Falklands the next day. The Foreign Office still argued, however, that whilst 'the evidence . . . was highly suggestive, it was not yet entirely conclusive and diplomatic action was being taken to prevent an attack'.[10]

Carrington, it seems, still believed that Argentina would not invade, and when during a meeting that evening the Prime Minister stated that Britain would have to fight, Carrington was horrified. As the meeting broke up, he is reported to have exclaimed: 'The woman's gone mad. . . . It can't come to that.'[11] He still believed that the diplomatic process would triumph.

The Argentinians landed on Friday, 2 April, although in London there was some uncertainty about the course of events. At first Humphrey Atkins made a statement in the House denying that there had been an invasion. It later transpired, however, that the Argentinians had landed prior to his speech but that he had been unaware of this. Whether Foreign Office officials had this information is unknown. The following morning Atkins returned to the Chamber and apologized for inadvertently misleading the House.[12]

John Nott, Secretary of State for Defence, also addressed the House about the invasion and gave what was considered to be a 'dreadful' speech.[13] Carrington, of course, was not accountable to the Commons, but in the evening he appeared with John Nott before the 1922 Committee, where he received a very hostile reception.

It was clear that both Secretaries of State and their Departments were held responsible for what had happened. They were strongly criticized for neither predicting nor preventing the invasion. This criticism was not confined to the Conservative back-benches, but extended to the public at large and was expressed forcibly in the Press.

On 3 April the Prime Minister announced that the Task Force would be sailing. On 5 April Carrington, Luce, and Atkins resigned from the Foreign Office. Nott at the Ministry of Defence offered his resignation, but did not persist when the Prime Minister rejected it.

[10] *Falkland Islands Review*, para. 249.
[11] Cosgrave, *Carrington: A Life and a Policy*, 32.
[12] HC Deb., 3 Apr. 1982, cols. 651–2.
[13] J. Prior, *A Balance of Power* (London: Hamish Hamilton, 1986), 147.

Factors Influencing Carrington's Resignation

Parliament

Carrington could not, of course, appear on the Floor of the House. The onus for accounting to the Commons fell on the junior ministers in the Foreign Office—Richard Luce, whose responsibilities included South America, and Humphrey Atkins. Both suffered on the Floor of the House as emotions rose and outrage grew over the invasion of the Falklands.

The invasion was clearly a humiliation for a Conservative party which traditionally supported strong foreign and defence policies. The Opposition parties could, and did, point to the actions of David Owen, who, as Foreign Secretary in a Labour government, had prevented a similar show of Argentinian aggression getting out of hand. There was, moreover, talk of the Opposition tabling a vote of censure against the government over the failure of its defence and foreign policy. Certainly, the atmosphere suggested that the government was on trial. Members of Parliament needed a target, and John Nott gave them one by his inadequate performance on 3 April on the Floor of the House.[14]

The Foreign Office was also attacked, and dislike and distrust for the department surfaced, as opinions verged on the hysterical. Teddy Taylor proclaimed that 'the Foreign Office was not working for Britain', while others suggested that the Foreign Office had not been a 'friend' to the Falkland Islands, and that it even wanted to get rid of 'a tiresome problem'.[15] Particularly strident were suggestions that the Foreign Office was staffed by appeasers: 'The whole story will inevitably lead some people to think that the Foreign Office is a bit too much saturated with the spirit of appeasement.'[16]

Perhaps if Carrington had been able to make a statement, he might have calmed members, but more probably his presence would have provided an additional focus for the anger and outrage. The failure to anticipate what was happening was seen as incredible: 'a blunder . . . a monumental folly . . .'[17] Carrington was accused of confusing diplomacy and foreign policy[18] and, together with the

---

[14] HC Deb., 3 Apr. 1982, col. 650.
[15] Ibid., col. 653 (Teddy Taylor), col. 656 (Russell Johnson), col. 656 (Sir John Eden).   [16] Ibid., col. 658.
[17] Ibid., cols. 651–2.   [18] Ibid., col. 648.

Secretary of State for Defence, of making a 'massive misjudgement'.[19] There was not, however, a concerted call for resignation, although David Owen suggested that 'Ministers must now consider their position'.[20] Others argued that the Foreign Secretary and the Secretary of State for Defence be charged with rectifying the situation, and, if they were unable to do so, then resigning.[21] Mr Silkin declared that, if the government were unable to provide satisfactory answers to the lack of anticipation and response, then Mrs Thatcher, Lord Carrington, and Mr Nott should all resign from office;[22] but this may be seen as no more than a predictable call for resignation by the Opposition.

Richard Luce, who had sat through the debate and had experienced the atmosphere in the House, was the first of the Foreign Office trio to suggest resignation. He clearly believed that both he personally and the department had lost the confidence of the House. Resignation was a matter of honour.[23] Carrington, however, refused to let him resign alone; either both would resign or neither.[24] The extent to which the attitude of the House of Commons was a factor in Carrington's resignation is hard to gauge. However, it is likely that he found the jingoistic fervour expressed there abhorrent and that he wanted no part in it. It is also clear from subsequent comments that he considered the attack upon the Foreign Office to be unacceptable, particularly the accusations of appeasement. It may be that 'these bitter words' were in part responsible for his resignation.[25]

The 1922 Committee

The attitude of party back-benchers is reasonably considered of more importance in its influence on resignations than the opinion of the House of Commons as a whole. A minister may expect ritualistic calls for his resignation from the Opposition, but, providing he has the support of his back-benchers, particularly senior ones, he is safe. For the Conservatives this means that the 1922 Committee is all important, and for Carrington this was especially true. Meeting with the Committee was the only opportunity he

[19] Ibid., col. 651 (Rowlands).   [20] Ibid., col. 647.
[21] Ibid., col. 651.   [22] Ibid., col. 664.
[23] Jordan, 'Individual Ministerial Responsibility', 134.   [24] Ibid.
[25] K. Harris, *Thatcher* (London: Weidenfeld and Nicolson, 1988), 113.

had to make his case to back-benchers, and indeed the only opportunity they had to bring him to account. However, his meeting with the 1922 Committee was disastrous. Carrington was not a party man, and the back-benchers knew it. 'The noble lord, for all his eminence and his thirty years of service had always despised the party and not always troubled to conceal its unimportance in his priorities.'[26]

He was generally disliked by back-benchers, who saw him as aloof and arrogant. Mrs Thatcher's loyal supporters were particularly hostile to him, mainly because of his pro-European views and his failure to align clearly with Israel, but, in addition, some had not forgiven him for the Zimbabwe (Rhodesia) settlement.[27] His views in fact coincided with the inclinations of the Foreign Office, and thus he was also suspected of being captured by a department that many back-benchers distrusted, even hated—as had become apparent in the debate in the House. The invasion of the Falklands gave the 1922 Committee the opportunity to give vent to their hostility towards Carrington. A minister respected and regarded with affection might have retained their support, but Carrington stood no chance. The reception he received upset and shocked him and seems likely to have been an important factor in his decision to resign.[28]

The effect of back-bench attitudes upon Carrington may be viewed in constitutional or in political terms. If Carrington resigned because he believed he was under an obligation to do so as he no longer had the support of the majority party in the House of Commons, then his motivation for resigning may be seen as having a constitutional basis. Indeed it could be argued that the 1922 Committee conveys the confidence, or otherwise, of the House, and therefore acts as an agent for the constitution. This view has its attractions in a system which is dominated by party. But it raises questions about how large a government majority has to be before its back-bench committee is seen as always representing the opinion of the House, how many of the committee must support that opinion, and the extent to which the opinion is controlled by the executive of the committee. Moreover, strictly and directly, such a committee has no constitutional authority.

[26] H. Young, *One of Us* (London: MacMillan, 1989), 265.
[27] Cosgrave, *Carrington: A Life and a Policy*, 20.
[28] Prior, *A Balance of Power*, 147

On the other hand, if Carrington resigned because he believed the 1922 Committee would insist on his going and this would embarrass the government, or because he felt unable to continue in office when so many of his party were hostile to him, then his considerations were political. Most probably it was a combination of the constitutional and the political, but it is interesting to note that, much as he was disliked by the 1922 Committee, it did not campaign for his resignation (as it did, for instance, with Brittan and Currie). Cosgrave reported: 'Whilst it would be true to say that a great many people . . . thought that Carrington should resign, the number who believed he actually would was far smaller. . . . His friends wanted him to remain at his post, and his enemies feared that he would do so.'[29]

It may be that, powerful though the Committee is, it does not consider itself powerful enough to insist upon the resignation of a Foreign Secretary. Alternatively, it may be that Carrington resigned of his own accord before the Committee could muster its forces.

The Prime Minister

Mrs Thatcher, it seems, sought the views of Cabinet over whether Carrington should, or should not, resign. She was of the opinion that he should not, but 'the weight of Cabinet opinion was against her'.[30] However, despite the verdict of her colleagues, the Prime Minister tried strenuously to prevent Carrington from resigning, as her reply to his resignation letter indicated: 'I did my utmost through Saturday and Sunday to dissuade you from this course . . .'[31] In the end Carrington's resignation was announced by the Foreign Office rather than Number Ten, an indication that he had had to insist on relinquishing office.

The Press

The lack of support for Carrington in the party and in Parliament was both roused by the Press and reflected in it. Nor was it just the tabloids that were hostile and seeking retribution; the quality Press too wanted explanations and expiation. For *The Times* the initial target was John Nott, who, it reported, would be called upon to resign by the Opposition in the debate on 3 April. *The Times* supported the use of force in its editorial and wanted an explanation of the government's passivity up to this point.

On Monday, 5 April, *The Times* reported on Nott's inadequate performance during the debate on the Saturday, expressing surprise that he was still in office. Elsewhere, however, it suggested that he had redeemed himself during a television interview by asserting that Britain should fight. Meanwhile, the editorial switched attention to Carrington, appealing both to his constitutional honour and the exercise of individual ministerial responsibility, and to his political duty in providing himself as a sacrifice.

Lord Carrington's standing as Foreign Secretary is now also questioned . . . if he felt that some mistakes had been made for which he as Foreign Secretary held responsibility, he would certainly accept that responsibility and honourably resign. It may be that the government's capacity to retain the domestic unity expressed by Saturday's debate requires some such act of expiation.[32]

Again it is not known to what extent Carrington was influenced by such calls for his resignation, which in other papers were expressed in a more forthright fashion.[33] However, James Prior believed that the articles that appeared in the Press that Monday 'were the last straw'.[34] Carrington had suffered at the hands of the Press before. He was attacked over the Vassall affair when he was First Lord of the Admiralty. The *Daily Express* then stated that Carrington had known of the existence of another spy in the Admiralty since the trial of the Portland conspirators a year earlier, but he had failed to take action.[35] Carrington denied the charge and was exonerated by a tribunal chaired by Lord Radcliffe, which concluded that the newspaper reports were unjustified. However, the day before the tribunal sitting ended, Carrington, it seems, was contemplating resignation, although he did not wish to resign.[36] Carrington's experience with the Press over the Vassall affair may have made him wary of facing another hostile campaign over the Falklands.

---

[32] Ibid. 5 Apr. 1982   [33] e.g. Andrew Alexander, *Daily Mail.*
[34] Prior, *A Balance of Power*, 147 (this view was supported by William Whitelaw in *The Whitelaw Memoirs* (London: Aurum Press, 1989)).
[35] Article by Percy Hopkyns, *Daily Express*, 8 Nov. 1962.
[36] Cosgrave, *Carrington: A Life and a Policy*, 68.

Carrington's Resignation Classified

Lord Carrington's resignation can be classified as voluntary in that he was not 'forced' to resign. Parliament did not pass a vote of censure or indicate that it would do so if Carrington's resignation was not forthcoming; neither did the 1922 Committee directly call for Carrington's resignation. However, both were likely to have influenced Carrington in his decision. Their attitudes and comments indicated a lack of support, even hostility, that was reinforced by the Press. Nevertheless, with the Prime Minister's support Carrington might have survived, as Nott did, at least until the Falklands episode was over.

There are two interpretations of Carrington's resignation. The first (put forward by both Geoffrey Marshall and David Judge) suggests that his resignation was a rare example of a minister accepting responsibility for departmental fault or misjudgement in which he was involved, or of which he knew.

Lord Carrington's resignation in 1982, accepting personal responsibility for misjudgement of the danger from Argentina to the Falkland Islands . . . provides a clear precedent for the existence of a rule requiring a Minister who is personally culpable of misjudgement or negligence to offer his resignation.[37]

Such an interpretation arises from a consideration of relevant constitutional history. If precedent indicates that in the particular circumstances a resignation is constitutionally required, then the manner in which the resignation is executed and the political rhetoric that accompanies it do not detract from its constitutional basis or prevent it from becoming a precedent for future resignations.

The alternative interpretation (put forward by both Robert Pyper and Grant Jordan) argues that the resignation should not be seen as a precedent for individual ministerial responsibility, but rather as a manœuvre to avoid government or collective responsibility. 'A more realistic interpretation of the FO resignations would be that they represent not an acceptance, but an attempt at avoidance of responsibility.'[38]

---

[37] Marshall, *Constitutional Conventions*, 65. See also Judge, *Ministerial Responsibility*.
[38] Pyper, 'The FO Resignations', 52. See also Jordan, 'Individual Ministerial Responsibility'.

Carrington's resignation is, therefore, seen as a device to remove pressure from the government, particularly the Prime Minister; his assumption of responsibility was intended to distract attention from the full extent of the government's failures. In this scenario Carrington's resignation was political and any reference to honour and the acceptance of responsibility diversionary and cosmetic. There was no constitutional content.

This interpretation of Carrington's resignation centres upon the cause of the resignation and the reasons offered for it. However, while the resignation of the Foreign Secretary did indeed appease and divert, in the short term at any rate, such diversionary tactics would seem to have substituted one type of responsibility (individual ministerial responsibility) for another (collective) rather than avoiding it altogether. Moreover, the interpretation fails to recognize that a resignation does not necessarily lack a constitutional basis because it is politically convenient and beneficial to the government.

The Pyper–Jordan argument rests on two factors: first, Carrington's failure to admit fault, which, they hold, indicates that his acceptance of responsibility was a sham; secondly, the nature of the policy towards the Falklands, which, they contend, concerned collective decision-making and therefore collective mistakes, for which the government as a whole was answerable. The interpretation also requires either that Carrington was prepared to be a political sacrifice, or that the Prime Minister and senior colleagues decided that he should fulfil that role and that he accepted their verdict. This is by no means certain.

Constitutional responsibility not political sacrifice

Carrington's decision to resign is likely to have been influenced by the Prime Minister, not because she pressed him to resign—indeed, she did the opposite—but because of her attitude to the Falklands. Carrington was not alone among members of the government in believing that the Prime Minister was not just prepared to fight if necessary, but actually preferred that course of action to diplomacy. This, it seems, Carrington could not understand, and he would no doubt have found difficulty in supporting such an attitude. Dispatching the Task Force was one thing, but going to war over the Falklands, without fully exhausting all diplomatic routes, was another: 'the fact that a somewhat incredulous world— and an almost as incredulous Westminster—increasingly accepted over this weekend that Mrs Thatcher was willing to go to war does seem to have played a major part in Carrington's decision to leave office.'[39]

Carrington must have felt out of step with the Prime Minister, most of the Cabinet, the party, and the country. He shared with the Foreign Office a non-nationalistic outlook, while Mrs Thatcher had a 'nationalist outlook on international life'.[40] It was her attitude that appealed to the country at that time, and Carrington, it seems, considered that his resignation, by expiating the need to find a scapegoat, would unite the country behind the Prime Minister.[41]

However, this does not mean that Carrington was offering himself as a political sacrifice to distract attention away from the role of others in the Falklands débâcle. He was recognizing a constitutional obligation to resign from the office of Foreign Secretary because of public outrage over what was seen as a failure by the Foreign Office: 'there was an undeniable feeling in the country that Britain's honour and dignity had been affronted . . . The wide sense of outrage and impotence was understandable and I was head of the Foreign Office.'[42]

This was an acceptance of his own culpability, but not an indication that he would accept blame for the errors of others. Indeed, he made clear that he had opposed the decision of the Secretary of State for Defence to scrap HMS *Endurance*, and was quick respond to an article in *The Times* which attributed the failure to send a nuclear-powered submarine to the South Atlantic to Carrington's concern that it would be too provocative. Lord Carrington wrote: 'This is untrue, as Mr Nott at the Ministry of Defence can testify.'[43] Mr Nott in fact never gave a responding testimony, but perhaps this says more about Mr Nott than about Lord Carrington.

Further indications that Carrington's concern was to fulfil his obligations as the minister responsible were supported by the

---

[39] Cosgrave, *Carrington: A Life and a Policy*, 36.   [40] Ibid. 160.
[41] This was the specific reason Carrington subsequently gave for his resignation. See Lord Carrington, *Reflect on Things Past: The Memoirs of Lord Carrington* (London: Collins, 1989), 370.   [42] HL Deb., 25 Jan. 1983, col. 159.
[43] Letter to *The Times*, 18 June 1983.

statements of his junior ministers. Carrington did not resign alone: with him went Richard Luce and Humphrey Atkins. Luce had been the first to suggest resignation after his experience in the House, and his and Carrington's resignations can be seen in tandem (Atkins, as Lord Privy Seal, did not have the same responsibility). Carrington, of course, never made a resignation speech in the Commons, but Luce did, and his comments suggest that certainly he found the criticism levelled at the Foreign Office, as opposed to ministers, unacceptable: 'it is an insult to Ministers of all Governments, of whatever colour or complexion, to suggest that officials carry responsibility for policy decisions. Ministers do, and that strikes at the heart of our parliamentary system.'[44]

Luce, therefore, took responsibility for the policy of the Foreign Office, and by implication its successes and failures, and it seems reasonable to assume that Carrington shared this view. David Owen made such an assumption, when he praised all three Foreign Office ministers for accepting responsibility: 'They all made the right decision and deserve the respect of the House for re-emphasising the responsibility of individual Ministers—not officials—for the decisions that are made.'[45]

Carrington clearly resented criticism which suggested that officials in the Foreign Office were more concerned with the process of diplomacy than with the policy, or even that they pursued their own policies: 'Those of us politicians who have worked with them [Foreign Office officials] know that there is no more dedicated or patriotic or skilful body of men in England; and I am overwhelmingly resentful of these unjustified criticisms . . .'[46]

In the light of Carrington's comments, it would seem reasonable to assume that his resignation, at least in part, was to stem the tide of often vitriolic criticism against the Foreign Office. Moreover, it could be argued that, far from distracting attention away from the Ministry of Defence and the Prime Minister, the removal of the Foreign Office from the arena of controversy caused the spotlight to fall upon them.

Certainly the Opposition indicated that it was not going to forget the Prime Minister's responsibility in what had happened. Healey maintained that she bore the 'overwhelming responsibility',

---

[44] HC Deb., 7 Apr. 1982, col. 976.   [45] Ibid., col. 986.
[46] HL Deb., 25 Jan. 1983, col. 159.

while Callaghan insisted that she had made 'a gross blunder'.[47] Thus while in the short term Carrington's resignation may have quietened the Conservative back-benchers, who now waited for Mrs Thatcher and John Nott to redeem themselves by repossessing the Falklands, in the longer term it did not succeed in settling the matter, and the Prime Minister was unable to resist the holding of a full inquiry into the Falklands affair. Thus, if Carrington's resignation was a political device to protect the Prime Minister, it was only partly successful.

Individual or collective responsibility

The rationale for the contention that Carrington's resignation was not an example of individual ministerial responsibility but a political gesture lies in part in the argument that the responsibility was a collective or government one, and the Prime Minister, as Chairman of the Defence and Overseas Policy Committee, had 'ultimate responsibility for the failure to prevent the Argentine move on 2 April 1982'.[48] However, this is questionable.

The Defence Committee consisted of the Prime Minister, who was in the chair, the Foreign Secretary, the Secretary of State for Defence, and the Chancellor. The Franks Report stated: 'The timing and agenda of meetings of the Defence Committee are ultimately a matter for the Prime Minister, advised by the Secretary of the Cabinet and the Cabinet Secretariat. Meetings are arranged as required.'[49] However, it was the responsibility of the Foreign Secretary, as his was the lead department on the Falklands, to initiate a meeting if he considered it necessary. This he failed to do. The Report made this clear.

We recognise that Cabinet Committees, such as the Defence Committee, usually meet to take decisions at the invitation of the Minister with proposals to put forward: and we have noted that, in September 1981, the prospect of further negotiations still existed on the basis of agreed government policy. Nevertheless, it was also evident at the time that the policy road ahead, last endorsed by Ministers in January 1981, could well be blocked with serious political repercussions. Officials in both the Foreign and Commonwealth Office and the Ministry of Defence were looking to

---

[47] HC Deb., 7 Apr. 1982, col. 9635, 974.
[48] Pyper, 'The FO Resignations', 83.
[49] *Falkland Islands Review*, Annex B, p. 93.

Ministers to review the outcome of the contingency planning they had done in view of a potentially more aggressive posture by Argentina. In the event Government policy towards Argentina and the Falkland Islands was never formally discussed outside the Foreign and Commonwealth Office after January.[50]

Carrington did circulate minutes to members of the Committee a number of times during the period September 1981 to March 1982. But, significantly, he decided not to present a paper for discussion.[51] As a result there was no meeting of the Defence Committee to discuss the Falklands until 1 April 1982—the day before the invasion—and the issue was not raised in Cabinet until 25 March. However, as indicated by the Franks Report, the deteriorating situation suggested that policy options needed to be reconsidered, and it was for Lord Carrington to inform his colleagues of this need. Franks commented:

We cannot say what the outcome of a meeting of the Defence Committee might have been, or whether the course of events would have been altered if it had met in September 1981; but, in our view, it could have been advantageous, and fully in line with Whitehall practice, for Ministers to have reviewed collectively at this time . . .[52]

For the Prime Minister to call such a meeting she needed to be aware that the situation regarding Argentina required reconsideration, and there is no evidence that she had the necessary facts. For these she relied upon her Foreign Secretary, and he seemed to prefer not to review collectively, but to handle matters himself.

The specific failure to meet in September, referred to by Franks, was due to Carrington's decision not to present a paper proposing a public education campaign on the advantages of leaseback. This was the line recommended by his officials, and supported by Ridley, the junior minister at the time, and Franks believed that it should have been considered—indeed, adopted—as a constructive way forward. The fact that it was not meant that Britain had nothing to offer in negotiations and thus the initiative passed to the Argentinians: 'We conclude that the Government were in a position of weakness, and that the effect of Lord Carrington's decision was to pass the initiative to the Argentine Government.'[53] This is a clear

[50] Ibid., para. 291. [51] Ibid.
[52] Ibid., para. 292. [53] Ibid., para. 290.

indication that Franks considered Carrington culpable, and there were other conclusions that also attributed fault to the Foreign Secretary or his department. The Report commented that the view taken by the Foreign Office early in 1982 of how the dispute would develop was a reasonable one, although 'in the event it proved to be a misjudgement...'.[54] It listed three 'important factors' in the misjudgement: a failure to recognize the urgency of the sovereignty issue to the Argentinians, an under-reaction to the increasingly aggressive Argentinian response, and a belief that any escalation would proceed logically through diplomatic and then economic measures before military action.

Franks considered that ministers had not received the best advice:

We believe that Foreign and Commonwealth Office officials did not attach sufficient weight at this time to the changing Argentine attitude at and following the February talks and did not give sufficient importance to the new and threatening elements in the Argentine Government's position. We conclude that they should have drawn Ministers' attention more effectively to the changing situation.[55]

Franks was also critical of the lack of co-ordination between different parts of the government machine, and, although the Report does not suggest that this was the Foreign Office's responsibility, the Foreign Office is central to both sets of relationships criticized. The Report indicated the need for 'a clearer understanding of the relative roles of the assessment staff, the Foreign and Commonwealth Office and the Ministry of Defence, and for a closer liaison between them'.[56] It also concluded that, had there been 'better liaison between the Foreign and Commonwealth Office, the British Embassy in Buenos Aires and the Government... Ministers would have been better able to deal with the landing on South Georgia when it occurred'.[57]

These conclusions of the Franks Committee indicate that there were constitutional grounds for resignation and that Carrington's resignation was indeed in accordance with the convention of individual ministerial responsibility. He was accepting responsibility for the actions of himself and his department, and hence for the misjudgements that were clearly made.

---

[54] Ibid., para. 296. [55] Ibid., para. 302.
[56] Ibid., para. 317. [57] Ibid., para. 323.

A failure to admit fault

Resignations on the basis of individual ministerial responsibility are an acceptance of fault. However, Carrington never directly reinforced his action by admitting such fault. It is partly on this basis that both Pyper and Jordan argue that the resignation does not belong within this category: 'the whole exercise in honourable sacrifice is marred by the insistence that there have been no errors of judgment.'[58]

Carrington's letter of resignation certainly did not admit to fault, although the statement that 'much' of the criticism was 'unfounded' perhaps suggested that a proportion might have some justification.[59] However, this was not an argument that Carrington was prepared to accept when he was interviewed on television on the evening of his resignation. He insisted that the interpretation of what was happening in the South Atlantic at the time was different from that which could be applied with hindsight, but this did not make it wrong. Nine months later, after the publication of the Franks Report, he still insisted: 'I do not really and honestly think that I can say that I would have done anything of substance differently.'[60]

However, this insistence that he would not have done things differently is not the same as saying that in retrospect there was no miscalculation or misjudgement. The position is rather that, without the benefit of hindsight, these misjudgements would be repeated, perhaps because of inadequate information or because the judgement process itself was faulty. This analysis accords with Richard Luce's statement to the House, in which he spoke for Carrington and Atkins as well, although whether with their permission is not known.

I must tell the House in all humility that in the past few days I have thought carefully about the events of the past few weeks. I can only say that . . . I do not see that in the circumstances of the time my Right Honourable Friends and I would have made any different decisions . . . But with the benefit of hindsight . . . we were wrong, and that is now a fact of history.[61]

---

[58] Jordan, 'Individual Ministerial Responsibility', 135.
[59] *The Times*, 6 Apr. 1982.   [60] HL Deb., 25 Jan. 1983, col. 159.
[61] HC Deb., 7 Apr. 1982, col. 976.

Luce's statement was therefore a recognition of fault, although clearly he was puzzled as to how the fault could have been avoided. Carrington was never that forthcoming, always expressing regret about what happened, but never indicating a shortcoming in himself or his department.

However, Carrington's failure to admit fault does not necessarily affect the constitutional validity of his resignation. It depends on whether it is a requirement of individual ministerial responsibility for the minister to say 'I have done wrong and therefore I resign', or whether it is sufficient for him to say 'you think I have done wrong and because of this I will resign', or even 'I do not recognize that you think I have done wrong, but nevertheless I will resign'. There would seem to be no conventional requirement for any recognition of fault by the resigning minister, and therefore any of these versions seems adequate.

Moreover, even though not admitting fault, Carrington believed, or appeared to believe, that he was acting in accordance with the constitution. He considered that the convention required his acceptance of responsibility for his department and that under the circumstances the only way in which this responsibility could be properly fulfilled was through his resignation. By resigning he was accepting any blame, whether he believed it to be justified or not, and protecting his civil servants.

Pyper argues that Carrington's letter strongly suggested that he had only resigned to restore confidence in the Foreign Office and the government, and that by implication he would have resigned even if there had been no constitutional requirement for him to do so. This seems a doubtful assumption, for there is no political requirement, or perhaps more significantly no political gain, for a minister to sacrifice himself for the good of his department, and only the retaking of the Falkland Islands would restore confidence in the government. Moreover, even if Carrington's actions served a political purpose, this does not negate the constitutional obligation that he appears to have felt.

This was not the first time that Carrington had tendered his resignation. He had been a Parliamentary Under-Secretary in the Ministry of Agriculture in the 1950s and was closely involved in the Crichel Down affair. When Dugdale resigned, Carrington too offered his resignation, but withdrew it when assured that the business was not his fault.[62] This previous instance of a resignation offered strengthens the argument that over the Falklands too it was constitutional rather than political requirements that were of most importance to him. Moreover, there is a further link that can be made between the two resignations. Carrington's resignation, like Dugdale's, can be classified as 'honourable', in the sense that he too took responsibility for his department's shortcomings instead of blaming his civil servants.

The convention of individual ministerial responsibility is frequently modified by political considerations, but in the case of Carrington there was no need for modification. Political considerations were in accord with constitutional requirements. Politically, the head of a senior minister was required. Luce's resignation alone would not have been sufficient. This meant that either Carrington or Nott had to go, and in the event it was Carrington. A number of reasons can be put forward as to why he was preferred. He had a poor relationship with back-benchers; he was not in the House of Commons; his attitude towards the Task Force was ambivalent; and his department was mistrusted in Westminster. However, the key reason must be that he did not allow a choice to be made. He insisted upon resignation. This, however, did not remove culpability from Nott, nor from the Prime Minister.[63]

Much has been made of Lord Carrington's progression from the Foreign Office to General Electric, where he was chairman, and subsequently to head of NATO. This prestigious post has been seen by some as a 'pay off' by the Prime Minister to Carrington for shouldering the blame and accepting the role of scapegoat for the invasion of the Falklands. However, Carrington demonstrated that he was ill-suited for the scapegoat role, refusing to accept any responsibility that was not his to accept, and thereby indicating that, while others might see him as a scapegoat, this was not how he saw himself.

Conjecture in this area is mainly based on the final conclusion of the Franks Report, which appeared to exonerate Carrington. However, a closer reading of the Report indicates that there had been misjudgement by Carrington and his department, and thus in

[62] Pyper suggests that Carrington and his fellow junior minister, Nugent, 'were at least as blameworthy, and possibly more so, than Dugdale himself' (Pyper, 'The FO Resignations', 51).　　　　　[63] See Ch. 7.1.

conventional terms 'fault'. Moreover, the significance in constitutional terms of his resignation is not reduced because personal considerations might have played a part. It is no doubt easier to resign and end a successful political career for the chairmanship of General Electric than for the obscurity of the back-benches (although this second option was not, of course, open to Carrington). However, it would seem unreasonable to insist that ministers must suffer personal and political loss before their resignations are considered to have constitutional validity.

Ministerial responsibility is derided because it is often overridden by political calculation. But there is no reason why personal or political considerations should not act to reinforce constitutional requirements. Indeed, the force of the convention originally was that it supported political practice while at the same time being sustained by it. Carrington's resignation seemed to do just that; it supported the political requirements, while they in this instance gave substance to the constitutional convention.

6.2. LEON BRITTAN: THE WESTLAND AFFAIR

Background

The Westland affair concerned the need to find a solution to the financial problems of the Westland helicopter company and illustrated the inherent conflict for Conservative governments between protecting the defence industrial base and allowing market forces to operate. Linked with this was the question of whether Britain had a commitment to European collaborative ventures in defence, or whether her relationship with the United States was inhibitory. Two options to Westland's problems emerged: first, a rescue by an American company, Sikorsky, which was favoured by the Westland Board; secondly, rather late in the day, the construction of a European consortium of which Westland would be a part.

Both the DTI and the Ministry of Defence had an interest in Westland and they came to support different solutions. The DTI, which was the sponsoring department, was headed by Leon Brittan. He moved from a position of proclaimed impartiality to support for the Sikorsky option. However, the Ministry of Defence, led by Michael Heseltine, provided most of the orders for Westland and favoured a European solution, arguing that it would better protect Britain's defence industrial base.

Government policy on Westland, as stated by the Prime Minister, was impartiality and non-interference; it was for Westland to make the decision on a commercial basis. By November 1985 the Sikorsky deal looked certain, but at this stage Heseltine began to campaign fervently among his ministerial colleagues for a European solution. However, he failed to get the full option discussed at the Economic Subcommittee or to get Westland on to the Cabinet agenda. He argued, therefore, that there had been no collective judgement made about the alternative proposal (indeed, that any discussion had been deliberately blocked by the Prime Minister) and so he was not bound by collective responsibility. This led to his controversial decision to make public his disagreement with stated government policy. As the Defence Committee reported: 'The Government was now treated to the unusual spectacle of one of its number, supported by the resources of his department, pursuing a policy which was diametrically opposed to the government's stated policy.'[64]

Heseltine's behaviour inevitably brought him into direct conflict with Leon Brittan at the DTI. Brittan soon found that the Prime Minister supported his line, but was not prepared to take direct action against Heseltine. He therefore moved to counter Heseltine himself, but his actions were even more controversial than those of the Secretary of State for Defence; for, while Heseltine may have shown complete disregard for declared government policy, his actions were at least open. Brittan, however, believed it was necessary to act more discreetly; subsequently his actions were to seem underhand and unworthy of a senior member of the government.

Heseltine campaigned to convince the public and the shareholders of Westland that a European solution was better both commercially and politically. Brittan publicly decried his actions, particularly his lobbying of Members of Parliament, but he too embarked on a campaign 'to give the facts',[65] although only the facts relating to the Sikorsky solution. Moreover, he considered it imprudent to be 'personally' involved (perhaps not surprisingly

[64] HC519 (1985–6), para. 105.
[65] *The Defence Implications of the Future of Westland plc: Minutes of Evidence, and Appendices* (1985–6), HC169, HMSO, Q801.

since he still insisted in public that he was impartial) and therefore left the matter to his civil servants.

As a result, Winston Churchill, a member of the Defence Committee, was lobbied by an official from the DTI on Mr Brittan's 'express instructions', and other Members of Parliament seem to have been contacted by civil servants acting 'on their own initiative' or because of a 'chance remark' from Mr Brittan.[66]

Brittan's use of his civil servants for political campaigning, and their apparent assumption that they could, or should, act on their own initiative, were strongly criticized by the Defence Committee inquiring into the Westland affair. The Committee suggested that the actions of the DTI indicated a belief that Heseltine's breach of the convention of collective responsibility meant that 'he could be thwarted by any means'. This, said the Defence Committee, 'cannot be justified.'[67]

However, such an assumption may have contributed to the disclosure of parts of a confidential letter from the Solicitor-General, Sir Patrick Mayhew, to Michael Heseltine. The letter was a response to one written by Heseltine to Lloyds Merchant Bank, who represented the European consortium. Heseltine's communication, as he intended, was made public by Lloyds. It stated that, if Westland joined with Sikorsky, the company might no longer be a welcome participant in European collaborative projects. Sir Patrick Mayhew was asked by Leon Brittan, who was acting for the Prime Minister, to give his opinion on the letter. He advised that, on the evidence he had seen, it might contain 'material inaccuracies',[68] and he informed Michael Heseltine in writing to this effect.

The Solicitor-General's letter was copied to the Prime Minister, the Foreign Secretary, the Chief Secretary to the Treasury, and the Secretary of State for Trade and Industry. Within hours of its dispatch extracts of the letter were leaked to the Press by an unknown party. The extracts were selective and, as the Defence Committee concluded, 'calculated to do the maximum damage to Mr Heseltine's case and his personal credibility'.[69]

However, public attention was temporarily distracted from the leaking of the letter by the resignation of Michael Heseltine three days later. On 6 January he dramatically walked out of a Cabinet

---

[66] Ibid., Q831.   [67] HC519 (1985–6), para. 109.
[68] Prime Minister's statement to the House, HC Deb., 27 Jan. 1986, col. 655.
[69] HC519 (1985–6), para. 162.

meeting after Mrs Thatcher ruled that in future all statements by ministers on the subject of Westland had to be cleared by the Cabinet Office. This was the occasion to which Heseltine referred during his campaign for the leadership in November 1990, when he accused Mrs Thatcher of reading the conclusions in advance of the discussion. It may be concluded, a little more charitably, that the Prime Minister had prudently included a draft conclusion in her brief (not an unusual procedure) and was impatient with discussion.

Heseltine's resignation

Heseltine's resignation and his subsequent statements revealed a considerable amount about the working of Cabinet government in the 1980s. It also had relevance for the convention of individual ministerial responsibility, not because it complied with any formulation of the convention (Heseltine did not resign for departmental or personal fault) but because of the insight it provided into the tension between collective and individual responsibility.

Heseltine insisted that his resignation was not brought about because he disagreed with the government's collective policy. In his view there was no collective policy. Nor was he sacked for failing to support the government line, although it is possible to see his resignation as constructive dismissal—the Prime Minister pushing him to a point where she knew he would have little option but to resign.

He gave three reasons for his resignation: first, the use by Brittan of his position to support Sikorsky; secondly, the Prime Minister's refusal to allow Heseltine 'the collective judgement of his colleagues' (and her failure to ensure that his protest was recorded in the Cabinet Minutes); thirdly, the unprecedented Cabinet procedure which required all statements on Westland, including reiterations of past positions, to be cleared with the Cabinet Office. Heseltine claimed that such vetting would work to the advantage of Sikorsky and that it would also interfere with 'my right as the responsible minister to answer questions on defence procurement issues in line with policies my colleagues have not contradicted'.[70]

Heseltine maintained that he was being prevented from

---

[70] P. Hennessy, 'Helicopter Crashes into Cabinet: Prime Minister and Constitution Hurt', *Journal of Law and Society*, 13/3 (1986), 427.

adequately fulfilling his function as a minister and from being accountable as the convention of individual ministerial responsibility required. His comments suggested that collective responsibility was not concerned with collective decision-making, but rather that it was a mechanism by which an individual minister could be prevented from following his preferred policy and from fulfilling his constitutional obligation. It therefore reduced, and even precluded, the accountability of the individual minister.

Sir Robert Armstrong's inquiry

The public and politicians may have been distracted from the leaking of the Solicitor-General's letter but the Law Officers had not been. They insisted on an inquiry into the leak and the Prime Minister had little option but to agree. The inquiry was conducted by Sir Robert Armstrong, Cabinet Secretary and Head of the Home Civil Service, and his report was presented to Mrs Thatcher on 22 January 1986. The Prime Minister gave the findings to Parliament the following day, but the full report was never made public, and when the Defence Committee investigated the disclosure, it was not given the co-operation necessary for all the facts to be uncovered. There are, therefore, still many unanswered questions.

The only official information on the leaking of the letter came from statements in the House by the Prime Minister and Leon Brittan, and from evidence given to the Defence Committee by Brittan, Sir Robert Armstrong, and Sir Brian Hayes, Permanent Secretary at the DTI. The government refused to allow the Committee to question the civil servants involved, namely, Mogg, Mitchell, and Bowe from the DTI, and Ingham and Powell from Number Ten, and the Committee, whilst expressing its displeasure, did not pursue the matter by bringing it before the full House.

According to Sir Robert, officials at the DTI believed it was imperative that the public should be made aware that Heseltine's letter contained 'material inaccuracies'.[71] Moreover, there was a particular urgency, because Westland was due to hold a press conference later that day. Therefore, when a copy of the Solicitor-General's letter came through to the Department, John Mogg, Brittan's personal private secretary, contacted the minister by

[71] HC169 (1985–6), Q1190.

telephone at his luncheon engagement. He read the letter to him and asked whether it should be made public, and, if so, whether this should be 'in general or specific terms'. 'The Secretary of State responded that he thought it should go into the public domain and that it should be done in specific terms but that Number Ten, the Prime Minister's Office, should be consulted.'[72] Sir Robert's paraphrase of Brittan's response to Mogg seems to underplay Brittan's concern that Number Ten should give its agreement. Brittan told the Defence Committee: 'I would particularly stress, it all had to be subject to the agreement of Number Ten.'[73]

Number Ten, however, would not countenance disclosure of the letter from the Prime Minister's Office, as Mogg discovered when he telephoned Powell. As well as their conversation, there was also one between Colette Bowe, press secretary at the DTI, and Bernard Ingham; they arrived at the same conclusion.

During these conversations, there was, according to Lord Armstrong, 'a difference of understanding' about what was being sought and what was being given. He insisted: 'I am absolutely clear that the officials at Number Ten did not believe, from the conversations, that they were being asked to convey an agreement on which the Secretary of State's authority was conditional. I think this is where the misunderstanding . . . arose.'[74]

This suggests that either Brittan's officials expressed themselves so badly that Powell and Ingham failed to understand the position, or that they did not comply with Brittan's requirements. There is, of course, an alternative. Perhaps Sir Robert was mistaken in his belief that the officials at Number Ten did not understand what they were being asked to do.

It is not known exactly how the telephone conversations concluded and whether the DTI officials believed they had the agreement of Number Ten or not. Sir Robert's statement on the matter suggested that Number Ten 'accepted' the disclosure of the letter from the DTI,[75] but the Defence Committee was somewhat sceptical, asking whether perhaps Number Ten 'insisted' rather than 'accepted' that the disclosure came from the DTI and also suggested the method of disclosure.[76] There is certainly an implication that Colette Bowe felt she was being pushed into doing something

---

[72] Ibid.   [73] Ibid., Q933.   [74] Ibid., Q1318.
[75] Ibid., Q1288.   [76] Ibid., Q1297.

she knew to be improper, for she made unsuccessful attempts to contact her permanent secretary, Sir Brian Hayes, for advice.[77]

Moreover, this view is supported by comments made in April 1989 by Sir Leon Brittan. He declared that Ingham and Powell gave their 'express approval' to the leaking of the letter and stated that there would have been no question of releasing the document without this approval.[78] He did not expand upon what he meant by the phrase, and subsequently insisted that he had said nothing new. However, he had said something new, for 'express approval' certainly means more than a general, non-specific agreement which might be misunderstood or misinterpreted. It suggests that Number Ten did indeed give specific authority.

Sir Bernard Ingham's later recollection of events would not seem quite to correspond with that of Sir Leon Brittan. Ingham stated that Colette Bowe asked him to leak the letter, something which he refused 'point blank' to do.

I told Colette Bowe that I had to keep the Prime Minister above that sort of thing. At no time was I asked to approve of the disclosure. I could not have done so without seeking Mrs Thatcher's specific permission, and I would not have been prepared to put such an idea to her.[79]

Ingham considered that the reason the DTI was subsequently able to claim Number Ten had approved of the disclosure of the letter was because of his failure to advise Colette Bowe against it. 'It was at best tacit acceptance in the sense that I did not actively object to a Ministerial decision to disclose it.'[80]

Whatever happened, the intention was to give extracts of the Solicitor-General's letter to the Press, and to give them unattributably. The selection of the extracts, according to Sir Robert, was made by two officials from the DTI (presumably Mogg and Bowe), and he thought it 'unlikely' that Mr Brittan had authorized the method of disclosure.[81] When the Defence Committee pressed Brittan as to whether he had authorized the release of the whole document, he replied: 'I am not in a position to answer your question.'[82]

He also refused to say who selected the passages or whether he

---

[77] Ibid., Q1324.   [78] *Sunday Times*, 4 Apr. 1989.
[79] B. Ingham, *Kill the Messenger* (London: HarperCollins, 1991), 331.
[80] Ibid.   [81] HC169 (1985–6), Q1249.   [82] Ibid., Q936.

knew the facts to enable him to answer the questions. He did, however, accept in the House on 27 January that 'the disclosure of that information—urgent and important as it was—should not have taken place in that way, and I profoundly regret that it happened'.[83]

Brittan's officials must also have recognized that the disclosure 'should not have taken place in that way', or indeed at all, for they must have been aware that convention requires that the advice of the law officers, and even the fact that advice had been given, should remain confidential. Brittan took full responsibility for what his officials did, but the question remains as to whether he was also taking responsibility for the actions of the officials at Number Ten and even the Prime Minister.

The Prime Minister always stated that she was completely unaware of Leon Brittan's part in the disclosure of the letter until she received Sir Robert Armstrong's report. This statement has caused considerable scepticism, requiring, as it does, the acceptance that Mrs Thatcher, who previously had been fully involved in the Westland affair, had not considered it necessary to demand an explanation from her officials, that they had chosen not to tell her what had happened, and that Leon Brittan had also not spoken to the Prime Minister on the matter. Even Sir Robert conceded that the Prime Minister's apparent lack of concern to investigate the matter was 'strange'.[84]

The findings of the inquiry failed to answer adequately the crucial question of whether Brittan had the authority of the Prime Minister—either explicit or implicit—to disclose the letter. Sir Robert said that he found no evidence that he did have this authority, but, as the Defence Committee suggested, this might mean no more than that the officials interviewed did not know of such authority.

Sir Robert never interviewed Leon Brittan. Indeed, it seems that Brittan remained silent throughout the investigation, allowing his officials to face an inquiry into their actions and to be named in Parliament and the Press. Yet, if his subsequent insistence that he had authorized these actions is to be believed, he could have prevented an inquiry by accepting responsibility. His behaviour as the

[83] HC Deb., 27 Jan. 1986, col. 671.   [84] HC169 (1985–6), Q1320.

responsible minister was criticized by the Defence Committee for being unprofessional.

If as the Prime Minister repeatedly told the House, the Department of Trade and Industry officials were confident that they had Mr Brittan's authority for the disclosure, and if, as Mr Brittan has confirmed, he gave them that authority, his silence during that time might be thought to have fallen short of the backing which a Minister normally gives his officials.[85]

Much hinges, of course, on what he gave authority for and to what extent the authority was conditional on approval from Number Ten. This has never been clear. When Brittan appeared before the Defence Committee, he refused to answer questions which would have revealed when he was first involved in discussions about releasing the information, and whether he spoke to anyone at Number Ten about disclosing the Solicitor-General's letter. He also refused to say whether he had any conversation with the Prime Minister about his authorization of the disclosure prior to her receiving the report.

Leon Brittan's refusal to answer the questions put by the Defence Committee inevitably led to speculation that his silence was because his answers would have conflicted with those given by Sir Robert Armstrong and Mrs Thatcher. This in turn implies that the Prime Minister had been involved in the disclosure of the letter, at least to the extent that it was known that she wished it to happen. Indeed, Brittan's later comments on Westland suggest that either the Prime Minister authorized the disclosure of the letter, in which case she was guilty of impropriety, or her officials authorized it without her approval and thus they improperly exceeded their authority.

On 23 January Mrs Thatcher revealed the findings of Sir Robert Armstrong's report to Parliament. She stated that the Solicitor-General's letter had been released by officials in the DTI on the authority of the Secretary of State, Mr Leon Brittan, and with the agreement of Number Ten, but without her knowledge. On the following day Brittan resigned. On 27 January an emergency debate on the disclosure of the Solicitor-General's letter was held and Mrs Thatcher's claim of non-involvement was accepted, if not entirely believed, at least by those who mattered—the Conservative back-benchers.

---

[85] HC519 (1985–6), para. 205.

Factors Influencing Brittan's Resignation

Parliament

The revelation that the Solicitor-General's letter had been disclosed on the authority of Leon Brittan was greeted with outrage by Parliament. His silence up to that point, together with the setting-up of the inquiry, had led to assumptions that the letter had been leaked by an official on his or her own initiative rather than being sanctioned by a minister. Moreover, the underhand method used was thought (perhaps naïvely) to be inappropriate in British political life, and more consistent with corrupt American practice.

Brittan might have survived if this had been his only misdemeanour. But the episode of the Solicitor-General's letter followed close behind another controversy, also involving a letter. On 8 January a meeting had taken place between Brittan and Sir Raymond Lygo, Managing Director of British Aerospace and also spokesman for the European consortium.

Michael Heseltine had at the time made public allegations that Brittan had exerted undue pressure on Sir Raymond Lygo, suggesting that he withdraw from the European consortium, in case the Airbus project, in which he was involved with the United States, was put in jeopardy. On 13 January Sir Austin Pearce, Chairman of British Aerospace, wrote to the Prime Minister confirming Heseltine's allegation and complaining of Brittan's behaviour.

Brittan was informed of Pearce's letter by the Prime Minister's office just as he was leaving for the House. However, when questioned about the existence of the letter in the House, his replies were evasive and misleading. Whilst never telling a direct lie (perhaps because nobody asked exactly the right question), the impression he gave was that no letter had been received. Moreover, as he was sitting beside the Prime Minister, there is a presumption that he was acting under her instructions, or at least not contrary to her wishes.

By the late afternoon it was clear that Brittan had been less than honest with Parliament and that evening he returned to the House to apologize: 'If it is thought that I have in any way misled the House, I apologize unreservedly.'[86] Brittan gave for a reason the

---

[86] HC Deb., 13 Jan. 1986, col. 872.

fact that the letter was marked 'private and strictly confidential' and therefore it was 'essential that I took great care in what I said to protect the strict confidence attached to it by Sir Austin Pearce'.[87]

It is interesting that Brittan should attach such significance to confidentiality in this instance when (unknown as yet to the House) only a few days previously he had given his authority to the disclosure of confidential material written by the Solicitor-General. The inevitable conclusion is that his attitude towards confidentiality varied with the occasion.

Nor was it only Leon Brittan's integrity that was brought into question by his actions in the House. The Prime Minister too was implicated in the episode. Roy Jenkins summed it up pointedly:

Is it not the case that, although the behaviour of the Secretary of State has been pathetic, the behaviour of the Prime Minister has been much more extraordinary? . . . For the Prime Minister to sit there for half an hour and allow the Secretary of State to mislead the House was a most extraordinary procedure. Although what the Secretary of State said may just be within the formal bounds of the truth, the margin is so narrow that we shall count our spoons quickly whenever they are together again.[88]

Parliament no longer trusted the Thatcher–Brittan duo, and this was before it knew of Sir Robert Armstrong's conclusions.

Even the subsequent letter written by Lygo and made public on 17 January did little to bolster Brittan's flagging reputation. For, although Lygo wrote of an 'unfortunate misunderstanding',[89] the damage had been done. It appeared that Leon Brittan with the Prime Minister's approval had tried to cover up Pearce's letter, and this could only be explained if its accusations were true. Lygo's revision of the interpretation of the meeting did little to change this view. It is, therefore, hardly suprising, given the prevailing attitude to Brittan, that, when his part in the release of the Solicitor-General's letter became known, he should find little support anywhere in Parliament.

The 1922 Committee

Brittan was not by all accounts a popular minister. He had no following in the House, owing his position in Cabinet to prime ministerial patronage rather than party support. During the evening

---

[87] Ibid., col. 876.   [88] Ibid., col. 874.   [89] HC169 (1985–6), p. 369.

of 23 January, after the Prime Minister had made her statement in the House, the 1922 Committee met. Its members declared their support for Mrs Thatcher, but called for the resignation, or, if necessary, dismissal, of Leon Brittan. Members were offended by the seemingly devious nature of his behaviour, which had demonstrated itself in the use of his civil servants to lobby Members of Parliament and to leak a confidential document, and by his failure to accept responsibility before such an acceptance became unavoidable. Most important of all, however, back-benchers could not forgive him for implicating the Prime Minister in a sordid affair which probably could have been avoided by his prompt resignation. Brittan's resignation was therefore seen as essential to distance him from Mrs Thatcher and enable the party to rally around her.

The opinion of the Committee was conveyed to Mrs Thatcher by the Chief Whip, John Wakeham, after he had been briefed by the Chairman of the Committee, Cranley Onslow. The following day Leon Brittan heard from both men of the lack of support from the party. It appears that it was this strength of party opinion against him that was most influential in Brittan's decision to resign. If he remained in office, then he would be required to make the winding-up speech for the Emergency Debate, scheduled for Monday, 27 January. Without party support, he would be humiliated.

The Prime Minister

Mrs Thatcher stood firmly beside Leon Brittan. She stated her belief that the disclosure of the Solicitor-General's letter was not 'a resigning matter' and indeed tried to dissuade him from this course of action, as her reply to his resignation letter indicated: 'I am very sorry that despite all the arguments I could use I was unable to dissuade you this afternoon from resigning ... It was my wish that you should remain as a member of the Cabinet.'[90]

Many suspected that her loyalty to Brittan was born out of a guilty conscience, but it must also be remembered that she had already lost one minister when Heseltine resigned. Losing two colleagues over the same incident was not good for her, or the government's, public reputation, not to mention their actual

[90] *The Times*, 25 Jan. 1986.

effectiveness. Howe and Whitelaw also believed that Brittan should stay, but, despite their representations to him, Leon Brittan resigned.

Brittan's Resignation Classified

Brittan's letter of resignation showed no recognition of a constitutional requirement for relinquishing office. His stated reason was political—he had lost the support of the party. His letter to the Prime Minister said:

Since your statement in the House yesterday, it has become clear to me that I no longer command the full confidence of my colleagues.

In the circumstances, my continued membership of your government would be a source of weakness rather than strength . . . it is for this reason that I have tendered my resignation.[91]

Brittan's letter gives no indication that his action was governed by any feeling of constitutional obligation. It is also clear that the Prime Minister saw no constitutional requirement for resignation, and the opinion expressed by the 1922 Committee owed more to personal animosity towards Brittan and the fear of political damage to the Prime Minister, and hence the party, than to constitutional propriety. Thus, if the constitutional character of a resignation is in part measured by the extent to which the political actors feel and express a moral obligation to resign, or to request a minister's resignation, then the departure of the Secretary of State for Trade and Industry barely registered on the constitutional scale.

However, the available evidence suggests that there was a constitutional requirement for Brittan's resignation. Brittan did not have the authority to order the release of a confidential letter from a law officer to another minister without the permission of both parties. He had, therefore, authorized something he had no right to authorize, and his officials had carried out his instructions. Indeed, it seems likely that his officials exceeded these instructions, either because they believed Brittan expected then to act on their own initiative, or because they came under pressure from Number Ten, or because they misunderstood the degree of cover they were being given. This suggests a combination of civil service and ministerial fault.

[91] Ibid.

The ministerial fault became more serious constitutionally because of Brittan's initial reluctance to accept responsibility for the actions of his officials when their actions were so closely bound to his own. In retrospect, when the findings of the inquiry were made public, Brittan's behaviour appeared to be that of a minister who was prepared to see his civil servants shoulder the blame in the hope that his part in the affair might be minimalized. However, he did finally come to accept responsibility for what had happened. In his resignation statement to the House he said: 'I . . . accept full responsibility for the fact and the form of that disclosure.'[92]

He also told the Defence Committee that he took full responsibility for what his officials had done: 'not just in some formal constitutional sense, but also in the sense that I am not suggesting that they went in any way beyond what I authorised them to do.'[93]

Moreover, Brittan expressed his regret at what had happened, thus recognizing that a serious misjudgement had been made: 'the disclosure of that information—urgent and important though it was—should not have taken place in that way, and I profoundly regret that it happened.'[94]

However, the acceptance of responsibility and the expression of regret by Brittan happened after his resignation. This and his refusal to answer certain questions put by the Defence Committee, which left his officials vulnerable and exposed again to criticism, gave his acceptance a hollow ring.

In any case, an acceptance of responsibility, even if exercised through resignation, is not sufficient to fulfil the constitutional requirements of accountability. It may be the final part of the process of accounting, but it is not a substitute for explanation. As the Defence Committee stated: 'Accountability involves ACCOUNTING in detail for actions as a Minister.'[95]

Brittan failed to account to Parliament, either before or after his resignation. This suggests that his concern was not with constitutional conventions but with political-damage limitation and loyalty to the Prime Minister.

How then should Brittan's resignation be categorized? There is little doubt that his resignation had a constitutional foundation. There had been departmental fault on the part of both the minister

---

[92] HC Deb., 27 Jan. 1986, col. 671.   [93] HC169 (1985–6), Q967.
[94] HC Deb., 27 Jan. 1986, col. 671.   [95] HC519 (1985–6), para. 235.

and his officials, and this was considered serious enough by Parliament and the party for resignation to be required. Brittan, in accordance with constitutional principles, accepted responsibility for his actions and the actions of his civil servants and resigned from office. To this extent his resignation is certainly in the tradition of the Dugdale–Carrington resignations for departmental fault in which the minister is involved. Moreover, Brittan also accepted that there had been fault—an acceptance never made by Carrington—which earns a few more points on the constitutional scale.

However, Brittan's acceptance of responsibility came too late to be seen as 'honourable', either in the sense of self-sacrifice or in preserving personal dignity and standing. His officials had already been named and blamed, although, if the facts are as stated, they were acting either specifically or generally upon Mr Brittan's orders.

Moreover, the classic statements of responsibility, instead of being accompanied by explanation, were used to evade accountability. The doctrine of individual ministerial responsibility therefore became a shield to protect the Prime Minister and the government, instead of a constitutional procedure to ensure accountability.

Brittan resigned because he lost the support of the party. His part in the disclosure of the Solicitor-General's letter was unacceptable, especially following his previous actions. Moreover, the party needed a scapegoat. There was nothing grand or honourable about his resignation. He went because he was pushed, and he went reluctantly. His resignation may be seen as an indication that resignations for departmental fault still occur and indeed support the constitutional convention, but it should be recognized that political expediency and not constitutional duty was in this instance the primary motivation.

7

Cases of Non-Resignation: Political Circumstances and Constitutional Obligations

7.1. SIR JOHN NOTT: THE FALKLANDS EPISODE

Background

The invasion of the Falkland Islands led directly to the resignations of Carrington, Luce, and Atkins from the Foreign Office, but Sir John Nott, Secretary of State for Defence, remained in office. His failure to resign has been seen by some as evidence that the Foreign Office resignations were not examples of individual ministerial responsibility, but rather that Carrington, Luce, and Atkins were taking the blame for a collective decision.[1]

It is more appropriate, however, to see Carrington and Nott as having separate responsibility. Both may have been culpable but not jointly culpable. Cosgrave suggested:

if the Foreign Office had been culpably blind in not reading correctly the political signals of a bellicose character emanating from Buenos Aires, then the Secretary of State for Defence could be said to have been a trifle careless in considering the military requirements of the Falkland Islands.[2]

The Franks Report recognized this 'carelessness' or misjudgement, being particularly critical of the decision to scrap HMS *Endurance*. It was also dissatisfied with the response of the Ministry of Defence to the worsening situation:

The decision to sail the first nuclear-powered submarine was taken on Monday, 29th March.

We consider that there was a case for taking this action at the end of the previous week . . . we would have expected a quicker reaction in the Ministry of Defence.[3]

---

[1] See Ch. 6.1.   [2] Cosgrave, *Carrington: A Life and a Policy*, 39.
[3] *Falkland Islands Review*, paras. 331, 332.

Carrington and Nott were therefore both at fault, but, while Carrington resigned, Nott remained in office. In the case of Carrington the constitutional and political requirements coincided, but with Nott an initial coincidence of the political and the constitutional gave way to a predominance of political considerations, which worked to prevent, or at least defer, his resignation.

Political Considerations

The reaction of the House of Commons to the invasion of the Falkland Islands was one of outrage. Members of Parliament were particularly annoyed about the decision to scrap *Endurance*, and they had the chance to express their feelings when Nott spoke in the debate on 3 April, the day after the invasion. He gave an unconvincing performance and Members from both sides of the House indicated their dissatisfaction by constant interruptions and cries of disbelief. *The Times* reported:

To anyone of a moderately generous frame of mind, the treatment of the Secretary of State for Defence was cruelty beyond human endurance. But there could have been few listening to his far from plausible attempts to justify the delay in responding to the early warning signals that an invasion was imminent, who would have felt that at that moment Mr Nott's departure from the government was not just around the corner.[4]

Nott seemed to have lost the support of the House. Most Members believed that he and his department were guilty of failing to prevent the Argentinian invasion, and the evidence suggests that they certainly misjudged the situation. The convention of individual ministerial responsibility required that Nott resign, and the political situation seemed to support it. However, later that day he appeared alongside Carrington before the 1922 Committee and seemed to redeem himself a little. His determination to retake the Falkland Islands, using force if necessary, struck the right chord with back-benchers, as it did subsequently with the Press. *The Times* announced that Nott's standing had been somewhat restored by his readiness to fight, which he had made plain in a television interview with *Weekend World*: 'We are going to restore British administration to the Falkland Islands. That was the Prime Minister's commitment. We mean to stick to it even if we have to fight.'[5]

[4] *The Times*, 5 Apr. 1982.   [5] Ibid.

Nott did qualify his comments by saying that the overriding objective was to restore sovereignty by peaceful means, but the emphasis of *The Times* report was on his willingness to use force. This suited the mood of the country.

Despite a slight mellowing of attitudes towards Nott, accompanied by increased hostility towards Carrington, the Secretary of State for Defence must have spent the weekend considering his position. He was clearly in touch with the Prime Minister at some time, as the letter in which he offered his resignation indicated: 'In view of the public reaction and now that the Task Force has sailed, I would like to confirm the message which I have already sent to you, that I wish to put my office at your disposal.'[6]

The Prime Minister rejected his offer, but it is interesting to speculate whether, if she had managed to persuade Carrington over the weekend to remain in office, she would have accepted Nott's resignation. It is possible that Mrs Thatcher recognized the political necessity of losing one of her ministers and that she would have preferred that minister to have been Nott rather than Carrington.

Nott's offer of resignation was different from Carrington's. First, Carrington did not offer to resign but stated that he was resigning. Nott clearly was prepared to stay in office if the Prime Minister wished him to do so. Secondly, there was no acceptance of responsibility by Nott, and no suggestion that he believed that constitutionally he was under an obligation to resign. It would seem to have been a political rather than a constitutional gesture. However, by the time the gesture was made, the political requirements had changed. Carrington and his junior ministers had resigned, and the Prime Minister clearly did not wish for further resignations. Moreover, the Ministry of Defence was now the key department. She needed its minister to be committed to her viewpoint, and to be as dependent upon success in the South Atlantic as she was. In addition, if Nott remained in charge, he would not be able to blame any shortcomings on his predecessors, as an incoming minister would have been able to do.

The dispatch of the Task Force and the resignation of Lord Carrington combined to quieten Conservative back-benchers, and relieve the pressure on Nott to resign. There were other pressures,

6 Ibid., 6 Apr. 1982.

however, for there is little doubt that Nott was on trial throughout the Falklands conflict. Although the Falklands Campaign succeeded in restoring British sovereignty to the Islands, in many ways it was not a success for Nott. Indeed, after the retaking of the Falklands, *The Times* suggested that the Prime Minister would be requiring his resignation, commenting: 'It was not Nott's war and neither is it likely to be Nott's peace.'[7]

The Prime Minister did not ask Nott to resign at this time. However, on 2 September 1982 Nott announced that he would not stand at the next general election. He was retiring from politics to resume a business career while he was still relatively young. This, he stated, had always been his intention.[8] (Indeed, he was one of a number of Conservative ministers for whom resignation or dismissal proved a path to affluence.) News of his decision was released from Downing Street and the Prime Minister expressed her regret.

Conclusion

Sir John Nott did, therefore, in the end resign. At first glance his resignation owed nothing to the convention of individual ministerial responsibility. He certainly never accepted responsibility or admitted fault (although recognition of fault would not seem to be a requirement of the convention). However, there would seem to have been a constitutional requirement for his resignation after the invasion of the Falklands, and it is therefore possible to see his departure from office as a delayed fulfilment of that requirement. Just as the line between resignation and dismissal is often blurred, so the timing of a resignation may confuse attempts at classification. However, if it is accepted that at times individual ministerial responsibility may be delayed in its operation, then Nott's resignation can be seen in this light.

7.2. JAMES PRIOR: THE MAZE PRISON BREAKOUT

Background

On 25 September 1983 thirty-eight Republican prisoners shot their way out of the Maze Prison in Northern Ireland, killing one prison

---

[7] Ibid., 17 June 1982.   [8] *Independent*, 3 Sept. 1982.

officer and injuring several others. Mr James Prior, Secretary of State for Northern Ireland, announced the setting-up of a full inquiry to be conducted by Sir James Hennessy, Chief Inspector of Prisons in the United Kingdom.

Parliament was in recess, but Prior immediately faced criticism from Unionist Members of Parliament in Northern Ireland. They contended that the lax security at the Maze was the general responsibility of the Northern Ireland Office and the personal responsibility of the Under-Secretary of State, Nicholas Scott, whose responsibilities included prisons in the province. The focus upon Scott was a continuation of a campaign against him which had begun in the summer, not long after he had taken office, and which stemmed from his offer to meet Noraid, the New York-based group of Republican fund-raisers. The meeting never took place, but Scott's resignation was sought by Ulster Unionists then, and it was sought again after the Maze break-out.

As pressure grew for Scott's resignation, Prior indicated that, if his Under-Secretary were forced from office, he too would go. This was similar to the position adopted by Carrington—either both went or neither did. This seems to be the accepted constitutional position where departmental fault is concerned. The responsibility belongs to the Secretary of State and, whatever delegatory arrangements he might make with a junior minister, he cannot devolve ministerial responsibility. Prior himself later illustrated the position in relation to another junior minister within his department: 'In discharging his duties, my hon. Friend acts on my behalf.'[9]

In the event, judgement about the need for resignation by either, or both, Northern Ireland ministers was withheld until the publication of the Hennessy Report. However, within a few days of the start of the inquiry, 'intelligence sources' were indicating that human error had been responsible,[10] and, when Parliament reconvened, Prior stated the terms on which his resignation would be forthcoming. He would resign if the Report found that government policy was to blame for the break-out, or if it considered that the incident had resulted from his failure to implement something which it was his duty to implement.[11] In view of the leaked information it seemed unlikely that the Report would reach either of these conclusions.

[9] HC Deb., 8 Feb. 1984, col. 623.   [10] *The Times*, 29 Sept. 1984.
[11] HC Deb., 24 Oct. 1983, cols. 23-4.

Prior's statement has been portrayed as an attempt to redraw the lines of ministerial responsibility by separating policy from administration and asserting that he, as the minister, was under no obligation to resign for errors arising in the second category of administration. Such a formulation requires a clear split between administration and policy and a presumption that any policy content can be isolated—a dubious proposition.

In the subsequent debate on the Hennessy Report, the difficulty of making this clear division was raised by Julian Amery with reference to the situation of the Secretary of State for Northern Ireland:

the line between administration and policy is very blurred. . . . Some Ministers—and the Secretary of State for Education springs to mind—are concerned with policy but do not, for example, control the schools. They are in the province of the local authority. However, the Secretary of State for Northern Ireland . . . is administrator and policy maker. . . .[12]

It may be possible, and indeed necessary, to make a clear divide between administration and policy when the responsibility is divided between two constitutionally or legally separate bodies, although, even then, the division of responsibilities, and hence accountability, is not always completely along the lines of policy and administration.

Using Amery's example, local authorities make policy about schools as well as administering them, and, with the ability of schools to opt out of local authority control, the minister may carry some responsibility for administration in these cases. The constitutional acceptability of ministers being unaccountable for all that happens within schools lies not in the easy split between policy and administration, but in there being some other body, namely local authorities (or increasingly Boards of Governors), which can be held politically accountable instead. This is not the case in many areas of government, where, if ministers refused to accept responsibility for administration, there would be no line of responsibility at all.

Enoch Powell succinctly expressed the constitutional problems for accountability if this view of ministerial responsibility were accepted:

[12] Ibid., 9 Feb. 1984, col. 1073.

I believe that this is a wholly fallacious view of the nature of ministerial responsibility . . . the responsibility for the administration of a Department remains irrevocably with the Minister in charge. It is impossible for him to say to the House and to the country, 'The policy was excellent and that was mine, but the execution was defective or disastrous and that had nothing to do with me.' If that were to be the accepted position, there would be no political source to which the public could complain about administration or from which it could seek redress for failings in administration.[13]

Powell was correct in terms of the overall convention of individual ministerial responsibility. It would be unacceptable for a minister to refuse to answer questions, to explain, and even to take amendatory action, if necessary. But, in the Maze case, Prior never directly indicated that he would not accept explanatory or amendatory responsibility for administrative actions. His stipulation seems to have been concerned with resignation. He was later to tell the House that it had not been his intention 'to map out some new doctrine of ministerial responsibility', adding: 'I do not accept . . . that there is any constitutional or other principle that requires ministerial resignations in the face of failure, either by others to carry out orders or procedures or by their supervisors to ensure that staff carried out their orders.'[14]

Certainly Maxwell Fyfe's division after Crichel Down indicated no requirement for a minister to accept vicarious liability for errors in which he had no part, and of which he could not reasonably have known. However, a minister can still be considered personally at fault for failing to be aware of extensive breaches in procedures. Much depends on the information that was available to him, and whether he could be considered negligent in failing to monitor certain areas of administration. This had importance for Prior, but also generally for the development of departmental executive agencies, where a clear split of responsibility is essential for their success.[15]

The Hennessy Report and the Parliamentary Debate

The Report was published on 26 January 1984 and was accompanied by the resignation of the Governor of the Maze Prison, Mr

[13] Ibid., cols. 1060–1.   [14] Ibid., col. 1042.   [15] See Ch. 12.

Ernest Whittington, who was held by the Report to be ultimately accountable. 'The extent of the deficiencies in management and in the prison's physical defences amounted to a major failure in security for which the governor, who carries the ultimate responsibility for the state of the prison, must be held accountable.'[16] He was not the only individual who was held to be culpable. A number of officers of various ranks were indicated as sharing responsibility for events at the Maze, including the Security Principal Officer, whose performance 'fell markedly below an acceptable standard', and the Assistant Governor, who, the Report recommended, 'should be deployed to other duties'.[17] The Report detailed the security lapses by staff and also the defects in the construction of the prison defences, which had made the escape possible. In all seventy-eight recommendations for the improvement of security were made.

Of the escape itself, Hennessy found that it had required extensive preparation and had involved a deliberate policy of conditioning staff to reduce their alertness. It was this conditioning that resulted in inadequate searches of the prison and of visitors and thus allowed guns to be smuggled in.[18] Hennessy also stated that the appointment of IRA leaders, in particular McFarlane, as orderlies was a serious error of judgement, for it allowed them to organize the break-out.[19]

The failure of the prison officers to carry out their duties in the acceptable manner may be seen entirely as an administrative or operational concern—indeed, a local operational concern resulting from poor management and discipline, which was entirely the responsibility of the Prison Governor. This was certainly how Prior presented it to the House: 'Let the House be clear; the Hennessy Report finds that the escape would not have succeeded if order and procedures had been properly carried out that Sunday afternoon.'[20]

Prior was correct in his assertion—the escape would not have taken place if prison staff had acted entirely properly. However, there would seem to have been some policy decisions which contributed to the security situation by substantially reducing morale in the prison service, and thus making the conditioning of staff,

---

[16] *Report on Security Arrangements at the Maze Prison* (Chairman, Sir Peter Hennessy) (1984), HC203, HMSO, para. 10.12.   [17] Ibid., para. 8.24.
[18] Ibid., para. 3.03.   [19] Ibid., para. 3.09.
[20] HC Deb., 9 Feb. 1984, col. 1042.

which Hennessy believed to be an important factor, possible. Moreover, in such a sensitive area as Northern Ireland, it could be considered appropriate for the Secretary of State to have a closer involvement with the prison and its administration than seems to have been the case.

A Constitutional Requirement for Resignation?

Whether there was a constitutional requirement for Prior's resignation depends on two factors: first, whether the division of policy and administration and the accompanying limitation regarding resignation was acceptable; secondly, even if it was, whether it was the case that administration alone had been responsible for the Maze Prison break-out.

Prior's division of policy and administration relieved him, he believed, of the obligation to resign. Moreover, he insisted that there was no precedent which required his resignation. He dismissed Crichel Down as having no constitutional validity. 'I do not believe that it [Crichel Down] is a precedent or that it establishes a firm convention. It is the only case of its sort in the past 50 years and constitutional lawyers have concluded that the resignation was not required by convention and was exceptional.'[21]

He did not say what precedent it failed to establish. It did not establish that a minister must resign because of vicarious responsibility for the actions of his officials, although the rhetoric at the time suggested that this was the case, but it is generally considered to have reinforced the rule that ministers are constitutionally required to resign for departmental fault or misjudgement in which they are involved, or of which they knew or should have known.[22] Moreover, Carrington's resignation in 1982 provided a further precedent.[23]

Prior, however, asserted: 'There is no clear rule, no established convention. Rightly it is a matter of judgement in the light of individual circumstances.'[24] This statement would seem to confuse constitutional requirements with political judgements. The convention that a minister may be required to resign for departmental fault in which he is involved is well established. It is part of the

---

[21] Ibid. [22] See Ch. 2. [23] See Ch. 6.1.
[24] HC Deb., 9 Feb. 1984, col. 1042.

morality of the constitution to which appeals can be made, and were made by some Members of Parliament, notably Enoch Powell, in the Maze Prison debate. Moreover, Prior himself recognized that, if he had been at fault, then he might have been required to resign; hence his determination to distance himself from any responsibility for administration and his insistence that the fault lay within that area.

The inference behind his separation of policy and administration was that administrative decisions are taken 'on the ground' (that is, locally, distant from the ministry, low in the hierarchy, or in the routine execution of policy), and have nothing to do with ministers. Many administrative decisions do indeed fall into this category and are often on the periphery of departmental responsibility. No minister, for instance, would be held accountable for the erroneous actions of a clerk in the Social Security Office, for the minister could not reasonably be expected to know of such actions. Ministers, however, may be involved in administrative decisions that are central to the department, and here they cannot be absolved from responsibility if these decisions cause, or contribute to, mistakes on the ground. There were many in the House who supported the contention of Peter Archer, Opposition spokesman for Northern Ireland, that this had been the situation at the Maze.

What happened was an immense administrative disaster. It was not a disaster in a peripheral area of the responsibility of the Northern Ireland Department. It was a disaster that occupied an area which was quite clearly central to the Department's responsibility . . . [It was] an administrative failure of the sort that goes from the bottom straight to the top.[25]

Moreover, some of the administrative errors may be seen as stemming from policy decisions concerning the treatment of prisoners at the end of the hunger strike at the Maze. In general terms prison staff believed that concessions had been made which undermined their position. The effect of this belief on morale was reported by Hennessy:

When the hunger strike ended, the changes introduced by the government were seen by many members of staff as concessions and as a surrender to the prisoners' demands. Thus, the effect on staff morale was considerable. Many members of the staff spoke to us of this period with great bitterness,

---

[25] Ibid., col. 1061.

suggesting that thereafter there was no point in attempting to resist the prisoners' demands; the best policy was to appease them.[26]

The attitude helped the development of the atmosphere in which the conditioning of H7 [the prison block involved] staff became possible. We believe that it was based upon a poor appreciation of the situation and of the government's wider aims in seeking to end the protests.[27]

Mr Prior, whilst telling the House that he accepted the Report in its entirety, had from the moment of publication sought to play down the issue of morale. During the debate on the escape, he told the House: 'If morale was as low as some people have since been trying to make out, we would not have seen such courage displayed by the prison officers during the escape . . . generally speaking morale was reasonable.[28]

The 'some people' mainly referred to the Northern Ireland Prison Governors and to the Northern Ireland Prison Officers Association, who had insisted that morale had been a key factor, and that this was the responsibility of the Northern Ireland Office. But they also made more specific allegations concerning the effect of government policy, which required that all men coming off hunger strike should be found prison employment. Indeed, they insisted that guidance directly from Stormont had been responsible for key members of the IRA, notably McFarlane, being made orderlies.

Prior confirmed that it was government policy to ensure that prisoners had work when they came off protest, and that an instruction was given to this effect. However, he insisted that, although there were discussions between the Northern Ireland Office and the prison authorities as to what work was available and its suitability, it was the Governor's task to 'work out the actual mechanics of this . . .'.[29]

Much, of course, depends on the detail of the discussions and how much was left to the Governor's discretion. Mr Peter Archer took up the matter of work allocation during the parliamentary debate, contending that a Minute, in which the work allocation was detailed, was sent to the Northern Ireland Office. McFarlane's position as an orderly was clearly given, along with the work allocated to the rest of the prisoners. Mr Archer maintained that, because this was an issue of political sensitivity and a policy matter

---

[26] HC203 (1984), para. 9.27.   [27] Ibid., para. 9.28.
[28] HC Deb., 9 Feb. 1984, col. 1045.   [29] Ibid., cols. 1043–4.

over which directions had been given, ministers, through their officials, should have kept themselves informed, and asked: 'It will not do to leave the matter . . . as a mistake made without the involvement of anyone at a senior level. If senior officials were not involved, why were they not involved?'[30]

This seemed a reasonable question, and there were others. Mr Archer asked why warnings given by prison staff about the security situation at the Maze were ignored and whether Minutes sent to the Northern Ireland Office, which expressed staff concern over H7, were read.

The Northern Ireland Office was not criticized by Hennessy for its apparent unawareness of problems that might arise over work schemes nor for its failure to liaise with prison officers. It was, however, criticized for not giving sufficient priority to proposals made in January 1982 to rectify weaknesses in security at the main gate, although successive governors of the Maze were also held responsible for not being 'sufficiently forceful in pressing for essential improvements'.[31]

However, the main criticism of the Northern Ireland Office concerned the officer in charge of the Security and Operations Division, one of the divisions under the control of Nicholas Scott. Hennessy, after first pointing out what improvements had been made since his appointment, stated: 'he did not appear to appreciate the extent of the many security weaknesses we found at the Maze. To this extent . . . he must be held responsible for some of the shortcomings at the Maze.'[32]

The Report acknowledged that any shortcomings within this division were the 'concern' of Nicholas Scott, but it exonerated him from personal blame, sympathizing with him for being 'overworked and under resourced'.[33] Scott, it would seem, failed to control or direct his divisions adequately. Moreover, being 'overworked' is not the sort of excuse that Parliament readily accepts for ministerial misjudgement or error. However, Scott was only a junior minister. Prior was the minister ultimately responsible, and Robert Maclennan commented: 'If the Under-Secretary is "overworked and under-resourced" whose fault is that if not the Secretary of State's?'[34]

So, while the obvious and immediate cause of the Maze break-

---

[30] Ibid., col. 1052.   [31] HC203 (1984), para. 6.15.
[32] Ibid., para. 10.16.   [33] Ibid., para. 10.17.
[34] HC Deb., 9 Feb. 1984, col. 1079.

out could be classified as administrative or operational, this did not necessarily absolve Prior from constitutional responsibility. First, the administrative fault was so widespread that Prior should have been aware of it, particularly when it was in an area of political sensitivity, over which it would have been reasonable to expect the Secretary of State to exercise a degree of ministerial oversight. Secondly, the faults in administration would seem to stem at least in part from faults in policy, or from a failure to perceive, and subsequently to heed, the effects of the policy. Thus, even if Prior's version of individual ministerial responsibility is accepted and he is excused responsibility on the first count, there would still seem to have been a possible constitutional basis for requiring his resignation.

Prior Remains in Office

A number of Members of Parliament from both sides of the House considered that the Report cast sufficient shadow over both Scott and Prior to warrant resignation. However, when the Hennessy Report was debated in the House, the only calls for resignation came from Ulster politicians, who believed that the Prison Governor had been made a scapegoat for the Maze break-out. Labour, and some Conservative back-benchers, were highly critical of Prior, but indicated that they believed he should remain in office.

The Prime Minister made clear her desire that Prior should retain his position and work to remedy the security defects. It is possible that she did not want his resignation because she considered herself more secure, or at least more comfortable, if Prior was in Northern Ireland rather than on the back-benches, from which he would be able to criticize the government's economic policies. Additionally, Prior's resignation, and the subsequent appointment of a new minister, would cause disruption to the improving relations with the Irish Republic. But in any case, Mrs Thatcher did not seem to like resignations (perhaps preferring reshuffles over which she had control) and this one would have caused her the particular problem of finding a suitable replacement.

The Prime Minister's support for Prior was very clearly communicated to Conservative back-benchers and was no doubt influential, as was the implication that attempts to force the resignation of the Secretary of State for Northern Ireland were unpatriotic. This was a suggestion that Prior made himself when he spoke of the break-out from the Maze in the House in October: 'The IRA may have had something of a success to tell over this particular escape, but it is nothing to the success they will have to tell if they forced the resignation of the Secretary of State in these circumstances.'[35]

This sentiment was echoed in the debate by Sir Humphrey Atkins, who stated that, if Prior were to resign, 'the loudest cheers would come from the IRA',[36] and Michael Mates, who intimated that even to criticize the minister was to the advantage of the IRA.[37] Such a statement suggests that ministerial accountability is inappropriate when it concerns Northern Ireland. However, this was refuted by Enoch Powell, who noted the argument that this was not the moment to insist on resignation because it would aid the IRA, but insisted: 'It is always the moment . . . for accepting responsibility.'[38]

However, Powell found his only support from the Ulster Unionists. Mr Kinnock took a similar position to Mrs Thatcher, although of course for different reasons. Labour was concerned about the possible replacement for Mr Prior, as Peter Archer indicated: 'I cannot envisage him being replaced from among members of the present administration by anyone more compassionate or more politically sensitive.'[39]

Thus a strong attack in constitutional terms upon Prior and the Northern Ireland Office from Labour's Northern Ireland spokesman was not supported by demands for resignation. Political judgement suggested that the Opposition would prefer Prior to remain in office. It was not just a question, therefore, of a minister refusing to yield and the Prime Minister and party supporting rather than opposing. It was also a question of the Opposition deciding it was expedient to stop short of demands for resignation. By so doing, the Labour Party denied any wavering Conservative back-benchers support, and left the Ulster Unionists isolated.

Conclusion

The failure of Prior to resign over the Maze Prison break-out does not indicate that Prior's reformulation of the convention of

---

[35] Ibid., 24 Oct. 1983, col. 23.   [36] Ibid., 9 Feb. 1984, col. 1060.
[37] Ibid., col. 1066.   [38] Ibid., col. 1064.   [39] Ibid., col. 1056.

individual ministerial responsibility was accepted, or that the convention was weakened in any way, or even no longer existed with regard to resignation.

The non-resignation of Prior demonstrates once more that there are constitutional and political aspects to any resignation. The constitution provides the morality, the precedent, and the rule. The rule, however, is not absolute but requires a political judgement as to whether the fault, misjudgement, or negligence is serious enough for the minister to feel obliged to resign, or for other political actors to press for the resignation. In addition, judgements are also made which relate not to the incident but to the wider political situation. These can act to modify the application of the convention.

In the Maze Prison break-out there are reasonable grounds for considering that the error was such as to provide both constitutional and political justifications for resignation. However, the requirement for resignation conflicted with the political requirements of the situation in Northern Ireland, as seen by the principal actors, including the Prime Minister and the Leader of the Opposition. Prior, therefore, remained in office, providing an example of the ability of purely political considerations (that is, considerations which are wider than party political considerations, or which for different reasons suit both government and Opposition) to influence the workings of the constitution, but no evidence that it has weakened its requirements. In practice, this means that the non-operation of the constitutional requirement has to be argued for; dispensation is not lightly arranged and is certainly not available upon request.

8

Cases of Non-Resignation: An Evasion of Ministerial Responsibility?

8.1. WILLIAM WHITELAW: NO CONSTITUTIONAL REQUIREMENT

Background

During July 1982 William Whitelaw suffered an uncomfortable few weeks as Home Secretary. Indeed, there were suggestions that he might resign. Two specific incidents concerning security at Buckingham Palace, and his responsibility for them, were the direct cause of Whitelaw's discomfort. However, it was the political dissatisfaction within the Conservative Party over his performance as Home Secretary which made these incidents so significant, for, if the incidents had provided a constitutional reason for resignation, they could have been used by Conservative back-benchers to fulfil a political requirement.

At the beginning of the year, the right wing of the Conservative Party at Westminister started a 'whispering campaign' to discredit Whitelaw.[1] Its displeasure with the Home Secretary arose directly from the announcement that the crime figures had increased by 10 per cent, an electoral embarrassment for the party of law and order, and from Whitelaw's refusal to adopt a hard line or tough approach. There had been a number of incidents which had caused public concern, the latest of which had been the decision not to prosecute in the Glasgow rape case (a decision which had resulted in the resignation of Nicholas Fairbairn),[2] and these had heightened anti-Whitelaw feelings. The discontent with Whitelaw was reflected in the popular Press (the *Daily Mail* referred to him as 'Mr Wetlaw') and in the constituencies. Whitelaw's position looked

---

[1] *Sunday Times*, 7 Feb. 1982.   [2] See Ch. 4.1.

increasingly tenuous as law and order became a prominent political issue.

However, Whitelaw survived. He had the Prime Minister's personal and open support and that of his fellow Cabinet ministers. The Opposition, fearing a hard-line replacement, refrained from attack, and, importantly, right-wing back-benchers failed to convince other Conservative Members that Whitelaw should be sacrificed. Moreover, there was no solid ground on which his opponents could found their case. They could not point to specific errors or misjudgements.

The crisis caused by the crime figures therefore passed, but law and order still remained an issue and Whitelaw's popularity with those on the right of the party showed no signs of increasing. They still believed that Whitelaw should be replaced, and awaited their opportunity. In July it looked as if it had arrived.

Security at the Palace

On Monday, 12 July 1982, the Home Secretary, William Whitelaw, made a statement in the House concerning an incident at Buckingham Palace the previous Friday. An intruder, Michael Fagan, had breached Palace security and gained access to the Queen's bedroom. He appeared in court on the Saturday charged with an earlier infringement of Palace security. Whitelaw stated that the operational responsibility for royal protection lay with the Commissioner of Police and announced that, in consultation with the Commissioner, he had set up an inquiry to be conducted by Assistant Commissioner Dewar.[3]

The House expressed concern and alarm over the safety of the Queen and security at Buckingham Palace; also over the fact that it had seemed to require an article in the *Daily Express*, listing a number of previous security breaches, before the security issue was taken seriously. Moreover, there was bewilderment, in which William Whitelaw shared, that Fagan was able to breach Palace security twice.

A week later, on 19 July, Whitelaw returned to the House to make another statement concerning security at Buckingham Palace. Commander Trestrail, the Queen's police officer with

---

[3] HC Deb., 12 July 1982, col. 645.

responsibility for her protection outside the Palace, had resigned his position after admitting a homosexual relationship with a male prostitute over a number of years. This statement was greeted with incredulity and ridicule by the Opposition and with anger from the Conservative back-benchers. Whitelaw later told Hugo Young: 'There was no statement in the world you could make. It was like playing cricket and standing there with no bat, and someone bowling at you . . .'[4]

The Home Secretary was asked by Mr George Cunningham: 'Are we to assume that this information was not known to the Security Services till now? Does this mean that no positive vetting was carried out on the Commander, or that there was a positive vetting, which failed to reveal these facts?'[5] Mr Whitelaw replied: 'He had been positively vetted.'[6]

It subsequently emerged through Trestrail's solicitor, that the Commander had been positively vetted only three or four months previously, and thus any inference that might be drawn from Whitelaw's reply that Trestrail had been subject to vetting from the time of his appointment was clearly not a correct one. As *The Times* stated: 'The natural inference for the House to draw from the Home Secretary's answer was a misleading one.'[7]

The Home Secretary denied that he had misled the House, stating that he had not been asked when, only if, Trestrail had been vetted; no doubt he was technically correct. However, his approach did not accord with the openness of which he had spoken earlier in his statement. 'I have made it clear throughout that it is my duty to the House to report everything to it at the earliest possible opportunity that I can find. This I have done on every occasion, and this I will continue to do.'[8]

The imprecision over Trestrail's vetting would seem to have come through clumsiness. It was not an attempt seriously or culpably to mislead the House, and it was never raised as such in Parliament. It did, however, add to the catalogue of Whitelaw misfortunes that seemed to be accumulating.

By 21 July, when there was a debate in the House, Whitelaw's position again appeared less than secure. Whitelaw, however, survived politically and fulfilled his constitutional obligations, both

---

[4] *Sunday Times*, 25 July 1982.   [5] HC Deb., 19 July 1982, col. 22.
[6] Ibid.   [7] *The Times*, Editorial, 27 July 1982.
[8] HC Deb., 19 July 1982, col. 21.

regarding the Fagan incident and the Trestrail resignation, which in fact were separate matters.

Responsibility for Fagan

The Home Secretary is the police authority for the Metropolitan Police District. Constitutionally, police authorities have the duty to ensure an adequate and efficient police force, but have no responsibility for operational control. This is vested in the Chief Constable, or, in the case of London, the Commissioner. The Home Secretary has an additional, not clearly defined, general power regarding the Metropolitan force. This enables him to give directions to the Commissioner on matters concerned with operational control, or at least to have some influence in operational policy; for instance, whether to adopt the methods of community policing, or perhaps in what areas to concentrate resources. However, this does not lessen the responsibility of the Commissioner for operations on the ground, as William Whitelaw made clear. 'I am specifically excluded from being responsible for police operations. If the Home Secretary is to take on board being constitutionally responsible for their operational work, you get into very great difficulty.'[9]

This statement failed to recognize that there is already 'great difficulty' with the present system of accountability for operational matters, for the police do not account directly to Parliament and any other line of accountability is somewhat tenuous. The Home Secretary can be asked detailed questions by the House about police conduct, thereby producing an indirect accountability. Whitelaw, therefore, owed informatory or reporting accountability to the House for the Fagan incident at Buckingham Palace. However, he would only be directly accountable if the intrusion had occurred because he had failed to ensure an adequate and efficient police force, in terms of personnel, equipment, and training facilities, or if he had given directions regarding policy which resulted in insufficient security at the Palace.

On 21 July Whitelaw gave the House the results of the Dellow inquiry. It found that, although there had been technical failures, the basic cause of the breakdown in security was a failure by the police to respond efficiently and urgently. Whitelaw stated:

[9] *Sunday Times*, 25 July 1982.

'Furthermore, the incident revealed slackness and weaknesses in supervision. The commander, A District, has resigned from the force and the chief inspector at the Palace has been transferred to other duties.'[10] Four other police officers were subject to disciplinary inquiries.

Whitelaw also announced an increase in security at the Palace, both in personnel and equipment. Moreover, a Deputy Assistant Commissioner had been appointed, who would have single responsibility for the protection of the royal family and their residences and would report directly to the Commissioner. Most significant of all was the establishment of a permanent group, comprising representatives of royal households, the police, the Household Division, and the Property Services Agency, to be chaired by a senior official. The group would meet regularly to examine the effectiveness of arrangements, although Whitelaw was at pains to stress that this would not lessen the operational responsibility of the new Deputy Assistant Commissioner or of the Commissioner. But he added: 'The group will report personally to me.'[11] Thus Whitelaw effectively ensured that, if there were future breaches of Palace security, he would not be able to escape personal responsibility, for he had assumed some operational oversight function.

During the debate there were attempts to implicate Whitelaw in the security breaches by suggesting that part of the problem had been lack of equipment, or improperly installed equipment, or indeed that the incident had arisen because of the poor organization of the Metropolitan Police. However, Whitelaw referred to Dellow's Report, which stated that individuals within the police force were to blame, not the police authority.

Whitelaw therefore fulfilled his constitutional obligations. He gave Parliament a full account of what had happened and expressed his regret. He then reported appropriate amendatory measures, both in terms of punishment and in ensuring that such an incident would never recur. He did not offer his resignation, much to the disappointment of right-wing Tory back-benchers, stating that to do so would be 'unconstitutional'.[12] His resignation was certainly not constitutionally required.

---

[10] HC Deb., 21 July 1982, col. 397.   [11] Ibid., col. 398.
[12] *Sunday Times*, 25 July 1982.

Responsibility for Commander Trestrail

Whitelaw's personal responsibility for the failure in the vetting system was never seriously suggested. He could not be held responsible for the fact that Commander Trestrail had not been positively vetted on his appointment, for he had not been Home Secretary. The subsequent failure of the vetting system to uncover Trestrail's relationship did fall within his area of responsibility, as the Director of M.I.5 is directly responsible to the Home Secretary, but Whitelaw was not, of course, responsible for individual vettings. Even the imprecision of Whitelaw's statement about vetting could not seriously be considered as an attempt at a cover-up, for Whitelaw announced another inquiry to be conducted by Lord Bridge, who would investigate the appointment of Trestrail as the Queen's police officer and his activities. His brief was to determine whether security had been breached or put at risk, and to advise on changes in the security arrangements. Whitelaw therefore offered both explanatory and amendatory accountability and again there was no requirement for his resignation on grounds of personal responsibility.

The two incidents did not provide the personal fault required by the constitution even to raise the question of resignation on constitutional grounds. There was no personal involvement, nor would it be reasonable to have suggested that the Home Secretary should have been aware of what was happening. Even using an absolute version of ministerial responsibility, which suggests that ministers are vicariously responsible for the actions of their officials, there would not be a requirement for Whitelaw's resignation. The mistakes were made not by Whitelaw's department but by the police and security services. Thus, despite the calls for resignation by some back-benchers and the popular Press, Whitelaw was constitutionally correct to remain in office.

A few months later, however, he was personally involved in yet another 'incident', and once more there were calls for his resignation.

Whitelaw and the Immigration Bill

Early in the morning of 16 December, the government was defeated by eighteen votes on its Immigration Bill. There were calls, yet again, for the Home Secretary's resignation, for it had been his responsibility to see the Bill through the House of Commons. Moreover, the defeat could have been avoided if Whitelaw had stood firm on the draft published in October, instead of trying to appease the right-wing of his party with concessions. This did not work, and Whitelaw ended up with the worst of both worlds— pleasing neither the Opposition nor his own party.

William Whitelaw had clearly made a misjudgement. However, his misjudgement was political, and he needed to account for it to the party leadership and his government colleagues and not to Parliament. *The Times*, indicating the situations in which it believed it was appropriate for a minister to resign, seemed to confuse constitutional situations with political ones, but did not consider that Whitelaw fell into any of the categories.

Not every minister who makes a mistake should leave office. He should only do so if he has acted dishonourably or improperly, or if his mis- judgement has been of such a nature as seriously to impair his value to the government. Mr Whitelaw's was a straightforward misjudgement. There are some who argue that it has destroyed his usefulness as a senior minister. But they fail to appreciate the contribution he has made to this government.[13]

The Prime Minister, however, and Cabinet colleagues did appreciate Whitelaw's behind-the-scenes contribution and the Home Secretary was given the collective protection necessary for his survival. Mrs Thatcher expressed her total confidence in William Whitelaw in Parliament and, through unattributable sources, to the Press. Conservative back-benchers were made aware, yet again, that Whitelaw was a protected person.

Conclusion

Attempts by Conservative back-benchers to secure Whitelaw's resignation failed, partly because he never provided them with a strong enough constitutional basis and partly because he had political protection from the Prime Minister and senior colleagues. There were also other factors, as indicated by George Cunningham in a Question concerning the incidents at the Palace: 'Does the Home Secretary appreciate that a Home Secretary of any other

[13] *The Times*, 17 Dec. 1982.

party would have been crucified by the House and by the media for this affair?'[14]

The Home Secretary did seem to appreciate this point. He did not suffer a sustained attack from the Opposition, whose leadership was, if anything, supportive of him, and party solidarity ensured that most of his own back-benchers stayed silent, although many were privately critical of him. Further, Whitelaw's own personality, courteous but solid, enabled him to accept the humiliation and ridicule which other Home Secretaries might have found unacceptable.

Whitelaw's failure to resign was not, therefore, a breach of the constitution, nor an indication that political considerations override constitutional requirements. His resignation was not constitutionally required. It may have been politically desired by some of his party, but it is seldom that a minister resigns under such circumstances.

8.2. LORD YOUNG: A TIMELY EXIT FROM GOVERNMENT

Background

The eighteen-month period from May 1988 to November 1989 was not a good time for the DTI. Three major incidents hit the headlines—Barlow Clowes, the House of Fraser take-over, and the sale of Rover to British Aerospace. In all three the DTI played a central and controversial part and Lord Young was Secretary of State at the crucial time. However, none of the incidents was resolved while he was still at the department, a fact which supports Finer's view that resignations may sometimes be avoided by a timely reshuffle.[15] This, of course, depends on whether Young's resignation would have been required if he had still been Secretary of State, which in turn is determined by the extent of his personal involvement in the incidents.

The Barlow Clowes affair

In May 1988 liquidators were called in to Barlow Clowes & Partners and Barlow Clowes Gilt Managers. It soon transpired

[14] HC Deb., 21 July 1982, cols. 401–2.
[15] Finer, 'The Individual Responsibility of Ministers', 393.

that some eighteen thousand investors had lost their money, not because their high-risk investments had failed, but because the funds had been misappropriated by Peter Clowes.

The company had been licensed by the DTI and there were immediate allegations that the department had been negligent in fulfilling its regulatory function. These were accompanied by calls for compensation from the government. Lord Young set up an inquiry, headed by Sir Godfrey Le Quesne. Young told the House of Lords that the purpose of the inquiry was to determine the facts regarding the department's handling of the matter and whether the department was to blame. He was later accused of misleading Parliament, for, when the Report was published in October, Sir Godfrey made clear that his terms of reference had restricted him to establishing the facts only and had not allowed him to pass judgement.

The lack of conclusions drawn by the Report enabled the government to draw its own, and Lord Young declared that, on the basis of the Report, he had decided the government had no legal liability towards investors in Barlow Clowes. There were no grounds for concluding that the DTI's handling of the affair was 'unreasonable or caused the losses experienced by investors' and thus there was 'no justification for using taxpayers' money to fund compensation'.[16]

This was not a popular conclusion. Many Conservative backbenchers had constituents who had lost money in Barlow Clowes. Others were uncomfortable that those involved were new investors who had been encouraged by the government to invest in the market for the first time. Lord Young therefore faced a hostile reception from the 1922 Committee at its meeting on 20 October. Indeed, it was reported that, of the eighty or so members present, none showed support for Young's decision.[17] The majority believed that the government had a moral responsibility to provide some compensation and that a commitment to that effect should be forthcoming immediately.[18] Lord Young, however, stood firm. He refused to offer an *ex gratia* payment, on the grounds that it would open the floodgates to claims by other investors who had

---

[16] HL Deb., No. 1406, 20 Oct. 1988, col. 1259.
[17] *Independent*, 21 Oct. 1988.   [18] *Sunday Times*, 23 Oct 1988.

lost money invested with security dealers licensed and regulated by the DTI.

Although not apportioning blame, the Report did not exonerate the department. It catalogued a series of warnings from the City and the Bank of England about the status of Barlow Clowes from 1984 onwards. These warnings were misread or their significance was misjudged, and, although the department was uneasy about the company, Barlow Clowes was given the benefit of the doubt and continued to be granted a licence. This licence was renewed as late as October 1987, a month after the Deputy Governor of the Bank of England had expressed the Bank's unease about Barlow Clowes, although the renewal was accompanied by an order for an investigation of the company by external inspectors.

As with the collapse of the Vehicle and General Insurance Company in 1971, which resulted in losses to policy holders of perhaps £20 million, it appeared that the regulators had failed to take prompt action despite signs that there was trouble.

Instead, the civil servants who were responsible for watching Barlow Clowes operated under a regulatory regime that gave them too little flexibility. They knew that some people thought Barlow Clowes fishy, but, without proof, they were loth to take the kind of action which they believed would drive the firm into early bankruptcy.[19]

Civil servants obviously made misjudgements. However, the Report gave little indication of whether or not these misjudgements were reasonable or whether they arose from negligent actions or inactions. In contrast to the Vehicle and General Report,[20] no individual civil servants were named and blamed. Lord Young insisted that any misjudgements were reasonable. Others, however, believed that the Report had been too generous to the department and that Lord Young was covering up to avoid the payment of compensation. He was suspected of protecting his civil servants, not for reasons of constitutional propriety but to save money. He was not, however, suspected of being personally involved in the affair. Indeed, most of the decisions concerning Barlow Clowes were taken before his appointment as Secretary of State. There were, therefore, no grounds on the basis of individual ministerial

[19] *Economist*, 22 Oct. 1988.   [20] HC133 (1971–2).

responsibility for his resignation, and, despite his political unpopularity, there were no serious calls for it.

The Barlow Clowes affair was referred to the Parliamentary Ombudsman, Sir Anthony Barrowclough,[21] but by the time he reported Lord Young was no longer a government minister. Sir Anthony found that there had been 'significant maladministration' on five counts. These involved licensing decisions, the failure of the department to heed the warnings given, and the inadequacy of its investigations. Sir Anthony was aware that his conclusion could be considered harsh for what might be seen by some as 'minor oversights'. However, he offered a justification for his decision.

A regulatory agency—which is what the Department was at the time in relation to the protection of investors—ought, in my mind, by definition to adopt a rigorous and enquiring approach as regards material coming into its possession concerning an undertaking about which suspicions have been aroused, and also as regards representations made to it on the part of the undertaking in question. And it was, in my view, the lack of a sufficiently rigorous and enquiring approach which led [to] . . . some of the . . . faults I have identified.[22]

The Report concluded that the failure of the department to provide the protection expected and required made it liable for compensation. It distinguished for compensation purposes between investments prior to 1984, for which the DTI was not liable, and those after this date, on the basis that, but for the maladministration by the DTI, these investments would never have been made. 'If matters had been handled properly in the 1984–85 licensing process, the operation of Barlow Clowes would have been brought to an end . . .'[23]

However, any report from the Ombudsman is only advisory, and in this case the conclusions drawn by Sir Anthony were rejected by the government. Nicholas Ridley, Young's successor at the DTI, stated: 'In the Government's view, the department's handling of the case was within the acceptable range of standards reasonably to be expected of a regulator.'[24]

---

[21] For a full account of the Barlow Clowes affair and the role of the Parliamentary Commissioner see R. Gregory and G. Drewry, 'Barlow Clowes and the Ombudsman', *Public Law* (1991), 192, 408.

[22] *Report from the Parliamentary Commissioner for Administration: The Barlow Clowes Affair* (1989), HC76, HMSO, para. 8.13.

[23] Ibid., para. 8.14.   [24] HC Deb., 19 Dec. 1989, col. 104.

Ridley conceded that there had been 'blemishes' but refused to accept that these amounted to 'maladministration', or that the government was liable for the losses of investors. Such a statement raised the question of whether the government was prepared to accept lower standards than the Ombudsman and more importantly indicated the inherent weakness of the Ombudsman, one of the constitutional checks upon executive power. However, Sir Anthony Barrowclough was not prepared to be disregarded or to let the matter drop, unpersuaded by the government's argument: 'Such indications I have seen of the grounds for questioning my findings had left me altogether unconvinced.'[25]

Subsequently, despite the government's refusal to accept any legal or constitutional liability, Nicholas Ridley announced that the government would pay £150 million compensation to the investors of Barlow Clowes, because of the 'exceptional circumstances' and in deference to the Ombudsman. Sir Anthony examined the settlement and concluded: 'I could not say, in all the circumstances, that the Government's proposals would not constitute a fair remedy for the injustice which had been suffered.'[26]

The government had executed a smart U-turn which defused the political campaign for compensation. It also served to fulfil in part the constitutional requirement for amendatory action for departmental fault, which Sir Anthony insisted existed and which the government refused to acknowledge in this case. Moreover, the DTI by this time had passed its function as a regulator to the Security Investments Board (SIB) and thus the incident could not be repeated. What was missing, however, was the minister who could be held responsible by Parliament for the cost of putting things right. It is not certain who that minister was, for the 'maladministration' or 'blemishes' had occurred over a number of years and under a succession of Secretaries of State. They had, of course, come to light while Lord Young was at the department, but he had no personal involvement in the affair nor an overseeing capacity. If he had still held his ministerial position, he would no doubt have been criticized for failing to pay compensation earlier, but this would have been an attack upon his political judgement rather than his constitutional propriety, and there would certainly have been no constitutional obligation for him to offer his

[25] HC76 (1989), para. 8.21.   [26] Ibid.

resignation. However, the affair did nothing to enhance Lord Young's reputation or that of the DTI, for it appeared that the department, under his leadership, was more concerned with protecting itself than with serving the interests of the public.

The House of Fraser Take-over

Long before Barlow Clowes was resolved and while Lord Young was still in office, the DTI became the centre of another controversy. This had its beginning in December 1981 when the Monopoly and Mergers Commission (MMC), backed by John Biffen, then Secretary of State for the DTI, disallowed a bid by Tiny Rowland's Lonrho Company for the House of Fraser Store Group. Rowland did not give up, however, and in May 1984 he attempted a boardroom *coup*, which resulted in Norman Tebbit, now head of the DTI, asking the MMC to investigate again. In November Rowlands appeared to lose interest in the House of Fraser and sold most of his shares to the Al-Fayed brothers, who the following March (1985) made an offer which the Board recommended should be accepted. Three days later Tebbit indicated that the MMC had cleared Lonrho to bid for the House of Fraser. In fact it seems that Norman Tebbit had received the MMC report several weeks previously.[27]

Lonrho now started a lobbying campaign to get the Al-Fayed brothers' take-over referred to the MMC. Tebbit refused and so, later in the year, did his successor, Leon Brittan. However, in March 1987 Paul Channon, now Secretary of State, appointed inspectors to look into the Al-Fayeds' acquisition of shares, which Lonrho alleged had been bought with money belonging to the Sultan of Brunei rather than their own funds. This Report was finally delivered in July 1988 to yet another Secretary of State at the DTI, Lord Young. He passed it to the Serious Fraud Office, stating that the Report could not be published while the Office was itself investigating.

Having waited so long for the Report, Rowland and the Lonrho company saw the further delay in publication as a confirmation that they had been cheated of control of the House of Fraser by the Al-Fayed brothers with the connivance of the City and the

---

[27] *Independent*, 31 Mar. 1988.

government. Rowlands, therefore, decided to take matters into his own hands and use his proprietorship of the *Observer* to further his cause. In March 1989 he printed a midweek edition of the newspaper which carried a copy of the Report he had somehow acquired. The distribution of the paper was prevented by injunctions granted to both the government and the Al-Fayeds; but it was subsequently published abroad and sufficient copies had been circulated for there to be an awareness that the Report indicated that there might have been malpractice.

Lord Young stated that the reason it could not as yet be published was because publication might prejudice the trial of people named in the Report, if legal action were to be brought against them. However, the validity of this reason was damaged when he added that the Report indicated wrongdoing, thereby himself making comments that were possibly prejudicial to a fair trial.

The return of Members to Parliament on 4 April put Young under increasing pressure to publish the Report. It had been four years since the Al-Fayeds had gained control of the House of Fraser, and it had still not been confirmed that the acquisition had been within the rules governing take-overs. This led to speculation that Lord Young was covering up either for departmental incompetence, or because of an embarrassing link between the Al-Fayeds, the Sultan of Brunei, Mrs Thatcher, and the Conservative Party.

In the House Tony Newton, government spokesman for the DTI, came under attack from both sides for not publishing the Report. Conservative back-benchers were particularly concerned that the government was about to become involved in another Spycatcher affair, with publication in Britain prevented by injunctions but taking place abroad.

However, just as with Barlow Clowes and the refusal to give compensation, Young held firm. The Report had not been published by the time he left office in July 1989, despite his comments that: 'It is my dearest wish that the report should be published. I want it out of the way.'[28]

This may have been the case, but he seemed to do little to ensure that his wish was granted, and there were suggestions that Young was content to be out of the way before the truth was known. However, as with Barlow Clowes, even if the Report did

[28] Ibid., 17 July 1989.

indicate departmental incompetence, or more seriously a deliberate campaign against Lonrho, as Rowlands suggested, Young had not been personally involved. Moreover, again most of the events occurred before his time at the department.

Lord Young's responsibility was for the decision not to publish or to delay publication. Thus, if it transpired that this was a deliberate decision by Young and the department to cover up wrongdoing—indeed, that it was government embarrassment rather than legal principle that was being protected—then the convention of individual ministerial responsibility might have given constitutional grounds for resignation. Whether or not this was required would, of course, have depended on how serious colleagues and the party considered the fault to be, and on the political situation at the time.

In December 1989 the Serious Fraud Squad announced that its inquiries were completed and that it was unlikely to be bringing prosecutions. However, it stated that there was still the possibility of a civil action being brought to disqualify the brothers from being directors of Harrods. This enabled Nicholas Ridley, having succeeded Young as Secretary of State, to continue with the familiar line that there would be no publication while there was the possibility of legal action.[29]

The Sale of Rover

The third incident involved the sale of the Rover car company to British Aerospace. This was hailed by the government as a triumph for Lord Young while he was Secretary of State. He had rid the taxpayer of a long-standing problem. From other quarters, however, concern was expressed that there had been only one bidder for Rover, and disappointment was voiced at the final price.

On 28 November 1989, several months after Young's departure from the DTI, the National Audit Office reported to the Public Accounts Committee (PAC) that Rover had been sold short by upwards of £100 million.[30] It made particular reference to surplus sites not required for the running of the business and to holdings

---

[29] The Report into the take-over of Harrods was eventually published on 23 Mar. 1990.

[30] *Report from the Comptroller and Auditor General: Department of Trade and Industry: Sale of Rover Group plc to British Aerospace plc* (1989), HC9, HMSO.

in nine associated companies, some of which could be sold without detriment to the rest of the business. It suggested that there should have been some 'clawback' provision to enable taxpayers to share in any benefit which accrued because of the sale of sites or companies. It pointed out, however, the difficulty in assessing the market value of Rover when the sale had not been open to the market and competition.

The government had granted British Aerospace exclusive negotiating rights from the beginning of March to the end of April. Its financial advisers, Baring Brothers & Co. Ltd, had indicated that it was essential to create a competitive market to ensure confidence that the best terms available were obtained. However, the Chairman of Rover favoured exclusivity to prevent any uncertainty over Rover's future that might occur with a competitive sale, and it was this approach that the government adopted.[31]

A deal was agreed with British Aerospace which, after some reduction by the European Commission of the subsidies given by the government, cost the taxpayer £422 million net. However, in a confidential memorandum from the National Audit Office to the PAC, it was revealed that there had also been an inducement of £38 million which had been kept secret. The following day Nicholas Ridley told the House that this inducement had been kept quiet to protect the Rover sale from a further inquiry by the European Commission, although he maintained that, in fact, the concession to British Aerospace did not come within the competence of the Commission because it would not affect the Rover Group's competitiveness.

Regardless of what Ridley said, however, it was clear that the House of Commons and the European Commission had been misled about the sale to British Aerospace. Moreover, it had been a deliberate deception which concealed the true cost to the taxpayer from Members of Parliament. This was subsequently confirmed by the Report from the Select Committee of Trade and Industry, which found after a two-and-a-half year inquiry that the cost of financial inducements to British Aerospace had been scattered through parliamentary accounts in such a way as to conceal them from Parliament's attention. The Report stated: 'Strict legal requirements may have been fulfilled, but the way in which they

---

[31] Ibid.

appeared in those financial documents, and the time delay before they appeared, were not adequate disclosure.'[32]

The Committee made clear its displeasure, both with the way in which financial accounting had been used to deceive and with the letter written by Lord Young to Professor Smith, Chairman of British Aerospace, in which ways were discussed of concealing the information from Parliament. 'We deplore the fact that attempts were made to conceal important aspects of the sale from the House of Commons.'[33] The Committee concluded: 'the House of Commons was seriously misled.'[34]

Conclusion

The minister responsible had been Lord Young and he was clearly personally involved in a deliberate act of suppression. The Rover incident confirmed a tendency for secrecy and covering-up within the DTI under Lord Young, which, after Barlow Clowes and the House of Fraser, many had suspected existed. In addition, it demonstrated a failure by the Secretary of State to account to Parliament. Indeed, the three incidents indicate an avoidance of accountability. In Barlow Clowes this was achieved through the non-disclosure of information because of an inquiry with limited terms of reference, in the House of Fraser by legal restraints, and in the sale of Rover by the Secretary of State giving misleading information. The deliberate misleading of Parliament over a matter of concern to the taxpayer, together with the embarrassment of Britain now being found out by the European Commission, might have ended Lord Young's ministerial career, had he still been a minister. After the publication of the Trade and Industry Report, *The Times* commented:

The answer is constitutional and fundamental. The fact that Parliament is often neglectful in discharging its function of monitoring the executive does not detract from the importance of this function. John Profumo lost office not because of his sexual misbehaviour but because he lied to Parliament. When Mrs Thatcher narrowly survived the Westland affair, the debate was on whether Parliament had been deceived. MPs are rightly jealous of their *de facto* prerogative to hound a minister from office, without

---

[32] *First Report from the Trade and Industry Committee: Sale of Rover Group to British Aerospace* (1990–1), HC34, HMSO.
[33] Ibid.   [34] Ibid.

which ministers could safely ignore the elected representatives. Only a peer could be so insensitive as to ignore it. Had Lord Young remained a minister, yesterday's report would surely have forced his resignation. All he has lost is his reputation.[35]

Suggestions that Lord Young would have been forced from office are, of course, speculative. Lord Young himself indicated that he would not have felt resignation necessary. He considered that the sale of Rover was the 'sale of the decade' and one of his greatest achievements, and that the end justified the means. However, to remain a minister Young would have required the support of his party and his colleagues, and his deliberate deception of Parliament might have put this in doubt.

Of the three incidents, it was undoubtedly the Rover sale which would have provided the constitutional grounds for resignation had Lord Young still been at the DTI. In fact he was no longer the minister, and indeed not even in government, when his misdoings were uncovered. This is not unusual. Indeed, the turnover at the DTI was such that during the House of Fraser take-over there were four different Secretaries of State. This inevitably makes it difficult to pin responsibility upon a particular minister, and it may mean that culpable ministers escape the sanction that otherwise might be imposed upon them by the House.[36] Thus, while there is no conspiracy by government or individual ministers to avoid ministerial responsibility through constant reshuffling, such manœuvres may nevertheless be effective in the limitation of resignations and the avoidance of accountability.

8.3. KENNETH BAKER: THE BRIXTON PRISON ESCAPE

Background

On Sunday, 7 July 1991, two IRA remand prisoners escaped from Brixton Prison after threatening prison warders with a gun on

---

[35] *The Times*, 22 Feb. 1991.

[36] Responsibility becomes even more difficult to locate when different governments are involved. In 1978–82 £80 million of taxpayers' money was invested in de Lorean car enterprises in Northern Ireland, most of which ended up in numbered Swiss bank accounts. The initial investment was made by Labour's Roy Mason. It was topped up by Humphrey Atkins (Conservative), and Jim Prior was the minister responsible when the company collapsed.

their way back from chapel. The initial statement on the escape was made by a Home Office official. The following day Kenneth Baker, the Home Secretary, gave details of the escape to the House of Commons and announced that Judge Tumim, Chief Inspector of Prisons, had been asked to conduct a full inquiry and to submit an interim report on the escape by the end of the month. Mr Baker promised this report would be published 'subject to the need to protect sensitive security material and to the possibility of criminal charges being laid'.[37]

The Chief Inspector had looked at security arrangements at Brixton Prison the previous year and had made a number of recommendations for their improvement in a report published in December.[38] The Home Secretary stated that he would be 'asking the inquiry to pay particular attention to the progress made in these areas'.[39]

He further indicated that such matters were the responsibility of officials not ministers. He said: 'the Home Secretary is responsible for policy in prison matters. The administration, development and running of the prisons are the responsibility of the director-general [of the prison service] and of individual prison governors.'[40]

Mr Baker also seemed to class the decision as to which prison high-risk Category A prisoners should be sent as lying within the responsibility of the director-general. One of the most significant recommendations made by the Chief Inspector had been that such prisoners should not be held in Brixton because the prison 'did not have the physical defences necessary for the job'.[41] The Home Secretary stated that this recommendation had been 'accepted' by the director-general.[42] Thus, even before the inquiry had started, Mr Baker was distancing himself from any culpability by indicating that all the matters that might be of concern were administrative and thus, he contended, not his responsibility.

Judge Tumim's Report on the Brixton escape was delivered to Kenneth Baker on 31 July and its conclusions were made public on 5 August, by which time Parliament was in recess. The full

[37] HC Deb., 8 July 1991, col. 650.
[38] *Report of a Review by Her Majesty's Chief Inspector of Prisons for England and Wales of Suicides and Self-Harm in Prison Service Establishments in England and Wales* (Stephen Tumim, Chief Inspector of Prisons) (Nov. 1990), Cmnd. 1383, HMSO. [39] HC Deb., 8 July 1991, col. 650.
[40] Ibid., col. 657. [41] Ibid., col. 650. [42] Ibid.

Report was not published on the grounds that it would damage security. Judge Tumim identified a number of failings which he considered had a bearing on the prison escape.[43] Many of these were matters of security detail. He noted the existence of an unguarded gate in the perimeter wall, inadequate searching and prisoner-escort procedures, shortcomings in communications with the control room, and the insufficient use of guard dogs.

More generally he was critical of a failure to treat the men as high-risk prisoners who were determined to escape, and most controversially he revealed that the Home Office's Directorate of Custody 1 (DOC1) had failed to heed a warning from the police about a planned escape. DOC1, headed by Mr Brian Bubbear, was the section responsible for the security of high-risk prisoners. According to Judge Tumim, DOC1 had received a report from the police in February that the prisoners were planning to get hold of a gun and escape after a Sunday Chapel service. This warning had not been passed on to prison officers. Judge Tumim also confirmed that he had previously given a warning about the unsuitability of Brixton for Category A prisoners. He added that he believed that Home Office inquiries after the riot at Strangeways had supported this view.

Shortly after the conclusions of Judge Tumim were made known, Kenneth Baker announced that the Governor of the prison, Reg Withers, would be taking early retirement and that Brian Bubbear, head of DOC1, had been relieved of his position. He was, in fact, transferred to immigration. However, this was not the end of the matter. In late November allegations were made that between October 1990 and February 1991 Staffordshire Special Branch had used a prison officer at Brixton in a covert plan to extract information from the remand prisoners. To gain their confidence, details of an escape plan were discussed.[44]

It was subsequently confirmed by Mr Baker that this information was contained within the unpublished parts of Judge Tumim's Report, and that the Governor too had been aware of the escape plan. However, the Home Secretary was adamant that neither he nor the Minister for Prison Services, Mrs Angela Rumbold, knew of the plan prior to the escape.

---

[43] See *Independent* and *The Times*, 6 Aug. 1991.
[44] *This Week*, Thames Television, 5 Dec. 1991.

I can give you that absolute undertaking—no information was passed either to the Prisons' Minister, Mrs Rumbold, or myself that information had been received by the governor and by a certain official in prison security headquarters about the prisoners being determined to escape.[45]

However, it would seem that Mr Baker was aware of at least some of these facts the morning after the escape, and thus knew of the involvement of Special Branch when he gave his statement to the House. He chose to make no reference to it then or a month later at the press conference, at which he blamed the Governor of the prison and the head of DOC1 for the escape. Despite Mr Baker's instigation of an internal inquiry into the role of Special Branch, his actions subsequently led to allegations by the Assistant General Secretary of the First Division Association that he was engaged in a 'cover up'.[46]

Mr Baker later told the Home Affairs Select Committee that he had not spoken on the matter because Judge Tumim had advised him that the information could endanger security. This was also the reason he gave for declining to answer questions about how much the prison service knew of the Special Branch covert action. The Home Secretary also refused to condone or condemn the Special Branch operation because of the police inquiry which was underway, and which 'may well come to me in my role as appellate authority as Home Secretary'.[47] The Select Committee therefore found its access to information and ministerial opinion restricted.

As far as Mr Baker was concerned he 'behaved properly and responsibly' over the Brixton escape;[48] there was no need for his resignation as matters of policy were not involved.

The Policy—Administration Divide

The Brixton Prison escape raised similar problems in apportioning responsibility as the Maze Prison break-out.[49] As in that instance,

---

[45] Transcript of Home Affairs Select Committee Hearing, 11 Dec. 1991 (broadcast in *In Committee,* BBC Radio 4, 15 Dec. 1991).

[46] Mr Derek Stubbs in *This Week,* 5 Dec. 1991, suggested that a civil servant, Mr Bubbear, had been publicly held responsible to cover up for the activities of Special Branch and divert attention from Mr Baker's own role.

[47] Home Affairs Select Committee Hearing (*In Committee,* BBC Radio 4, 15 Dec. 1991). [48] Ibid.

[49] See Ch. 7.2.

there were errors within the prison itself and within the department. Moreover, the responsible minister again made the divide between 'policy' and 'administration' and insisted that any errors or misjudgements were ones of administration and therefore not his responsibility. However, just as in the Maze incident, the division, even if accepted, was a difficult one to make. The decision as to which prison high-risk prisoners should be sent might be seen as a 'policy' rather than an 'administrative' matter. Likewise, the acceptance of Special Branch involvement within the prison might be considered a policy decision. Certainly neither of these issues was concerned with routine administration, operating at a distance from the minister. Both would seem to have been matters of sufficient political significance to be at least brought to his attention. It could, therefore, be argued that, even if Kenneth Baker was not involved in such decisions, he should at least have been aware of them.

An abdication of responsibility on the grounds of advice received

The Home Secretary used every opportunity to signal his non-culpability in the Brixton escape, even using the constitutionally dubious tactic of citing advice he had received from officials. By so doing he side-stepped responsibility for the implementation of Judge Tumim's earlier recommendations on security. He told the House: 'I was advised by the director-general of the prison service that they were all considered and that action was taken.'[50]

Mr Baker seemed to imply that, if the action taken proved to be insufficient, this was the fault of his officials. He was blameless. Moreover, he further implied that he was only able to report to the House what his officials told him. However, it is inappropriate for a minister with a direct departmental responsibility to offer only reporting or informatory responsibility in such a situation.[51]

In a similar attempt to abdicate responsibility, Mr Baker told the Home Affairs Select Committee that he could not reveal information because of advice given by Judge Tumim. He continued: 'I've had difficulty not being able to release as much as I know

---

[50] HC Deb., 8 July 1991, col. 653.   [51] See Ch. 2.

people want to know . . .'⁵² The implication was that Mr Baker would have liked to reveal more but was obliged to remain silent because of the advice he had been given.

Mr Baker also used the receipt of advice to abdicate responsibility after the Court of Appeal held him to be in contempt for failing to obey an order of the court. He justified his actions with reference to legal advice he had been given, causing Mr Hattersley, Shadow Home Secretary, to comment:

the Home Secretary will recall that, at the time of the Brixton escape fiasco, he claimed that no blame attached to him because he had not been consulted. In the case of the wrongful deportation of an asylum seeker, he admitted that he was consulted, but he hides behind the excuse that he did no more than accept civil servants' advice. Are there any circumstances in which the Home Secretary would feel it right to take the honourable course and resign from the office which he discharges so inadequately?⁵³

Mr Baker in these incidents seemed to suggest that he had no choice but to accept the advice he had been given. However, he, like any minister, was free to accept or reject it. Having chosen to accept it, he was responsible for the consequences of this choice.⁵⁴

The Home Secretary's willingness to reveal advice that he was given (and by implication blame the adviser if the decision taken proved to be wrong or unpopular), was contrary to the traditional constitutional position that civil servants advise and ministers decide. It suggested that he considered his responsibility was diminished or abrogated through the receipt of advice, and that he was placed under the implied direction of those whose responsibility it was to advise him. Such a position was not compatible with constitutional accountability.

---

⁵² Home Affairs Select Committee hearing (*In Committee*, BBC Radio 4, 15 Dec. 1991).

⁵³ HC Deb., 2 Dec. 1991, col. 31.

⁵⁴ Responsibility for the consequences of choosing to follow advice, even expert advice sought in time of war, was recognized by the Royal Commission on Mesopotamia, reporting in 1917. Its report stated:

But so long as the system of responsible departmental administration exists in this country, those who are political heads of departments . . . cannot be entirely immune from the consequences of their own actions. They have the option and the power of accepting or rejecting the advice of their expert subordinates. (From Jennings, *Cabinet Government*, 498.)

A constitutional requirement for resignation?

The Brixton escape was an example of departmental fault. The extent of ministerial involvement in, or knowledge of, the errors made was unclear. This was mainly because Mr Baker sought to limit the amount of information which became public, using a variety of means to justify the restriction. Thus the full story was not revealed, as Roy Hattersley subsequently pointed out during the debate on the Prison Security Bill:

We still do not know the full story of Brixton: therefore we do not know the truth. I take the opportunity to tell the Home Secretary once more that sooner or later he will have to be frank with the House and the country about what occurred at Brixton and about what he knew.[55]

Mr Hattersley would seem to have been optimistic; frankness is not normally a ministerial trait. Indeed, after incidents such as Westland and Rover,[56] it might be suggested that the half-told story has become a feature of British government and Mr Baker was merely continuing the trend. He never gave a full account of the escape and thus failed to fulfil the requirements of explanatory accountability. Moreover, because the full facts were not known, the amendatory actions taken by the Home Secretary were seen by many as unsatisfactory. There was suspicion that Mr Baker was hiding behind the faults of officials.

It is difficult to assess the extent to which Mr Baker was personally involved in the misjudgements of his department. However, it would seem that he was at least culpable of failing to exercise the required degree of control over his department. Moreover, the Brixton escape had not been the first incident which made his department seem ill-managed. There had been public unease about the handling of the prison service throughout much of Mr Baker's time as Home Secretary, and he had been strongly criticized for his reaction to law-and-order issues, particularly joy-riding and the legislation concerning dangerous dogs. In addition, by the time the Special Branch involvement had been made known, Mr Baker had been held in contempt by the Court of Appeal for failing to obey an order of the court not to deport an asylum-seeker before his case had been reviewed.[57]

[55] HC Deb., 3 Dec. 1991, col. 176.   [56] See Chs. 6.2, 8.2.
[57] See n. 53.

However, cumulative fault based on mismanagement rather than personal fault rarely results in resignation. More usually the minister finds himself without a department after a Cabinet reshuffle.[58] Thus, despite calls for resignation from the Opposition and the Press, and dissatisfaction on the government back-benches, Mr Baker remained in office.

It is probable that the lack of concrete evidence against the Home Secretary saved him from the sustained political pressure necessary to persuade him to tender his resignation. In addition, the protracted nature of the incident and its timing were to his advantage. The escape took place just before Parliament went into recess and thus the House was no longer sitting when Judge Tumim reported to the Home Secretary. Mr Baker was, therefore, able to announce selected findings of the Report and take disciplinary action without having to face a full examination in the House.

The part played by Special Branch did not come to light until November, when Mr Baker was able to announce that there was already an inquiry being conducted. In any case, by this time political interest in culpability for the escape had waned. The House of Commons would seem either to have a short attention span, being able to retain interest in an incident only for a limited period, or to see the resignation of a minister in the same light as the punishment of a small child, and thus only appropriate as an immediate response to misdoing. It is, therefore, always to the advantage of a culpable minister to delay giving explanations for as long as possible.

However, although there was no resignation, Kenneth Baker's continuation in office was to be short-lived. He was not given a seat in Mr Major's new Cabinet (April 1992). This might suggest some sort of expiation for mismanagement or lack of competence, but other political explanations are pertinent.

A Precedent for Non-Culpability in Cases of Administrative Fault?

The Brixton escape indicated a further development in the policy–administration divide, whereby ministerial responsibility was seen as limited to matters of high policy. Such a division is unsatisfactory,

---

[58] For example, Paul Channon, Secretary of State for Transport, who lost his ministry in a Cabinet reshuffle after he had come under criticism for his handling of a series of disasters—Lockerbie, King's Cross, Clapham.

for within the gap between 'high policy' and 'routine administration' there would seem to be matters which reflect on the overall effective implementation and efficient management of the department or which have a serious impact on the public interest beyond the immediate circumstances. Ministers should retain full responsibility for such matters.

When James Prior made his distinction between policy and administration after the Maze Prison break-out, it was strongly contested by the House of Commons.[59] However, when Kenneth Baker made the division, his contention was not questioned, even seeming to receive support from a former Home Secretary, Merlyn Rees.[60] This suggests that Members of Parliament now accept such a division as part of the convention of individual ministerial responsibility, or are indifferent as to whether it is or not. If so, constitutional change will have occurred by default and through the misinterpretation of a previous precedent.

[59] See Ch. 7.2.   [60] HC Deb., 8 July 1991, col. 653.

9

Conclusion

9.1. THE COINCIDENCE OF CONSTITUTIONAL AND POLITICAL REQUIREMENTS

The 1980s and early 1990s provided substantial evidence that the convention of individual ministerial responsibility requires resignation for departmental fault in which the minister was involved, or of which he knew or should have known (Carrington and Brittan), and for personal fault, either when acting as a minister without the backing of the department (Fairbairn, Currie, and Ridley), or in his private capacity (Parkinson, Nicholls, and Mellor).[1]

These resignations demonstrate the relationship between constitutional and political factors and the necessity for them to coincide and mutually reinforce before a minister is required to relinquish office. The constitution prescribes that, in cases of serious error in which the minister has been involved, he may be required to resign. It provides the rule, the precedent, and the morality to which appeals can be made. However, the application of the rule depends upon both the narrow judgement of whether the ministerial fault is serious enough to warrant resignation, there being no constitutional definition of 'serious', and the broader judgement of whether in the political circumstances resignation is appropriate.

A Constitutional Basis

The requirement for a constitutional basis explains why attempts to force resignation on ministers who are politically unpopular but

---

[1] Michael Mates's resignation (1993) can also be categorized as personal fault while acting in his private capacity, both as a private individual and as an MP.

constitutionally blameless are generally unsuccessful. Thus William Whitelaw remained in office despite a strong campaign against him. He denied his opponents' constitutional grounds and thereby enabled the Prime Minister and senior colleagues to continue to support him and provide collective cover. Whitelaw's survival contrasts with the demise of Brittan and Currie, who were initially afforded collective cover and prime ministerial support, neither of which was sustainable.

There must, therefore, be identifiable fault for the political pressure for resignation to be successful, and resignations without this constitutional requirement are rare. Ministers who are politically inept, unlucky, or unpopular usually struggle on until either they retire or there is a Cabinet reshuffle. However, it is possible to see some instances as the delayed operation of individual ministerial responsibility. Thus, Paul Channon, unlucky in a series of disasters —Lockerbie, King's Cross, Clapham—and open to the charge of mismanagement in his handling of them and subsequent incidents, lost his ministry in a Cabinet reshuffle, and John Nott retired from politics six months after the invasion of the Falklands.

Such retirements, whether voluntary or not, may be preferred by the prime minister to resignations, for their timing may be more controllable. However, they do not contain the elements of visible responsibility and obligation or punishment, which satisfy Parliament and the public but in practice provide only minimal accountability. The extent to which a resignation is regarded as a ministerial obligation, thereby carrying the ring of honour, duty, and dignity, or as a punishment, depends on the speed with which it is executed, the mistake involved, and the rhetoric surrounding the resignation. Using these criteria, Carrington's resignation rates highly on the scale of honour, while the resignations of Brittan, Currie, and Mellor merit low ratings, suggesting, certainly in the cases of Currie and Mellor, the loss of office as a punishment rather than an exercise of ministerial duty.

A 'Serious' Judgement

Once the constitutional foundation for resignation is present, a judgement is required to ascertain whether or not the fault is serious enough to warrant resignation. This judgement cannot be made in isolation from the social and political mores of the time.

It is not an absolute judgement, and herein lies the flexibility of the convention which enables it to adapt to circumstances without constant restatements of individual ministerial responsibility.

Precedents provide a measure of what may be serious enough to require resignation, but in the end the judgement is of a particular situation and is made by the political actors involved. These actors include the erring minister, his Cabinet colleagues, the prime minister, and the party, and whether or not the fault is considered serious enough for resignation depends largely on the effect of the error or misjudgement upon their interests. Resignation is, therefore, likely to be sought if the minister's actions have embarrassed the government and appeared to discredit it, if they have provided the Opposition and the media with sufficient ammunition to mount a sustained attack upon the minister in particular and the government in general, or if they have clearly offended the electorate, or an important part of it.

Finer suggested that for a resignation to occur 'the Minister [had to be] yielding, his Prime Minister unbending, his party out for blood'.[2] Recent cases indicate that some modifications are required to this statement. First, Finer did not define what he meant by 'yielding', but, if it is taken to imply a lack of resistance on the part of the minister to pressure for resignation, then this is not always the case. With the exception of Carrington and perhaps Fairbairn, ministers during the 1980s complied only when they realized they had no option. Secondly, the prime minister did not always exhibit the firmness suggested. Indeed, except in the cases of Fairbairn and Ridley, Mrs Thatcher was reluctant to accept resignations or the need for them, perhaps indicating an indifference to constitutional or even political requirements, or perhaps a reluctance to let her ministers go. Similarly, John Major was unwilling to accept that there was a need for David Mellor to resign, refusing Mellor's offer of resignation the first time, and thereafter indicating that the minister had his support.

The forthrightness of the prime minister in giving personal support to ministers under attack was a feature of many of the resignations. Mrs Thatcher tried to persuade Carrington not to resign, refused to accept Nott's resignation, indicated her belief that it was not necessary for Prior, Parkinson, or Brittan to resign,

---

[2] Finer, 'Individual Ministerial Responsibility', 393.

and would appear to have regretted the resignation of Currie. Her reluctance to countenance resignation by these ministers made the lack of support offered to Fairbairn from Number Ten appear akin to constructive dismissal. Likewise Mrs Thatcher's position regarding Nicholas Ridley, that it was for him to decide whether resignation was appropriate, can be seen in the same light, particularly when accompanied by a dissociation from his remarks. Such dissociation was a clear withdrawal of collective cover and an implied recognition of fault. It indicates the need for ministers to be sheltered beneath the umbrella of collective responsibility if they are to remain in office, a point also demonstrated in the case of Edwina Currie, whose resignation coincided with the redrawing of the collective line which left her without government support. However, it would be a mistake to see collective responsibility as a benign convention whose concern is the welfare of individual ministers. Its function is to protect the government as a whole, and the collective cover will not be extended if the protection of a particular minister puts the government or the prime minister at risk. This accounts for the lack of cover given to Ridley, and the eventual withdrawal of cover from Currie and Brittan.[3]

Moreover, the price paid for collective protection is that the individual minister must follow the collective line. This may not always be to the minister's advantage. Edwina Currie had to remain silent, but it is possible that, had she been allowed to answer her critics, she might have survived. Similarly, Leon Brittan's evasiveness did nothing to forward his cause. For Michael Heseltine, following the collective line in Westland, which he maintained had been imposed without discussion, was unacceptable. He asserted that to do so would prevent his fulfilling his responsibility as a minister and as a result resigned, thereby demonstrating the tension that exists between the conventions.

The third factor that Finer cited as likely to be influential in forcing a resignation was the party, and the evidence from the 1980s indicates that the party, in the form of the 1922 Committee,

---

[3] John Major similarly used 'collective cover' to protect Norman Lamont, Chancellor of the Exchequer. After the withdrawal from the ERM, Major made clear to the House that Lamont was following agreed government policy. He was not to be made a scapegoat. This contrasts with the policy to close thirty-one pits, which was identified as belonging to Michael Heseltine (President of the Board of Trade) and his responsibility.

particularly its Executive, is the main force behind resignations from Conservative governments. It certainly ensured the resignation of Brittan, Currie, Ridley, and Mellor and was highly influential in Carrington's decision to resign.

It is not easy, therefore, to ascribe to Parliament, or more accurately the House of Commons, a principal role in enforcing resignations. However, although resignations are not forced by Parliament—there are no votes of censure—it is the arena in which mistakes may be brought to light in the first place and where ministers may find themselves facing sustained public questioning.[4] In addition, any affront to the dignity of the House, either through a deliberate attempt by a minister to mislead it or through the denial of information, will result in united condemnation, as illustrated by the reaction to Brittan and Young.

Nevertheless, the evidence is such as to suggest that the strength of the 1922 Committee means that a minister's performance before this body may be more important than his performance on the Floor of the House. Indeed, for some ministers, notably Lord Carrington, this is the only arena in which they can perform before the party. It is certainly here that Conservative members are most likely to let their true feelings be known, and these feelings find official expression through the Executive of the Committee to the Chief Whip and hence to the prime minister. In practice, power is concentrated within the eighteen-strong Executive, and, although the decisions of this group are usually a reflection of the wider party position, the Executive has at times acted without taking official soundings. The fate of Currie, Ridley, and Mellor was decided by the Executive acting alone.

The Press may have emerged as a further factor in resignations

---

[4] As happened with Michael Heseltine on 19 and 21 Oct. 1992 over the pit closures. It seems certain that, had the government lost the vote in the House, Heseltine would have resigned. The policy was his responsibility. However, there is an interesting difference between Britain and Australia. In Britain neither the House of Commons nor the House of Lords puts forward motions censuring individual ministers. This contrasts with the Australian experience, where during the period 1976–89 there were '41 motions covering 26 separate cases where ministers might be considered liable for censure under the application of individual ministerial responsibility. All but one of these motions was lost on the floor of Parliament' (B. Page, 'Ministerial Resignation and Individual Ministerial Responsibility in Australia 1976–89', *Journal of Commonwealth and Comparative Politics* (Nov. 1990), 145).

since Finer was writing, although the part it plays is not easy to assess. There were suggestions that Carrington was influenced in his decision to resign by newspaper editorials, but there is no hard evidence. Research into the role of the Press in ministerial resignations in Australia has demonstrated that editorial opinion in the media is a significant indicator (if not a cause) of ministerial resignations.[5] It has not been established whether the Press is reflecting political opinion or creating it, but either way it would seem that the Press is a factor that should be included when considering the circumstances of resignations.

In Britain editorial opinion is often divided. For instance, not all papers campaigned for Mrs Currie's resignation, or that of Nicholas Ridley. In the latter case there would seem to have been a division between the quality Press and most of the tabloids, a division which has shown itself on other occasions—for example, in attitudes to William Whitelaw. Just as important as editorial comment is the extent to which newspapers give sustained coverage to an issue, thereby keeping ministerial mistakes in the public eye. In the case of Cecil Parkinson this prevented government's good news from taking the headlines, while the coverage of David Mellor distracted attention away from government problems. This did not, however, work in Mellor's favour, as he was seen as imposing an additional burden upon the beleaguered Prime Minister. Moreover, the nature of the coverage of David Mellor was undoubtedly a factor in the consideration by the political actors of whether the minister's misjudgements were serious enough to require resignation.

The seriousness of a mistake or misjudgement clearly depends on its context and its outcome. Thus Fairbairn's indiscretion in talking to the Press about the Glasgow rape case might not have been considered serious enough for resignation had it not occurred against a background of public concern about the police attitude towards rape and the lack of prosecutions. Parkinson too might have survived if revelations about his affair with Miss Keays had not coincided with the Party Conference. Similarly, and obviously, the Foreign Office's misinterpretation of the signals emerging from Argentina, and Carrington's failure to alert his colleagues to the

[5] Ibid. 155.

changing situation, would not have constituted serious fault if Argentina had not invaded the Falkland Islands, and Currie's statement about salmonella in eggs would probably not have been categorized as serious had it not resulted in a substantial drop in egg sales. These were by any standards disastrous consequences of misjudgements.

A Wider Political Judgement

The 1980s have demonstrated that usually, if a fault is considered serious enough to warrant resignation and thereby satisfy the conventional requirement of individual ministerial responsibility, there is also a requirement for it in the wider context. The political circumstances seldom work against resignation.

Inevitably, all the resignations that have been examined—Fairbairn, Carrington, Parkinson, Brittan, Currie, Ridley, Mellor—have demonstrated a coincidence of constitutional and political requirements. There was fault; the fault was considered serious; and the circumstances did not work against resignation. In the case of Whitelaw there was no constitutional basis for resignation and it is therefore incorrect to consider that he was saved by political factors. Even Lord Young, whilst in office, provided no evidence that would support a constitutional call for his resignation at that time, and the evidence against Kenneth Baker was protracted and cumulative, and the extent of his culpability uncertain.

The cases which provide the greatest focus for the supposition that the convention has given way to political consideration are those of Nott and Prior. However, their failure to resign did not undermine individual ministerial responsibility. In both instances there was a recognition of the constitutional position, if not by the ministers themselves, then by the other political actors and by political commentators. Both ministers would probably have been required to relinquish office but for the political situation, which was not just a partisan consideration concerned with the fortunes of the party and the government, but included a wider national concern. Moreover, their failure to resign cannot be seen as having created precedents for non-resignation. Since then there have been the resignations of Leon Brittan for departmental fault, and Edwina Currie, Nicholas Ridley, and David Mellor for personal fault.

9.2. PRECEDENTS FROM THE 1980s

Resignations Confined to High Policy

In 1984 James Prior insisted that he was under no obligation to resign for administrative errors. To an extent he was correct, for most administrative errors are too remote from the minister to be considered within his area of knowledge or control, and resignation would therefore be an acceptance of vicarious liability. However, the phrasing used by Prior was too wide. It implied that the minister's responsibility was confined to matters of high policy and that he should never resign for errors within administration, regardless of their nature or scale or of the minister's involvement. His contention was not accepted at the time. However, there was a possibility that it could subsequently be cited wrongly as a precedent for the principle that ministers never resign for administrative fault, just as Dugdale's resignation was for some time misinterpreted. This indeed happened. Kenneth Baker in a similar situation followed Prior in asserting that administrative or operational matters were not his responsibility and thus resignation was not appropriate. Moreover, when questioned in the House, the manner in which the minister responded was more characteristic of reporting or informatory accountability than of the explanatory accountability that was constitutionally required.

In contrast to the Prior situation, Members of Parliament did not resist the policy–administration division made by Baker or question the consequences that flowed from it. It might, therefore, be concluded that such a division is acceptable and that a precedent of non-resignation for administrative errors is established. It is probably too soon to draw such a conclusion. The facts relating to the Brixton escape were not sufficiently clear for Members to determine whether or not there was ministerial culpability, relating to policy or administration, and it is likely that a major administrative error or misjudgement, which was close to the minister and caused the government considerable embarrassment, would still be seen as a resigning matter. However, the Maze and Brixton incidents do provide a basis, albeit a doubtful one, for a minister to claim that resignation is not a constitutional requirement.

Responsibility of Junior Ministers

The resignations of the 1980s may also provide genuine, rather than misread, precedents which relate to the constitutional position of junior ministers. Fairbairn, Luce, Atkins, and Currie were all junior ministers who resigned, while Scott from the Northern Ireland Office came under considerable pressure to join them. In the debate on the Hennessy Report, which arose out of the Maze Prison break-out, Enoch Powell gave the orthodox constitutional position.

It is . . . a total misconception to imagine that any of the responsibility can be devolved to a Junior Minister. A Junior Minister may choose, if his chief resigns, to resign in solidarity with him; he may choose to resign himself for a variety of reasons. But there is no constitutional significance in acceptance by him of a responsibility which is not his. The locus of the responsibility is beyond challenge. It lies with the Secretary of State as a whole.[6]

The position of junior ministers, both ministers of state and parliamentary secretaries or under-secretaries of state, arises out of the fact that they have no legal status as ministers of the Crown.[7] A junior minister cannot, therefore, accept responsibility for the faults of the department of which he is a part, because this responsibility lies with the Secretary of State. Whatever delegatory arrangements he might make with a junior minister, he cannot devolve ministerial responsibility. The junior minister, like officials within the department, is therefore accountable to his minister, and accounts to Parliament only on behalf of the minister. The convention of individual ministerial responsibility therefore 'both protects and enfeebles' junior ministers.[8]

However, some junior ministers occupy very visible positions

[6] HC Deb., 9 Feb. 1985, col. 1060.

[7] The House of Commons Disqualification Act 1975, s9 (1), defines a minister of state and a parliamentary secretary thus: 'Minister of State means a member of Her Majesty's Government in the United Kingdom who neither has charge of any public department . . .'; 'Parliamentary Secretary includes a person holding Ministerial Office (however called) as assistant to a Member of Her Majesty's Government in the United Kingdom but not having departmental responsibilities' (quoted in R. Brazier, *Constitutional Texts* (Oxford: Clarendon Press, 1990), 311–12). The above refers only to legal responsibilities. Most parliamentary secretaries (or parliamentary under-secretaries, as they are styled if the head of their department is a Secretary of State) are delegated specific departmental responsibilities.

[8] K. Theakston, *Junior Ministers in British Government* (Oxford: Blackwells, 1987), 68.

and are associated by the public with particular areas of responsibility. It may in some instances be unsatisfactory if they cannot be held publicly and personally accountable for those areas. Moreover, where a Secretary of State sits in the Lords rather than the Commons, the junior minister is particularly exposed to the needs of accountability. Thus Richard Luce had to take the brunt of the Commons' anger over the invasion of the Falklands and defend Foreign Office action. Moreover, it is clear that he felt an obligation to resign on the grounds of individual ministerial responsibility, for it was his section of the Foreign Office that was under attack, and his resignation was certainly seen as more than a gesture of solidarity with Lord Carrington. Indeed, it presents an interesting contrast with that of Humphrey Atkins, whose resignation comes into that latter category of an honourable gesture of solidarity, but not constitutionally necessary.

Luce's resignation might, therefore, be classified as an acceptance of the conventional requirement for resignation where the minister was involved in departmental fault, and suggests an extension of the convention to junior ministers in some cases. Similarly Nicholas Scott's resignation was sought by Ulster Unionists because they believed that he, as the junior minister responsible for prisons in Northern Ireland, should bear the responsibility for the Maze Prison break-out. His survival probably owes more to the need to keep his Secretary of State in office, and perhaps to the fact that he had been a minister for only three months, than to a constitutional observance of the position of junior ministers.

In both instances, however, the relevant Secretary of State—Carrington or Prior—adopted the traditional position and insisted that it was inappropriate for a junior minister to accept responsibility for departmental fault. In the end Carrington resigned with Luce, while Prior and Scott remained in office.

Junior ministers are not, of course, constitutionally discouraged from taking responsibility for personal fault, as the resignations of Nicholas Fairbairn and Edwina Currie demonstrate. They may, however, find their public accountability restricted, as Edwina Currie did, thereby demonstrating the rule that junior ministers are still first and foremost accountable to senior ministers.

Resignations and Accountability

The 1980s may be seen as a good decade for resignations on the grounds of individual ministerial responsibility and for symbolic accountability but less so for actual accountability. The cases examined indicate a number of instances where accountability was evaded, or delayed, by various means. A series of changes of minister at the DTI made accountability for the Barlow Clowes affair and the House of Fraser take-over impossible to locate, although presumably this was not the intention of the frequent changes of Secretary of State. More seriously, the withholding of information from Parliament by Lord Young about the terms of the Rover sale can be seen as an exercise in accountability avoidance.

A particular feature of the cases studied was the inquiry. Inquiries are generally considered to enhance accountability by establishing the facts and apportioning blame. This was not the case with the inquiry conducted by Sir Robert Armstrong into the disclosure of the Solicitor-General's letter during the Westland affair, for its full findings were never made public. Crucial facts still need to be revealed so that responsibility can be adequately determined. The Quesne inquiry into Barlow Clowes established the facts, but it too failed to apportion blame, being specifically precluded by its terms of reference from making any conclusions concerning culpability.

There are other limitations upon inquiries as accounting mechanisms. The publication of a report may be withheld for legal reasons—as with the Report into the House of Fraser take-over, which was delayed by eighteen months because of the possibility of legal proceedings—or only parts of it may be made public. Judge Tumim's Report into the Brixton Prison escape was not fully published on the grounds that some information within the Report was damaging to security. An inquiry may be unwilling to embarrass the government—an accusation made about the Agriculture Committee and its inquiry into salmonella—or its conclusions may appear to exonerate the government, although closer reading of the contents of the report may indicate that there was significant fault. Both the Franks Report into the Falklands and the Hennessy Report into the Maze Prison break-out are open to such criticism.

The special professional expertise or experience of the person conducting the inquiry may also affect accountability, indicating the area on which the report will concentrate and its confidence in making criticisms. Thus Prior's choice of Hennessy, Chief Inspector of Prisons, to inquire into the Maze Prison break-out, whilst suitable, made it likely that the Report would be more confident in its criticisms of prison officers than of senior government officials or ministers. This was also the case with the inquiry by Judge Tumim into the Brixton escape.

Accountability is also diminished by using resignation instead of, rather than as well as, explaining. This was a particular feature of the resignations of Brittan and Currie, who both resigned but refused to account fully for the actions which had led to their resignations. Indeed, in the case of Leon Brittan, his resignation, accompanied by a bare acceptance of responsibility, may be seen as obstructing accountability. These resignations in particular suggest an absence of any graciousness or honour related to resignations on the grounds of individual ministerial responsibility, which history, or perhaps mythology, suggests existed. This may in the long run be detrimental to the convention, because it suggests an insensitivity to the demands of the constitution and an impatience with its requirements, particularly the requirement for accountability.

The 1980s were characterized by a lack of constitutional rhetoric surrounding ministerial resignations or calls for resignation. The only 'constitutional' debate concerned the Maze Prison break-out, and the only letter of resignation that was worded in terms of constitutional significance was written by Lord Carrington. This has resulted in suggestions that the resignations of the 1980s have little to do with constitutional considerations and much to do with political requirements.

However, the political requirement for resignation would seem to be met only when backed by, or indeed arising from, the morality of the constitution. Politicians call for constitutional requirements to be fulfilled at least in part for political reasons, but by so doing they reinforce the constitutional morality, which in turn gives the system legitimacy. The convention of individual ministerial responsibility is, therefore, still a determining factor in ministerial resignations. There are times when circumstances militate against its operation, but this does not reduce its significance. It does, however, illustrate that, for resignations to occur, there needs to be a coincidence of constitutional requirements and political desirability. The constitutional requirement is for fault which is considered by the political actors to be serious. If these conditions are met, then resignation may be required. However, this requirement needs to coincide with the desirability of such a resignation in the wider political context.

The period 1982–92 produced ten resignations on the grounds of individual ministerial responsibility, only three of which were required because of private indiscretion. Five of these resignations were by senior ministers, and one—that of Currie—by a junior minister with a high public profile. This contrasts with the previous decade, 1972–82, when there were only two resignations by senior ministers, both of which resulted from the fault or indiscretion of the minister while acting in a private capacity.[9] Such a comparison confirms that the convention of individual ministerial responsibility remains an operational feature of the British Constitution, at least in providing symbolic, if not actual, accountability.

[9] These were R. Maudling (1972 Poulson investigation), Lord Jellicoe (1973 associating with prostitutes). There were also two other resignations by junior ministers: Lord Lambton and Lord Brayley. These again were for private indiscretion. They contrast with the resignations of Luce and Atkins over the Falklands invasion.

PART THREE

Changes Affecting the Operation of
Individual Ministerial Responsibility

The Reform of the Select Committee System:
An Attempt to Redress the Balance

10.1. INTRODUCTION

In 1979 the system of select committees based on the Expenditure Committee and descended from the former Estimates Committee was reformed to provide a series of specialist committees 'to examine the expenditure, administration and policy of the principal government departments . . . and associated public bodies'.[1] This reform was intended to redress the balance between the executive and Parliament by improving Parliament's ability to scrutinize the executive and hold ministers to account. Over a decade later, however, fundamental questions about the powers of the select committees have still not been resolved.

In order to assess these powers and the limitations upon them, it is necessary to examine both their origins and recent developments. Such an examination of the theoretical and practical operation of the powers of select committees will also assist in providing an understanding of the relationship between the committees and the executive, and the inherent conflict between them.

The government has maintained that 'Select Committees exercise their formal powers to inquire into policies and actions of departments by virtue of the accountability of Ministers to Parliament.'[2]

The Treasury and Civil Service Committee (TCSC), however, has seen this as too narrow a view:

Select Committees exercise their formal powers to inquire into policy and actions of departments because Parliament is sovereign and has established

---

[1] Standing Order No. 130, 25 June 1979.
[2] *The Government's Response to the Fourth Report from the Defence Committee on 'Westland plc: The Defence Implications of the Future of Westland plc: The Government's Decision-Making'* (1986), Cmnd. 9916, HMSO.

the select committees to monitor Government departments on its behalf, giving them the traditional powers to send for persons and papers.[3]

The differences are fundamental. The government, by focusing upon ministerial accountability, suggests that the powers of select committees are limited by the convention. Thus select committees can require ministers to account but only within the conventional framework of restrictions developed by modern government. This presupposes that policy matters are for the government alone, and that the adversarial and majoritarian model of Parliament prevails; government back-benchers have the duty to support the government and Opposition members have the right to oppose and defeat it, if they can. Usually, of course, they are unable to do so. Thus accountability depends upon ministers who are normally well protected by the government's majority in the House.

This view contrasts with that expressed by the TCSC, which emphasizes the sovereignty of Parliament and its inherent right to scrutinize and control the government, not because ministers are conventionally accountable to Parliament, but because Parliament is supreme. The inherent conflict between government and select committees is well displayed in the dispute between them over the right of the committees to send for persons, papers, and records, for this is a crucial power for the committees and relates especially to the differences in opinion concerning the appearance of civil servants before select committees.

10.2. THE POWER TO SEND FOR PERSONS, PAPERS, AND RECORDS

The strength of select committees lies in their power to send for persons, papers, and records. Historically this power resides in Parliament, which, as a High Court, had the right to require information, and to punish for contempt if this information were withheld. This statement needs examination, however, for, whilst the House of Lords may have a historical status as a High Court, it is not clear how this power transfers to the House of Commons. Erskine May states that the ability to punish for contempt is a

[3] *First Report of the Treasury and Civil Service Committee* (1986–7), HC62, HMSO.

privilege enjoyed by each House collectively 'as a constituent part of the High Court of Parliament'.[4] This view was supported in *Kielley* v. *Carson*,[5] where it was held that the power to punish for contempt is inherent in each House of Parliament, not as a body with legislative functions, but as a descendant of the High Court of Parliament. Again this would seem historically inaccurate as far as the Commons is concerned. The answer may lie in a medieval misconception that constitutional authority could only reside in a court of justice. Such a belief enabled the Commons to assert its rights on the same basis as the Lords.

If the source of the Commons' privilege to punish for contempt arises out of its misperceived, rather than its actual, position as a court, then the power to send for persons, papers, and records may have arisen there as well. Origins have become cloudy, however, as the role and composition of Parliament have changed and as the Commons has become dominant within the institution of Parliament. The power to send for persons, papers, and records is more easily, and perhaps more accurately, associated with the fundamental right of Parliament to information, not in any judicial capacity but in its scrutinizing role as a legislature.

It remains one of the most important sources of parliamentary power and in theory it is unlimited. Indeed, for those writing at the begining of the century: 'In the unlimited character of the claim for information, which may in principle be made at any time, there lies a fundamental parliamentary right of the highest importance.'[6] Such a belief was based on previous practice. During the nineteenth century it was common for back-benchers to move for the return of papers. However, as a result of changes in procedure, culminating in the Balfour reforms of 1902, this power virtually disappeared, the control of parliamentary time passing to the government in negotiation with the Opposition.[7] Thus, while in theory the claim by Parliament for information is 'unlimited', in practice back-benchers do not have the opportunity to make such a claim. In addition, procedural requirements, privileges, and conventions protect many of those from whom information is required. Indeed, as the Select Committee on Procedure stated,

---

[4] E. May, *Treatise on the Law: Privileges, Proceedings and Usage of Parliament* (20th edn., London: Butterworths, 1983), 71.   [5] 4 Moore PC63, 1842.

[6] J. Redlich and C. Ilbert, *Procedure of the House of Commons*, ii (London: Archibald Constable, 1908), 40.   [7] See Ch. 1.3.

'The powers both as exercised by the House and its Select Committees are . . . circumscribed by qualifications, apparent contradictions, and lack of opportunity to exercise the powers which undoubtedly exist.'[8]

The powers of select committees are, therefore, limited by many of the factors, both procedural and political, that limit the whole House. In addition, there are restrictions which derive from the fact that select committees exercise delegated rather than original power and from the nature of their work.

10.3. LIMITATIONS IMPOSED BY PARLIAMENT ON THE POWER OF SELECT COMMITTEES

Terms of Reference

The powers delegated to committees are always limited in their use by the terms of reference set down by the House, either at the time of the appointment of the committee or on a later motion by the chairman. A committee attempting to exercise its powers beyond these terms would be acting *ultra vires*—hence the relevance of Edwina Currie's question to the Select Committee on Agriculture, which was inquiring into salmonella in eggs: 'is this an inquiry into what I said on 6th December or an inquiry into salmonella in eggs?'[9]

A Lack of Formal Authority

The power of select committees to send for persons, papers, and records is held to be 'unqualified',[10] and enables select committees to order the attendance of witnesses or the production of documents. Moreover, because the refusal to obey an order issued by a committee is a contempt of Parliament, non-compliance can be raised in the House as a matter of privilege and thus takes priority over other business. However, select committees can exercise such unqualified power only with regard to private individuals and, in very limited circumstances, the sending for papers from

---

[8] *First Report from the Select Committee on Procedure*, vol. i (1977–8), HC588-I, HMSO, Memorandum from the Clerk to the House, p. 15.

[9] HC108–II (1988–9), Q609.   [10] CJ (1849) 75.

departments. Otherwise the power is qualified to prevent a conflict 'with the privileges of the Crown and of the Members of the House of Lords, or with the rights of Members of the House of Commons'.[11]

The power of select committees is, therefore, restricted by parliamentary privilege and by parliamentary procedures, which arose historically to protect the privileges of the Crown. As a result, the formal authority to insist on the provision of necessary information, either in written or in oral form, remains with the House. This is a serious restriction upon select committees, for both prestigious and practical reasons.

Parliamentary Privilege and Attendance before Committees

Select committees cannot order Members of either House of Parliament to appear before them. Such an order would conflict with the privileges of Parliament. Committees are therefore limited to issuing invitations, both to Peers and Members of Parliament, whether ministers or not. A further restraint applies to a committee wishing to secure evidence from a Member of the other House. It is required to seek the permission of that House. Thus a Commons' select committee must obtain leave from the House of Lords to invite a Peer to attend before it. Leave is granted only if the Peer concerned consents to give evidence, and, whilst the Commons has modified its procedure and given a general leave for any of its Members to attend as witnesses before a Lords' Committee when requested to do so,[12] the only concession made by the Lords has been the granting of general leave to Peers who have been invited to attend Commons' committees on European legislation.[13]

Such considerations do not, of course, prevent a select committee from requesting the attendance of a Member of the House of Lords, but they do raise questions about the theoretical inability of a committee to call to account a reluctant minister who is a Peer, or indeed to call an ex-minister or ex-civil servant to give evidence. Thus, when Lord Young indicated that he would decline any invitation by the Trade and Industry Committee to give evidence on the sale of Rover to British Aerospace, for which he had been the responsible minister, the committee could take no direct

---

[11] May, *Treatise* (20th edn.), 697. [12] SO No96 CJ (1979–80) 95.
[13] LJ (1978–9) 35.

action.[14] It could not request an order from the House of Commons, as the making of such an order is a breach of the privileges of the House of Lords. The committee, therefore, had to rely on political persuasion to change the ex-minister's mind.

The position of select committees is stronger when Members of the House of Commons are concerned. If a Member should refuse an invitation issued by one of its own committees, the committee can seek an order in the House for his attendance. However, in accordance with a Resolution of 1688, select committees can still take no authoritative action on their own initiative: 'if any member of the House refuse, upon being sent to, to come to give evidence or information, as a witness, to a Committee, the Committee ought to acquaint the House therewith, and not summon such Member to attend the Committee.'[15]

Such instructions provide a reminder that the powers of select committees are delegated by the House, which retains for itself the authority to make an order for the attendance of a Member before a select committee. There have been few instances of such orders being necessary,[16] and none this century. This suggests an established convention that Members accept invitations. A chain of precedents support this position, the purpose of which is to facilitate the work of the committees and to prevent Parliament having to be called upon to use its formal powers.

This convention applies to ministers as well as back-benchers. There have been occasions when a minister has failed to attend before a committee, but these should be seen as exceptional. Harold Wilson refused to allow one of his ministers, Harold Lever, to give evidence to the committee inquiring into the Chrysler affair, on the basis that he was not the departmental minister responsible and that the doctrine of collective responsibility meant that a committee could not examine the part played by ministers in a collective decision. There were, however, particular circumstances

---

[14] See Ch. 8.2.   [15] CJ (1688–93) 51.

[16] e.g., first, when four members of the South Sea Company refused to attend the Committee of Secrecy, and 'The House ordered that Sir Robert Chaplin, Sir Theodore Janssen, Francis Eyles, Esquire, and Jacob Sawbridge, Esquire, who were directors of the South Sea Company and Members of the House should attend the Committee of Secrecy' (CJ (1718–21) 403); secondly, when Alexander Baille Cochrane refused to attend before the Select Committee on Election Procedure, although during the debate he agreed to attend and the motion was withdrawn (CJ (1842) 458).

surrounding the Prime Minister's refusal. The committee had not, in fact, decided to issue an invitation to Mr Lever, but the possibility that it might do so had been leaked, thereby enabling Wilson to indicate the government's attitude. A united committee might have insisted upon the right to call any person it chose, but the committee members were divided over both Wilson's action and the need to call Lever.[17] It would, therefore, be unwise to see this as a precedent relevant to the government's, or the prime minister's, capacity to prevent ministers from appearing before committees.

The other recorded instance of a minister refusing a request to appear before a committee was in 1979, shortly after the reform of the select committee system. The Attorney-General declined to appear before the subcommittee of the Home Affairs Committee. The Committee reported: 'Whilst we do not wish to press the matter in this instance, we feel that the refusal by Ministers to give evidence could raise an important issue which might need to be resolved early in the lifetime of the new Select Committee system.'[18]

The law officers are to an extent in a different position from other ministers because of their independent status. Hence no departmental select committee was established in 1979 to scrutinize their department or that of the Lord Chancellor for fear of undermining this independence.[19] However, this does not, or should not, diminish the accountability of the law officers to Parliament nor provide them with immunity from appearing before committees. The refusal of the Attorney-General to attend before a committee is, therefore, the same as the refusal of any other minister, and, similarly, could be pursued in the House.

In neither instance was an order requested by the select committee from the House. Indeed, there is no recorded instance of an order for the appearance of a minister being made,[20] although for a while in 1989 it looked as if one might be necessary to secure

[17] D. Ellis, 'Collective Ministerial Responsibility and Collective Solidarity', *Public Law* (1980), 367.

[18] *First Report of the Select Committee for Home Affairs* (1979–80), HC434, HMSO, para. 6.

[19] HC Deb., vol. 969, 25 Jan. 1979, cols. 38–9. However, the Lord Chancellor has given evidence to the Home Affairs Committee: for example, during its inquiry into the prison service in 1981, and into legal aid in 1993.

[20] HC588–I (1977–8), Memorandum from the Clerk of the House, para. 15.

the attendance of Edwina Currie, the ex-Secretary of State for Health, before the Select Committee on Agriculture. Mrs Currie was technically a back-bencher, having resigned as Minister for Health the previous week.[21] However, her attendance was required because of her responsibilities when she was a member of the government. She initially declined the invitation, and only agreed with great reluctance to attend after the Committee wrote to her stating that, if she continued to refuse, it would 'have no option but to take formal steps in the House to seek... [her] attendance'.[22]

Edwina Currie's compliance, even though reluctant and not immediate, supports the conventional position that Parliament is not called upon to make an order for attendance. Thus, whilst select committees can only issue invitations, these invitations would seem to be sufficient to secure attendance.

Parliamentary Privilege and Answering Questions

Attendance before a committee is of little effect unless accompanied by an obligation to answer questions. However, whilst the rules relating to attendance by a Member, whether or not a minister, would seem to be clear, those concerning the answering of questions are uncertain. Erskine May states: 'When a Member submits himself to examination without an order of the House he is treated precisely like any other witness...'[23]

This suggests that there is no difference between a Member and a private individual. Precedents indicate that private individuals are obliged to answer all questions put by a committee, and that there are no exceptions to this obligation. Witnesses cannot plead that they are in fear of their lives,[24] nor that their answers might be self-incriminating.[25] If May's statement is correct, then Members

---

[21] See Ch. 4.2.

[22] HC108–I (1988–9), Letter from the Chairman of the Committee to Edwina Currie, p. 185.   [23] May, *Treatise* (20th edn.), 741.

[24] Elizabeth Robinson refused to answer questions put to her by the Liverpool Bribery Committee because she said she was in fear of her life. She was called to the bar and, when she still refused to answer, was committed to custody (CJ (1833) 218).

[25] William Prentice was reported by the Select Committee looking into Petitions alleging Bribery at Elections at Great Yarmouth and York because he refused to answer a question on the grounds that it might incriminate him. He was informed by the Speaker that he must answer. When he again refused, he was ordered to be held (CJ (1835) 501). However, in 1992 the Maxwell brothers appeared before the Select Committee for Social Services which was inquiring into the Maxwell pension

of Parliament are similarly obliged. However, May's contention can be questioned on two grounds. First, a Member cannot be 'treated precisely like any other witness' because, whilst a select committee may order a private individual to answer its questions, it has no authority likewise to order a Member. This authority, along with that for the attendance of a Member, resides with the full House.

Secondly, precedents relating to Members would suggest that they are in a different position from that of private individuals. In two nineteenth-century cases[26] Members were reported to the House for refusing to answer questions put by a select committee. In neither case did the House order the Member to answer, or even indicate that, in its view, Members were obliged to answer all questions put by a committee. However, the House stated that it was for the committee to decide which questions to ask and the Member 'should explain his objections to them'.[27] This offers support for a further statement made by May that a Member is 'not at liberty to qualify his submission by stipulating that he is to answer only such questions as he pleases'.[28]

This would seem to distinguish between a reasoned and reasonable objection by a Member to a specific question and obstruction. It is assumed that such a distinction also applies to ministers. Here, too, there is some debate concerning their obligations before committees. The Procedure Committee, reporting in 1978, stated 'it is doubtful whether if he [a Minister] does attend voluntarily, he is obliged to answer questions.'[29]

This is a broad statement which presumably should not be taken to mean that a minister is within his rights to stay silent before a committee in order to conceal wrongdoing or to mislead, for such a right would conflict with the constitutional requirement that ministers account to Parliament. However, ministers are protected by parliamentary privilege in the same way as backbenchers. In addition, the government claims there are conventional considerations, operating through individual ministerial

---

fund. They pleaded a 'right to silence'. Despite strong reservations from the Committee, no formal action was taken against them.

[26] Fleming's case, 1842; Barwell's case, 1882 (HC588–I (1977–8), Memorandum from the Clerk to the House, para. 9). [27] Ibid.
[28] May, *Treatise* (19th edn., 1946), 687. (Subsequent editions do not contain this statement.) [29] HC588–I (1977–8), para. 58.

responsibility, which impose limitations upon the information ministers can give to committees (see below). This suggests a paradoxical situation in which the conventional mechanism through which ministers account to Parliament also acts to restrict that accountability as exercised before committees.

There have been examples since the reform of the select committee system of ministers, or ex-ministers, refusing to answer questions and by so doing obstructing the work of a committee. Leon Brittan refused to answer many of the questions put to him by the Defence Committee, which was inquiring into the Westland affair, and Edwina Currie, having reluctantly agreed to appear before the Agriculture Committee, failed to provide the necessary answers.[30]

In cases of apparent obstruction select committees have voiced their displeasure, most publicly in 1986 when the Trade and Industry Committee demanded time for a debate on the refusal of the Secretary of State to answer questions on the tin crisis: 'We formally call upon the Leader of the House to provide time for the House to express its view on the refusal of the Secretary of State for Trade and Industry to provide full answers to our questions on the role of the Government in the tin crisis.'[31]

Neither the Defence Committee nor the Agriculture Committee sought formally to bring to the attention of the House the inadequacies of Brittan's or Currie's answers. They may have considered that, as the ministerial careers of Brittan and Currie had already ended, there was little to gain. However, both committees expressed their dissatisfaction. The Defence Committee made clear in its report that it found Brittan's behaviour reprehensible and his account of what had happened insufficient. It further stated: 'Accountability involves ACCOUNTING in detail for actions as a Minister.'[32]

The Agriculture Committee, too, indicated its displeasure, and gave a statement of what it expected of Members of Parliament, particularly former ministers:

We believe Members of Parliament have a clear duty to assist select committee inquiries; indeed the House will rapidly fall into disrepute if it

---

[30] See Chs. 6.2, 4.2.
[31] *Second Report from the Trade and Industry Committee: The Tin Crisis* (1985–6), HC305–I, HMSO.   [32] HC519 (1985–6), para. 235.

expected everyone else to be accountable in this way, but not its own Members. This is particularly true of those who may be asked to account for their actions as former Ministers.[33]

The Committee subsequently suggested that 'the problems posed by the inability formally to summon ex-Ministers to give evidence had not been fully considered when the departmentally-related system was established.'[34]

This point was pursued by the Procedure Committee in its 1990 Report on the Working of the Select Committee system. It stated:

We see no acceptable reason for a Member to refuse a request from a Select Committee to assist in an inquiry, still less to decline to answer questions put to him or her. If a Committee wishes to investigate an issue where the actions of a Minister led to his resignation, that Committee is perfectly entitled to seek evidence from the relevant *former* Minister about the way in which he exercised his responsibility whilst in office.[35]

The Procedure Committee did not, however, recommend that formal powers should be given to committees to enable them to summon ex-ministers or suggest a mechanism by which a select committee could bring an ex-minister's failure to answer questions to the attention of the House.

Departmental Papers and the Need for an Address to the Crown

Just as select committees have no formal powers to secure ministerial attendance or answers to their questions, so their power with regard to obtaining documents is limited. They have the authority to order papers from departments headed by a minister. However, most departments are headed by a Secretary of State, and it is the accepted procedure that Parliament can obtain documents from these departments or the Privy Council only through an Address to the Crown.[36]

---

[33] HC108–I (1988–9), para. 102.

[34] *Second Report from the Select Committee on Procedure: The Workings of the Select Committee System* (1989–90), HC19, HMSO, para. 130.

[35] Ibid., para. 163.

[36] The restriction creates an anomaly, for the Chancellor of the Exchequer is not a Secretary of State but a 'Deputy Lord High Treasurer in medieval language . . .' and therefore in theory can be ordered by select committees to produce documents (Michael English MP, HC Deb., 20 Feb. 1979, col. 1673).

This arises historically because of the protection claimed by the sovereign for the Secretary of State and for the use of the royal prerogative. This procedure has resulted in a limitation upon select committees, which was first noted by Erskine May in 1857,[37] such that select committees can take no formal steps themselves to order a Secretary of State to produce papers. The position is similar to that of the refusal of an invitation to appear by a Member of Parliament, whether or not a minister. A committee has to find an opportunity to bring the matter to the attention of the House, and, in the case of documents, it is then necessary to move for an Address to the Crown. This obviously imposes severe limitations upon select committees, given the amount of documentation required by them in the course of their business. Moreover, whilst the refusal by a minister to appear before a committee is likely to result in media attention and hence political pressure to reconsider his position, the denial of documentation to a committee may receive little public attention.

During the period 1964–78 there were five recorded cases where a minister refused the request by a committee for a specific document.[38] The papers concerned were mainly departmental reports or reviews and minutes of meetings. They were refused on the grounds of confidentiality, and the committees took no formal steps to secure access to them. Since the select committee system was reformed, there have been a number of further occasions when committees have been refused access to papers by departments, sometimes for questionable reasons. The Ministry of Defence refused to provide the Defence Committee with copies of documents on defence spending which had already been leaked to the Press. The committee secured copies from the Press Association instead.[39] A similar incident involved the DTI, which denied the Trade and Industry Committee access to documents originating from the International Tin Council (ITC), even though these documents were obtainable from another source.[40]

The Department of Education and Science refused to provide

---

[37] May, *Treatise* (4th edn., 1857).

[38] HC588–I (1977–8), Memorandum from the Clerk to the House, p. 30.

[39] *Third Report from the Defence Committee: The D Notice System* (1979–80), HC773, HMSO, 640–i–v, and R. L. Borthwick, in G. Drewry (ed.), *The New Select Committees* (Oxford: Clarendon Press, 1985).

[40] HC305–I (1985–6), para. 7.

the select committee with a copy of an interim report, on the basis that it was not finalized.[41] The chairman of the committee considered that such an argument was irrelevant. The interim report was still a paper and the committee was entitled to it. The Department was criticized for being obstructive.[42] Concern was also voiced at the government's refusal to let committee members see documents from the Central Policy Review Staff (CPRS) unless, or until, they were published. In this context the Transport Committee was refused permission to see a relevant report by the CPRS during its inquiry into main-line railway electrification. The Liaison Committee in its Report of 1982–3 reacted strongly to this refusal, recommending that 'the CPRS should as a matter of course inform the appropriate select committees of the conclusion they reach in each of their investigations, and should be allowed to make available to committees the evidence which they have gathered'.[43]

In none of the above cases could select committees take any authoritative action of their own to secure the documentation they required. They were prevented from so doing by historical restrictions that have little relevance today.

The Effect on Select Committees of a Lack of Formal Authority

The lack of the formal authority to order a minister to appear and answer questions or to order the disclosure of papers from a department of state affects select committees in several ways. First, it reduces the status and political standing of such committees, suggesting a lack of trust by the House in its own committees and a reliance on ministerial goodwill. Secondly, it reduces the effectiveness of the committees. If a minister or ex-minister fails to cooperate with a committee's requests, it is open to the committee to seek a motion in the House for an order to attend or an Address to obtain documents. However, such a motion is not a matter of privilege and so does not take priority over other parliamentary business; moreover, there are not the opportunities that existed in the nineteenth century for back-benchers to raise a motion for an

---

[41] *First Special Report from the Select Committee for Education, Science and Arts* (1979–80), HC606, HMSO, para. 1.
[42] Chairman of Education, Science, and Arts Committee, HC Deb., 16–22 Jan. 1981, col. 1653.
[43] *Report from the Liaison Committee* (1982–3), HC92, HMSO, para. 50.

Address. In modern times, when the House of Commons is dominated by the executive and the parliamentary timetable is fully
subscribed, the chairman of a committee is unlikely to be given
debating time on a motion which the government opposes. The
lack of formal authority therefore works in favour of the executive, which the select committees are meant to scrutinize.

A further effect of this lack of formal authority has been the
need for committees to develop alternative tactics in order to secure
information. Committees have resorted to the Press Association
for documentation on defence spending and have even gone to the
United States of America to obtain information originating from
the ITC which was refused by the DTI.

More controversially, in 1978 the Select Committee on Nationalized Industries sought information from a private individual after
the Secretary of State for Industry refused a request for papers
concerning the future prospects of British Steel.[44] The chairman first
sought a debate on a motion of Address to require the Secretary
of State to release the papers, but he failed to secure parliamentary time. As a last resort the committee ordered the Chairman of
the British Steel Corporation, Sir Charles Villiers, to produce the
documents. Sir Charles was a private individual and thus the
Committee could exercise unlimited power 'to order the production of papers . . . relevant to its work . . .'.[45] This power has been
seldom used in modern times, and the order placed Sir Charles in
a difficult position. It was clear from the evidence he gave to the
committee that he was under instructions about answering questions from the Secretary of State, to whom he was responsible for
the running of British Steel. Compliance with the order would
contravene these instructions. However, failure to comply would
mean Sir Charles was in contempt of Parliament. He chose to
release the necessary document. Select committees have tried similar tactics more recently when departments have refused to release
information, but have been thwarted by the government's claim
that the material is 'confidential' (see below).

The lack of any formal authority to use against government
departments means that select committees are largely dependent
upon the government to co-operate. This dependence relationship

---

[44] *Fifth Report from the Select Committee on Nationalized Industries* (1977–8),
HC238, HMSO.   [45] HC588–I (1977–8), para. 7.6.

is illustrated by the statement made shortly after the reform of the select committee system by Francis Pym, then Leader of the House. He argued on behalf of the government that select committees were not hindered by their inability to order papers from departments of state:

I can . . . give the House a categorical assurance that whatever the formal position may be we certainly have not made, and shall not in future make, any distinction in considering whether particular papers should be made available to Select Committees on the question whether or not the Minister concerned is a Secretary of State.[46]

However, even whilst assuring the House of the government's co-operation, Mr Pym indicated its dominant position. The government decides which papers are released to select committees and to that extent it is irrelevant whether committees have the formal power to make an order or not. It is obviously in the interests of the government to maintain the limitation upon the formal powers of committees. Any extension might result in select committees taking formal action when initial requests are refused.

The inability of select committees to order papers from the Secretary of State or to demand attendance clearly weakens the power of the committees. This was recognized by the Procedure Committee, reporting in 1978, which recommended in relation to attendance that 'Select Committees should be empowered by the House to order the attendance of Ministers to give evidence to them'.[47] Regarding papers, the Committee considered 'Select committees should be empowered to order the production of papers and records by all Ministers, including Secretaries of State.'[48] The Committee recognized that the power to order needed to be enforceable, and that, if the object were to secure information, punishment in the form of contempt proceedings would be inappropriate. The Committee, advised by the Clerk of the House, suggested that the solution was 'to restore to select committees, in certain specified circumstances, the right, which formally belonged to any backbencher, to move for an Address or an Order for a return of papers'.[49]

Such a move would provide committees with formal access to

[46] Francis Pym, Leader of House, HC Deb., 16–22 Jan 1981, col. 1702.
[47] HC588–I (1977–8), para. 7.21.   [48] Ibid., para. 7.22.
[49] Ibid., para. 7.24.

the House when required, instead of only for contempt. However, when the Procedure Committee reported in 1990, it did not support the recommendations of its predecessor, concluding that it did not 'consider that new or additional procedures are necessary or would be workable'.[50]

The Committee considered that there was little demand for increased powers from select committees, and in any case, because of the government majority in the House, the powers would be meaningless. This would seem an inadequate reason. It is correct that the ability to order attendance would still rely on the House for enforcement, and that a move for an Address or an Order would not guarantee that a committee would succeed in obtaining the papers it required. The government might convince the House that there were reasons why a document should be withheld. In any case, it is likely that it would be supported by its own side. Nevertheless, the status of select committees would be enhanced and parliamentary access would be available. As it is, committees have to rely upon government assurances that, if the matter is sufficiently serious, a debate on the Floor of the House will be granted—a clear limitation on the effectiveness of the committees.

10.4. INDIVIDUAL MINISTERIAL RESPONSIBILITY: A CONSTITUTIONAL RESTRAINT OR A GOVERNMENT IMPOSITION?

The second restraint upon select committees arises from the application of the convention of individual ministerial responsibility as it relates to civil servants. The relationship between civil servants and select committees is an uneasy one and it is here that the conflict between the government and the committees is most evident. Civil servants frequently appear before select committees and give evidence. They are instructed by the government 'that it is the duty of officials to be as helpful as possible to Committees'.[51] However, there are limitations to this helpfulness, mainly based on the convention of individual ministerial responsibility.

[50] HC19 (1989–90), para. 162.
[51] *Memorandum of Guidance for Officials Appearing before Select Committees* (1980), Gen 80/38, Civil Service Department (often referred to as the Osmotherly Rules after its author).

Confidentiality

In 1976 the first *Memorandum of Guidance for Officials Appearing before Select Committees* was issued by the Civil Service Department.[52] This and subsequent documents impose limitations upon the evidence that officials can give to select committees. Particularly significant are limitations upon the disclosure of advice given by civil servants to ministers, inter-departmental exchanges concerning policy, and alternative policy options. Such limitations are held by the government to be necessary to uphold the conventions of individual ministerial responsibility and collective responsibility. However, their effect is to preserve the secrecy of decision-making and at times to hinder the workings of select committees.

Limitations upon the disclosure of government information are not new. Restrictions on what civil servants can publicly divulge have operated as part of the convention of ministerial responsibility, and Richard Crossman, as Leader of the House, wrote to select committee chairmen in 1967 outlining these limitations, which, he stated, were largely derived from existing practice.[53] The most significant of these limitations was the requirement, noted in the nineteenth century, that any order or address from Parliament must be for papers of 'a public and official nature' and not 'private and confidential' documents.[54] The interpretation of what is 'private and confidential' has been contentious.

The first Memorandum outlined those areas which the government considered to be confidential and thus beyond the scope of select committee inquiries. Most notable were advice given by civil servants and inter-departmental communications. However, there has been doubt since the issue of this Memorandum about the status of these broader limitations. It is clear that, as far as officials and ministers are concerned, they are conventional and obligatory. They govern the behaviour of civil servants before committees and have their origins in the relationship between officials and ministers.

---

[52] *Memorandum of Guidance for Officials Appearing before Select Committees* (1976), Gen 76/78, Civil Service Department.

[53] This practice was recognized by Erskine May from 1857, when he indicated the types of information that Parliament and therefore the Committees should not expect Ministers to reveal (May, *Treatise* (4th edn., 1857)).

[54] Ibid.

Not surprisingly, select committees have been less prepared to be bound by rules which reduce their powers and hence the power of Parliament. Indeed, the Chairman of the Select Committee on Education and Science, Christopher Price MP, contested the validity of the Memorandum on the basis that there had been no agreement between the government and Parliament.[55] His contention was reinforced by the 1990 Procedure Committee Report, which stated: 'It is important to note that the Memorandum of Guidance has no Parliamentary status whatever.'[56]

Prior to 1979 and the reform of the select committee system there seems to have been little invocation of the 'conventions' by those giving evidence before committees. Indeed, the Clerk of the House of Commons stated that examples were 'not frequent or typical' and cited only five cases between 1964 and 1977.[57] This covers a period before the issuing of the first Memorandum and before the committee reform. Since then the situation may have changed, as indicated by the Report of the Chairman of the Energy Committee, Ian Lloyd MP, to the Liaison Committee, in which he stated that the committee had had no problem: 'Apart from the usual difficulty from time to time over particular internal memoranda . . .'[58]

Limitations upon the grounds of confidentiality may therefore now be 'usual'. Moreover they affect oral and written evidence and apply to departmental and inter-departmental information. The government may express them in terms of conventional necessities, but select committees frequently see them as obstructive to their inquiries. The conflict between the government and the committees over this matter was evident in the First Special Report from the Education, Science, and Arts Committee, published in 1980. The committee complained that the minister, Mr Mark Carlisle, had refused to disclose information about the co-ordination of policy concerning overseas students between the Department of Education and Science (DES), the Overseas Development Agency, and the Foreign Office. But Mr Carlisle believed his position to be the correct one:

the Government takes the view that just as Select Committees are not able to know what advice officials give to individual ministers, but

[55] *The Times*, 24 July 1980.   [56] HC19 (1989–90), para. 153.
[57] HC588–I (1977–8), para. 7.11.   [58] HC92.

ministers must be responsible for what actions they take, equally, we would be wrong to give evidence as to inter-departmental advice.[59]

However, as far as the Education Committee was concerned, its inquiry into the funding and organization of courses in higher education had been hampered by the lack of information concerning 'the nature and extent of inter-departmental consultations'. Indeed, the committee reported: 'We do not feel we can fully discharge our responsibility to Parliament until we have access to more of the information that is available to the DES in formulating its decisions.'[60]

A similar complaint was made by the Foreign Affairs Committee, whose investigations were also concerned with overseas students: 'Great difficulty was presented by a rigid interpretation of the so-called convention by which Ministers and officials are prohibited from informing the House about the ways in which government decisions are made...'[61]

The 'rigid interpretation' to which the Committee referred concerned both advice to ministers and inter-departmental exchanges, and came from the Treasury as well as the DES. The Treasury wrote: 'It would not be appropriate for the Treasury to give evidence on the advice given by officials to Ministers or on the inter-departmental exchanges which led up to a decision by Ministers.'[62]

The letter from the Secretary of State for Education and Science contained the same sentiments:

I know that the members of your sub-committee will of course accept that since the decision was a collective one ... they cannot expect to receive information about the advice given to Ministers by officials or the processes through which a particular decision was reached, including the processes of inter-departmental consultation.[63]

Both committees believed that they had a right to information concerning policy-making, whether departmental or inter-departmental. They did not consider that they were bound by convention not to ask for the information, nor did they consider that ministers and officials were obliged not to reveal such information when it was vital to the inquiries being undertaken by the

---

[59] HC606, para. 4.　　[60] Ibid., para. 1.
[61] *Third Report from the Foreign Affairs Committee* (1979–80), HC553, para. 16.　　　　　　　　　　　　　　　　[62] Ibid., Appendix 31.
[63] Ibid., Appendix 32.

committees. They were not asking what advice was given, but what information was available. However, the government consistently equated 'information' with 'advice'.

The TCSC echoed the call for more information: 'It must be right for the Committee to be made aware of the basic information upon which the judgements of Ministers are made . . .'[64]

These incidents occurred within the first year of the new committee system, and the conflict between committees and government was heightened with the issuing of an updated *Memorandum of Guidance*, which has subsequently become known as the 'Osmotherly Rules'.[65] This re-enforced the restrictions upon select committees in a way which prompted Edward du Cann, speaking in the subsequent debate from the government back-benches, to state: 'It is a poor and miserable document. Its whole flavour is wrong. The attitude of whoever wrote it is wrong.'[66]

Christopher Price MP suggested that the requirement of select committees for background information could be met by the government without compromising the confidentiality of official advice, '[if] the Government—this means the Civil Service—[had] . . . a positive attitude to creating documents that can be given to Committees'.[67]

Such an attitude had been encouraged in the Croham Directive, which was sent by the Head of the Civil Service, Lord Croham, then Sir Douglas Allen, to heads of departments in 1977. In the Directive Sir Douglas stated: 'when policy studies are undertaken in future, the background material should as far as possible be written in a form which would permit it to be published separately.'[68]

The possibility of separating the substance of advice from the factual information on which it is based was subsequently acknowledged by Sir Geoffrey Howe, when Leader of the House. He considered that 'generally facts are disclosable' because 'the facts are common ground to the discussion that takes place in public'.[69]

However, judging by the experiences of select committees, this does not seem to have been a practice always adopted by civil

---

[64] *Second Report from the Treasury and Civil Service Committee* (1979–80), HC584, para. 5.   [65] Gen 80/38 (Osmotherly Rules).
[66] HC Deb., 16–22 Jan. 1981, col. 1666.
[67] Ibid., Christopher Price MP, col. 1658.
[68] *Croham Directive*, 6 July 1977.   [69] HC19 (1989–90), Q135.

servants. The Trade and Industry Committee was refused background information during its inquiry into the tin crisis. There were several factors which the committee found frustrated its investigation, but in its report it stated that the most serious obstruction was caused by officials, including Sir Brian Hayes, the Permanent Secretary, adhering strictly to the *Memorandum of Guidance* and refusing to answer a series of questions on the grounds that they concerned advice. 'The principal basis of the refusal to reply appears to have been the section of the Memorandum which states that "in order to preserve the collective responsibility of Ministers, the advice given to Ministers by their Departments should not be disclosed".'[70]

In evidence Sir Brian Hayes stated: 'I gave them [officials] specific instructions that they were to observe very carefully, in answer to questions put to them, the Memorandum of Guidance.'[71]

In addition, the committee was unable to secure the answers from the Secretary of State, Mr Paul Channon, who claimed he was obliged to abide by the 'constitutional conventions'. 'What I cannot do, for reasons the Committee I believe understands, is discuss the advice given by officials to Ministers or instructions given by Ministers to officials. I think this is well understood under normal conventions.'[72]

The existence of the convention was understood by the committee, but it pressed for information, wanting to know in 'general terms how much advance information about the impending crisis was received from officials'.[73]

Mr Channon, however, refused to be drawn either on this matter or on details of inter-departmental discussions, employing a blanket restriction on information which his civil servants were bound to follow. Moreover, it was not just the conventions concerning advice and inter-departmental communications that were strictly adhered to by civil servants, but those applying to *sub judice* rules and government relations with other countries, both of which are covered by the Memorandum. Again there was no attempt by the government to separate background information from information that could properly be considered confidential.

A similar restriction of information occurred during the inquiry

---

[70] HC305–I (1985–6), para. 10.   [71] Ibid., Minutes of Evidence, Q696.
[72] Ibid., para. 11 and Q839.   [73] Ibid., Q842.

into Westland. The Defence Committee requested the release by the DTI of a set of documents which became known as the 'October Documents'. The department refused the request, stating that it was not 'appropriate or in accordance with the normal conventions to make available inter-departmental correspondence of this kind . . .'.[74]

Instead, the Committee was provided with a Memorandum from the Permanent Secretary, Sir Brian Hayes (again playing a leading role), summarizing the documents.[75] After strong protests from the committee, a compromise was agreed whereby some members of the committee saw the original documents in confidence.

The appeal by the government, both through ministers and officials, to the 'normal conventions' and the expectation that select committees will accept the restrictions imposed by such conventions have been major features of the relationship between committees and government since 1979. At times the refusal by civil servants to answer questions is over-cautious, and the appearance of the minister before the committee resolves the matter. This was the case in the Defence Committee's inquiry into the future of the Gurkhas, in which officials refused to give information about the progress of a departmental study, seeing this as in the category of official advice to ministers. The committee chairman, Mr Michael Mates, insisted that he was seeking only factual information and expert assessment and suspended the sitting of the inquiry. Again the dispute concerned what was 'advice' and what was 'information'. The dispute was resolved in this particular case because the minister was prepared to provide the required information.[76]

The extent to which committees are prepared to accept the limitations of government-created conventions depends on the composition of the committee, its chairman, the political sensitivity of the issue involved, and its importance to the inquiry being undertaken by the committee. In the Agriculture Committee's inquiry into salmonella in eggs, Mrs Currie made clear even before her attendance that her answers to the committee would be

---

[74] HC169 (1985–6), Letter from the Permanent Secretary at the DTI to the Committee.

[75] Ibid., Memorandum from the Permanent Secretary at the DTI to the Committee.

[76] *First Report from the Defence Committee* (1988–9), HC68.

restricted. 'I cannot convey to you any conversations which I had with officials; these must remain confidential.'[77]

She was to confirm this approach when giving evidence. 'As I am sure you realise, as a former Minister, the content of any discussions that I might have had with officials, or any papers that I might have seen other than published information, is subject to the usual convention that is that I would not discuss it now.'[78]

The response of the Chairman, Mr Jerry Wiggins—'we quite understand that'—was surprising. For Mrs Currie was not just talking about advice being protected by the convention, but any information that had not been published. The Chairman was therefore accepting a considerable limitation which a number of committees had striven to resist. The situation was perhaps exceptional because of the controversy surrounding Mrs Currie, the fact that she was no longer a minister, and her reluctance to appear before the committee. Nevertheless, Mrs Currie's refusal to answer a number of questions on the grounds of confidentiality was condemned by many back-benchers, although it clearly won the approval of the Prime Minister.

In its 1990 Report the Select Committee on Procedure made recommendations concerning both inter-departmental communications and the release of factual information. It commented:

We doubt whether the fabric of constitutional government would suffer fatal injury if witnesses were more forthcoming about the level at which decisions are taken and the extent of involvement of different Departments.[79]

Similarly . . . it is difficult to see why . . . Committees cannot be told in purely factual terms, what options are under consideration and their cost implications. We regard as unsustainable the Government's argument that experienced and trained officials cannot distinguish between the subject on which Ministers sought advice on the one hand, and the substance of that advice on the other.[80]

However, the Committee was not prepared to enter into a contest with the government over the Osmotherly Rules. It took instead a 'pragmatic' approach, believing that 'discretion' rather than

---

[77] HC108–II (1988–9), Mrs Currie's letter to the Chairman of the Committee, p. 184.   [78] Ibid., Q593.
[79] HC19 (1989–90), para. 157.   [80] Ibid., para. 160.

confrontation was 'the sensible approach'.[81] Whilst recognizing that there was a risk of 'accusations of defeatism', the Committee's concern was 'that a wholesale review at Parliament's behest could simply result in a new set of guidelines which, whilst superficially less restrictive, would be applied rigorously and to the letter'.[82]

The Committee's fears may have been well founded, although it is arguable that less restrictive rules, strictly applied, are preferable to the Osmotherly Rules, even when they are not followed to the letter. However, the Procedure Committee's claim that it had received no evidence that the Rules 'had placed an unacceptable constraint on Select Committees'[83] is surprising. The restrictions on select committees may have been small in numerical terms, but the situations in which information has been withheld and the consequences this has had for some inquiries would seem to be grounds for concern.

The Widening of the Application of Confidentiality

It is not only what constitutes 'advice' that is at times disputed, but also who are the 'advisers'. The Memorandum concerns the actions of officials, but the government has broadened the field to include advisers from outside the service. This was evident when the Welsh Office instructed the spokesman for a firm of accountants, which had advised the Welsh Office on the finances of the Welsh Water Authority, not to reveal information to the Welsh Affairs Committee on the basis that the information had been supplied to the government in confidence. The Committee saw this as an 'infringement of its constitutional rights' to take evidence from witnesses, but the Welsh Office claimed that the same or similar considerations applied whether advice to ministers was from civil servants or outside consultants.[84] The outcome was a compromise whereby some of the information was revealed, but the Committee was clearly unwilling to concede that there were occasions when private individuals did not have to answer questions put by a committee, for to do so would be to allow a fundamental right of Parliament to drift away.[85]

'Confidentiality' was also the basis for the blocking by the

---

[81] Ibid., para. 157.　　[82] Ibid.　　[83] Ibid.
[84] *Report of the Select Committee on Welsh Affairs: Water in Wales* (1981–2), HC299, p. 336.　　[85] Ibid., p. 340.

government of select committee attempts to obtain papers from the Bank of England. The Trade and Industry Committee had unsuccessfully requested papers originating from the ITC from the DTI (see above). It subsequently made an order to the Bank of England for a list of documents in its possession relating to the Council. However, the government stated that the Bank was acting as its adviser and thus claimed the right to 'control which papers and details of papers the Bank of England was able to retain against the Committee's Order in so far as they were papers passed to the Bank of England in its unique capacity as adviser to the Government'.[86]

In both these cases there was a professional relationship which, it could be argued, relied upon the confidentiality of advice. However, there was not the same consultant–client relationship between the University Grants Council (UGC) and the government, yet Sir Keith Joseph considered that advice from the Council was also confidential and should remain private.[87] He equated the position of the chairman of the UGC with that of a senior civil servant: 'the position of the chairman of the UGC is as a second permanent secretary in the department and therefore he is an adviser to the Government.'[88]

This statement is not entirely convincing. The chairman is neither a civil servant nor a professional adviser who owes a duty of confidentiality to his client. Such interpretations by the government, which seek to extend adviser status beyond the civil service, are not readily accepted by select committees and may be contested. The Liaison Committee sounded a warning note:

at a later date we may wish to consider the question of whether . . . the same or similar considerations apply to committees securing details of advice given to Ministers by outside consultants as now apply to advice given by civil servants. Important constitutional questions are involved relating to the ring fence which the executive seeks to erect around itself to exclude parliamentary scrutiny.[89]

The Committee also disputed the government's insistence that the Central Policy Review Staff (CPRS) was covered by the restrictions

---

[86] *First Report from the Trade and Industry Committee (a supplementary report)* (1986–7), HC71, HMSO, para. 13.
[87] *Education, Science and Arts Select Committee: Minutes of Evidence* (1981–2), HC24, para. 2. [88] Ibid., para. 3.
[89] HC92 (1982–3), para. 49.

of confidentiality in the same way as departmental officials. It considered this claim to be wrong because the advice from the CPRS was 'of a different kind from the internal advice which, under the Memorandum of Guidance, is denied to Committees'.[90]

Both statements by the Liaison Committee recognize that advice given by civil servants is protected and may not be revealed to select committees. Individual select committees may have fought against the restrictions imposed by the Memorandum of Guidance, particularly if it has been rigorously applied, yet overall the select committees have succumbed.

However, this suggests an inherent political weakness rather than an acceptance of government practices. In fact, when select committees have been prepared to mobilize against the government, they have met with some success. After the Westland affair the Government indicated an intention to restrict further the information that would be made available to select committees, but when the chairmen of the select committees made clear their displeasure, the government moderated its approach, or at least adopted a more conciliatory attitude.

Much depends on the readiness of committee chairmen to act against party interests, when their party is in government, and the ability of the chairmen to mobilize the House behind them. Confrontation is contrary to the ethos of the committee system, which has always worked informally and through co-operation with the government rather than by instigating formal proceedings to acquire government information. However, the failure to use the existing procedures and powers may result in their reduction, a danger that was recognized by the Procedure Committee reporting in 1977: 'powers which have fallen into complete or partial disuse may come to be regarded as obsolete; and informal practices and conventions may come to be regarded as binding limitations.'[91]

The Power to Call Named Civil Servants

One of the principal areas of debate since the reform of the select committee system has been whether or not named civil servants can be summoned to attend before select committees. The

---

[90] Ibid., para. 50.   [91] HC588–I (1977–8), para. 7.9.

divergence of positions was apparent long before 1979,[92] but it has become more acute and of greater constitutional significance since that time. Two main arguments would seem to support the contrary positions. The first centres upon the convention of individual ministerial responsibility and the constitutional position of civil servants. It is argued that, because civil servants have no constitutional personality of their own, but act only as an extension of their minister, they appear before a select committee only if their minister requires them to do so on his behalf. It therefore follows that it is for the minister to decide who attends before a select committee, and not for select committees to summon named individuals.

The second argument focuses on the powers of select committees which are delegated by Parliament to enable the committees to scrutinize government departments. These powers, including the power to call for persons, are unqualified, and it is therefore for select committees to decide whom they require to appear before them. Parliamentary privilege protects Members of Parliament, and therefore ministers, from being ordered to attend by the committees, but this privilege does not extend to civil servants, and therefore they can be summoned individually to appear.

The inherent conflict between the two positions has not been recognized generally because select committees, which seldom exercise their formal powers, have refrained from issuing an order for a named civil servant to attend. Committees have preferred to issue informal invitations on a general basis to government departments and to rely on departmental co-operation in the selection of witnesses. Indeed, the committees themselves recognize there to be 'a long standing practice that committees requiring evidence from a Government department usually leave it to the department to nominate witnesses'.[93]

However, despite the respect which is normally shown for departmental choice, select committees still believe that they can, if they wish, summon a named official, a view supported by the Clerk of the House in 1977: 'There is no doubt . . . that a committee possessing PPR [power to send for persons, papers, and records] could summon a named official if it so wished.'[94]

---

[92] See the Sachsenhausen affair and the *Reports from the Select Committee on the Parliamentary Commissioner for Administration* (1967–8), HC258, and (1967–8), HC350.   [93] HC588–I (1977–8), para. 7.
[94] Ibid., Memorandum from the Clerk of the House, para. 15.

The government has been reluctant to accept this position without any qualifications. Prior to the reform of the committee system, the *Memorandum of Guidance for Officials Appearing before Select Committees* stated:

> If . . . a Select Committee summoned by name any other official to appear before them, and insisted on their right to do so, it would be for Ministers to decide what course to follow. The formal constitutional position is that although a committee's powers under their terms of reference to summon persons and papers is normally unqualified, such a summons is effectively binding only if backed by an Order of the House.[95]

There seems to be some confusion within this statement. A committee can only summon those individuals whom it can order directly to attend, that is those not protected by parliamentary privilege, diplomatic immunity, or the royal prerogative. It is not a question of the summons being made 'effective' by an Order from Parliament. If it is a legitimate summons, then it stands in its own right, and failure to obey it is a contempt of the House. It may be that the Rules of Guidance recognized both the theoretical powers of select committees to summon named officials, and the practical power of the government to refuse such a summons. In that case the only effective way for a select committee to ensure the appearance of a named official would be through the House. However, this is not, as the guidance states, the 'formal constitutional position'.

Subsequently, the Osmotherly Rules stated:

> Officials appearing before select committees do so on behalf of their Ministers. It is customary, therefore, for Ministers to decide which officials . . . should appear to give evidence. Select committees have in the past generally accepted this position. Should a Committee invite a named official to appear, the Minister concerned, if he did not wish that official to represent him, might suggest that another official could more appropriately do so, or that he himself should give evidence to the Committee. If a Committee insisted on a particular official appearing before them they could issue a formal order for his attendance. In such an event the official would have to appear before the Committee.[96]

This would seem to be a definite recognition of the right of select committees to order a named official to attend, although

---

[95] Gen 76/78.   [96] Gen 80/38 (Osmotherly Rules).

there is the implication that the government will concede this right only reluctantly and if it is formally exercised. The government's reluctance, and indeed its lack of co-operation, was demonstrated when, during the Westland inquiry, the Defence Committee requested five named officials to appear before it.

The committee was dissatisfied with the evidence given by Leon Brittan and by the internal inquiry conducted by Sir Robert Armstrong. There were still many questions unanswered. However, the attendance of the officials was blocked by the DTI and the Cabinet Office.

The Defence Committee was clear about its powers to order the attendance of the officials, if necessary. It cited Standing Orders 93 and 93 (a) of 1983 as giving a select committee the right to send for 'persons, papers and records, as confirmation that 'its power to secure the attendance of individual named civil servants [was] unqualified'.[97]

However, the Committee did not in the end test its powers. It seems that political pressure was brought to bear and a compromise was arranged, whereby the government Chief Whip, John Wakeham, negotiated with the Chairman of the Committee, at that time Sir Humphrey Atkins, for the Head of the Civil Service, Sir Robert Armstrong, to give evidence instead.[98] There were pragmatic considerations too. If the Committee did summon the officials to appear, they would undoubtedly be under instructions from their ministers not to give any further information to the Committee.[99] The convention of individual ministerial responsibility would ensure their silence over the important issues. Thus a select committee would have clashed with the government over a matter of principle but achieved nothing to forward its inquiries.

It did look after Sir Robert's first session of evidence that the Committee might insist that Bernard Ingham, the Prime Minister's Press Secretary, should appear before it. However, in the end the Committee took no action. Political and pragmatic considerations outweighed any advantage in securing Ingham's appearance.[100] The Committee settled for a second session with Sir Robert Armstrong,

[97] HC519 (1985–6), para. 228.
[98] P. Jenkins, *Mrs Thatcher's Revolution: The Ending of the Socialist Era* (London: Jonathan Cape, 1987), 202.   [99] Ibid.
[100] M. Linklater and D. Leigh, *Not with Honour* (London Sphere Books, 1986), 202.

although in its Report the Defence Committee stated that the request for the named officials still stood.[101]

The failure of the Defence Committee to use its power to summon the named officials did little to resolve the conflict over whether such officials could in practice be made to attend. It seemed to suggest that, even if the committees had a theoretical power to summon, the force of government opposition would mean that practical or political considerations would be likely to prevail and prevent its operation.

More recently, however, there have been signs that the government may be softening a little in its attitude. When Sir Robin Butler, Robert Armstrong's successor, gave evidence before the TCSC on the revised Civil Service Pay and Conditions of Service Code, he was asked whether he accepted that an official had a duty to appear before a select committee when summoned. He responded: 'Yes, there is a duty and it appears in the Osmotherly Rules and it is one that is accepted by Ministers.'[102]

Seeking clarification, Sir Robin was further asked whether this applied to a specific civil servant, to which he acknowledged this to be the case. In his responses Sir Robin seemed to support the contention of both select committees and the First Division Association, a representative of which, appearing before the same committee, stated: '[a civil servant] is obliged to turn up when summoned by a Select Committee; he may refer certain answers to his Minister but he is obliged to be present.'[103]

The importance of Sir Robin's answers lies in his assertion that the right is recognized by ministers, something that was much in doubt after Westland. The TCSC clearly sees it as an advance: 'We . . . welcome the clear statement of the Head of the Home Civil Service that ministers recognise the right of committees to summon those individual civil servants whom they wish to examine.'[104]

However, Sir Robin's statement needs to be treated with caution. The fact that ministers 'recognise the right of committees' does not necessarily mean that they will always be prepared to

---

[101] HC588–I (1977–8), para. 230.
[102] *Fifth Report from the Treasury and Civil Service Committee: The Civil Service Pay and Conditions of Service Code* (1989–90), HC260, HMSO, Q75.
[103] Ibid., C. Dunabin, FDA Executive Committee, Q17.
[104] Ibid., para. 22.

exercise their corresponding duty and ensure the attendance of summoned officials. Moreover, it is by no means certain that all ministers would agree with Sir Robin's assertion. Sir Geoffrey Howe, when giving evidence to the Procedure Committee as Leader of the House, 'attached particular importance to the convention that Ministers exercise discretion in choosing which officials should give evidence on their behalf'.[105]

Another Westland affair is required to see if there is any practical difference in the relationship between the government and the select committees. It seems likely that, regardless of constitutional theory, ministers will still try at times to block a committee's attempt to secure the attendance of particular officials, and committees will still be reluctant to push to the limit and issue the necessary summons.

'Conduct' and 'Actions'

One of the questions raised during the Westland affair was whether it was acceptable for a select committee to inquire into the conduct of civil servants. As far as the Defence Committee was concerned, the conduct of certain officials had been 'called into question' by the failure of Leon Brittan to answer questions in front of the Committee.[106]

Both the TCSC and the Liaison Committee sought to distinguish between the 'conduct' and 'actions' of officials. From a committee viewpoint 'actions' could be defined as: 'those activities which are carried out on the instructions of, or are consistent with, the policies of the Minister concerned'.[107] 'Conduct', on the other hand, fell outside this definition and may amount to 'misconduct'.[108]

There are, therefore, two distinct types of 'actions'. The first concerns those induced by either a specific or a general instruction from the minister. The second relates to actions which are consistent or compatible with ministerial policy. This suggests that, as long as officials are acting in accordance with policy objectives, they are always acting with the authority of the minister. However, this would seem too broad a definition of 'actions', for it takes no

---

[105] HC19 (1989–90), para. 123.   [106] HC519 (1985–6), para. 235.
[107] HC62 (1986–7), para. 15.   [108] Gen 76/78.

account of any misuse of discretion by officials in implementing policy. In such situations it is therefore necessary to consider whether the minister gave, or would have given, his approval of the behaviour in order to determine whether the 'action' or the 'conduct' (more easily understood as 'misconduct') of an official is at issue.

In the Defence Committee's inquiry into Westland the Committee sought to discover whether the Solicitor-General's letter was leaked by DTI officials on the instructions of their minister, Leon Brittan, or whether officials at the DTI, in concert with those at Number Ten, had taken the initiative in leaking the letter, or at least made their own decisions about the mechanisms for making it public.

Leon Brittan maintained that his officials had acted on his behalf and he accepted full responsibility for what had occurred, thereby in part fulfilling his obligations under the convention of individual ministerial responsibility. However, his failure to explain what had happened, and his refusal to answer certain questions, cast suspicion over the involvement of his officials. If they had gone beyond the actions that Leon Brittan sanctioned, or would have sanctioned if asked, then their 'conduct' was at issue. Also at issue was the behaviour of officials at Number Ten. If Powell and Ingham had acted on their own accord, it was their 'conduct' that was in question. However, if they had behaved in a way that was consistent with the policy of the Prime Minister, and she approved, or would have approved had she been asked, then their activities would be categorized as 'actions' and therefore a matter for which she owed full explanatory responsibility.

However, the Committee was unable to determine whether the five named officials had acted with ministerial approval or whether they had gone beyond the authority given to them. The government refused to allow them to give evidence on the grounds that 'A Select Committee inquiry into actions and conduct of an individual civil servant, conducted in public and protected by privilege, would give the civil servant concerned no safeguards and no rights, though his reputation and even his career might be at risk.'[109]

Such an assertion disregarded the fact that the civil servants had already been named in the House. An appearance before the select committee would not, therefore, have threatened their anonymity,

---

[109] Cmnd. 9916 (1986), para. 44.

and their reputations may already have been damaged. Moreover, Leon Brittan's reticence meant that, without evidence from the officials concerned, the Defence Committee's attempt to find out what had happened was bound to fail. The government accused the Defence Committee of attempting to act as a disciplinary tribunal, a charge that was rebutted by the Defence and Liaison Committees, both of which agreed that this was not the role of select committees. However, the Liaison Committee commented: 'But this does not mean that a Select Committee should be prevented from seeking to establish the facts if there is reason to believe that an identified civil servant has done something which is not compatible with his Minister's instructions or policy.'[110]

Moreover, the Committee was concerned that the government sought to exclude select committees from inquiring into 'actions' as well as 'conduct'. This, it insisted, was not congruent with 'the clear responsibility of a Select Committee to examine the administration of departments which necessarily involves taking evidence from officials directly involved in administration'.[111]

The Report from the Defence Committee on the Westland affair, with its strong criticism of the restrictions placed upon it and the lack of co-operation it received from government, was greeted with an attempt by the government to restrict further the committees. In its Response to the Committee the government stated: 'The government proposes to make it clear to civil servants giving evidence to Select Committees that they should not answer questions which are or appear to be directed to the conduct of themselves or other named officials.'[112]

The Liaison Committee condemned such a proposal outright and noted that, if such a restriction had been in operation at the time of Westland, Sir Robert Armstrong might have felt more inhibited in his answers, for many of the questions might have appeared to be directed to the conduct of named officials. This would have limited the information made available to the inquiry even further.

Moreover, the TCSC was concerned that any restrictions imposed by the government would apply to 'actions' as well as 'conduct', which in its view would be 'entirely unacceptable'.[113] Its concern

---

[110] *First Report from the Liaison Committee* (1986–7), HC100, para. 14.
[111] Ibid., para. 6.   [112] Cmnd. 9916 (1986), para. 44.
[113] HC62 (1986–7), para. 16.

was understandable, for such restrictions could provide a further limitation to the information made available to select committees, and in addition could foster an ethos of over-cautiousness, even suspicion, on the part of civil servants appearing before the committees.

The Committee recognized that officials giving evidence before a committee were already restricted by the convention of ministerial responsibility and that therefore 'there is an implicit assumption that the relevant Minister has given his authority for the answers to be given . . .'[114]

It follows from this that there will be occasions when civil servants are unable to answer questions because the minister refuses such authority. Indeed, this has been clearly expressed by Sir Robin Butler:

> ministers are in a position to approve or disapprove the evidence which a civil servant would give on their behalf . . . [This] might extend to the minister instructing the civil servant that there was certain information which the minister did not want the witness to reveal to the select committee.[115]

Besides being restricted, civil servants are also protected by the convention of ministerial responsibility. However, in return for respecting this protection, select committees require that the minister himself should give evidence where necessary. It is not sufficient for him simply to accept responsibility. He must give an account of what has happened, or, if he is unable to do so, explain why this is the case. Indeed, in the light of Westland, the Liaison Committee recommended that 'the Government gives an undertaking that in future it will always ensure that a Minister will be accountable to the appropriate Select Committee'.[116]

Where the conduct of a civil servant is concerned, however, the minister, although still bearing responsibility for his department, may not be able to give an explanation of what has occurred without exposing the misdeeds of the official. Indeed, he may not know the details of what has happened, for the individual official has acted beyond his instructions. This creates a possible gap in accountability which may only be filled if select committees can require individual civil servants to account directly for their conduct

---

[114] Ibid.   [115] HC260 (1989–90), Q123.
[116] HC62 (1986–7), para. 18.

in those circumstances. This also removes the possibility of the minister refusing to answer questions on the grounds that this would expose misdeeds of his officials, when it is his own misdeeds that he fears exposing. The direct accountability of civil servants to select committees has been rejected by the government, which insists that ministers alone are responsible, hence the move by the government to reinforce its position after Westland by issuing guide-lines to civil servants.

However, the united hostility of select committee chairmen to these guide-lines compelled the government to adopt a more conciliatory line, or at least to make reassuring noises. John Biffen, the Leader of the House, assured Parliament that there was no intention of reducing the effectiveness of select committees.

It [the Response of the Government to the Defence Committee Report] has been represented as a way of making any future select committee inquiry ineffective. It does not, and is not intended to, do anything of the sort. As now, if something has gone amiss, a Select Committee will be free to seek an account from the Minister concerned or from a senior official representing the Minister. This could cover what has gone amiss, why it has gone amiss, what has been done to correct and remedy what has gone wrong and to prevent a recurrence. In short, we do not seek to prevent Select Committees from pursuing their inquiries into the expenditure, administration and policies of Departments.[117]

At first sight this may seem sufficient and go some way to satisfying the Liaison Committee's recommendation that a minister should always be accountable to a select committee. However, after Westland there remains the problem of what a committee can do if the minister refuses to explain and so blocks the committee's inquiry. This is not addressed by the statement, the emphasis of which is on the committee's ability to ask questions, not the obligation of the minister to answer them.

In its Response to the Reports of the Liaison and TCSC Committees the government appeared to give ground a little to the committees' sensibilities by accepting the need to distinguish between 'actions' and 'conduct' and by offering a reassurance that the guide-lines would not apply to 'actions'. However, the government suggested that the main distinction to be made was in the

---

[117] HC Deb., 29 Oct. 1986, col. 415.

type of question asked by the committees, not in the behaviour of officials.

The Government believes that the most important distinction to be drawn in this context is between questions which seek to establish the facts of what has occurred ('actions') and those which explicitly or implicitly seek to assign criticism or blame to individual civil servants.[118]

This statement would seem to suggest that, even if an official has acted outside the boundaries of his authority, he may still be questioned on what happened, providing the purpose behind the questions is to establish the facts and not an attempt to apportion blame. However, in certain instances the appearance of seeking to assign criticism or blame may be an inevitable outcome of a select committee's attempt to establish the facts. Thus select committees are likely to find themselves blocked from seeking answers on any activities of officials that are questionable.

The government guide-lines to civil servants were appended to the Government's Response.[119] They reinforce the principle that it is the minister who must answer for the behaviour of his civil servants, even if this has involved unauthorized conduct. 'On such occasions, the principles of Ministerial accountability are still applicable, even if officials have acted outside or contrary to the authorization given to them by their Ministers.'[120]

Moreover, the guide-lines are quite specific that select committees cannot inquire into the conduct of civil servants: 'the understanding is that the Select Committee should not pursue their own investigation into the "conduct" of the person concerned or act as a disciplinary tribunal, but should pursue the matter with the Minister, for whom it would then be to deal with it . . .'[121]

It is recommended that the minister should 'deal with it' as he sees fit, through a formal departmental inquiry if necessary. He should then inform the select committee of the outcome and what has been done to rectify the matter and prevent a recurrence.

Civil servants are clearly instructed to avoid answering any questions concerning 'conduct'.

---

[118] *Government's Response to the First Report from the Treasury and Civil Service Committee (HC62), and to the First Report from the Liaison Committee (HC100)* (1986–7), Cmnd. 78, para. 5.   [119] Ibid., Appendix, para. 2.
[120] Ibid.   [121] Ibid., para. 5.

If, when officials are asked to give evidence to a Select Committee, it is foreseen that the inquiry may involve questions about the 'conduct' of the individual officials in question or about other individual named officials, it should be suggested to the Committee that it would be appropriate for a Minister or a senior official designated by the Minister to give evidence, rather than the named officials in question. Any question which appears to relate to the 'conduct' of individual civil servants, such as the allocation of blame for what has occurred, can then be answered by the Minister or designated senior official.[122]

Moreover, civil servants are instructed that, if there is any doubt as to whether 'conduct' is concerned, they should act cautiously and refuse to answer questions about their behaviour or that of other named civil servants.

The government's stated objective for issuing the guide-lines was the need to protect individual civil servants from committee inquiries and the allocation of blame for mistakes made. To this end it insists that questions concerned with the conduct of individual officials should be addressed to the relevant minister or senior civil servant. Westland, of course, indicated that this may not provide a committee with the information it requires. Ministers may not answer the questions, and the protection of the conduct of individual civil servants from committee scrutiny may also mean that certain facts are protected. The failure of the government to address these issues may lead to the conclusion that a secondary objective of the guide-lines was to impose a further restriction on the ability of select committees to secure information, particularly information that may be potentially embarrassing to the government.

10.5. CONCLUSION

There is clearly considerable discrepancy between the theoretically unqualified power of Parliament to send for persons, papers, and records and the ability of select committees to gather information. Some of the differences arise because of the parliamentary status of select committees. Their powers are delegated by the House, and Members of Parliament receive considerable protection from

[122] Ibid., para. 6.

their application. Thus select committees cannot order Members to attend, nor can they order the submission of papers from a department of state. In both instances a resolution is required from Parliament.

However, more restrictive are the limitations imposed by the government through the convention of ministerial responsibility. The convention throughout the twentieth century has acted as a check on the information that can be revealed to Parliament, but the reform of the select committee system has resulted in a more formal application of the convention. Two sets of guide-lines, which the government states should be read in conjunction, now limit the information that can be made available to select committees. Civil servants must refrain from answering questions concerning the advice they have given, information about inter-departmental communications or policy alternatives, and any confidential matters. They are also restricted from answering questions that might relate to the conduct of an individual civil servant. Ministers too insist that they are bound by the conventional requirements of confidentiality, and thus may well refuse to answer questions on the activities of their officials, whether these are in accord with ministerial instructions and policy or go beyond what the minister authorized, or would have authorized.

Moreover, these limitations, whilst regretted by select committees, are generally accepted by them. Objections may be made, but in the end the committees, dependent as they are on the co-operation of the government, would seem to be incapable of resisting, even recognizing that their attitude may be seen as 'defeatist'.[123]

Individual members of committees may, of course, also be unwilling to resist, for it seems likely that government whips use their influence to persuade Conservative committee members not to support critical reports which will embarrass the government, and to manage the election of select committee chairmen. There is evidence that at least one Member has been offered an appointment to a committee 'on condition that he took a certain view about the forthcoming election of the Chairman of that Committee'.[124]

It also seems likely that the Selection Committee, which allocates

---

[123] HC19 (1989–90), para. 157.

[124] Michael Mates, Chairman of the Defence Committee, in evidence to the Committee of Procedure, HC19 (1989–90), Q363.

the eleven places on each committee, listens to the concerns and recommendations of the Whips' Office. Thus troublesome backbenchers who might be inclined to contest restrictions imposed by the government may be sidelined.

In addition, recent developments suggest that resistance from a committee, whether to the restrictions imposed by the government or to government policies, may result in the responsible committee chairman losing his position. A rule introduced in July 1992 limits the service of a Conservative Member on a select committee to three terms of Parliament. It was introduced, according to Sir Marcus Fox, the Chairman of the Selection Committee, in the interests of fairness, to ensure there were seats on committees for the new Conservative intake.[125] The introduction of a time limit was against the recommendation of the Procedure Committee, which had reported: 'The normal rate of turnover of Committee membership is . . . sufficient to ensure a fairly regular influx of new ideas and personalities and we do not favour any rigid ceiling on length of service.'[126]

However, the introduction of the rule conveniently meant that Nicholas Winterton, the Conservative Chairman of the Health Committee, which had been critical of the government's reforms in the health service, was no longer eligible to serve on the Committee. Sir Marcus Fox, who also chairs the 1922 Committee, insisted in the House that Conservatives on the Selection Committee had not been influenced by the whips, but refused to explain the procedures of the Committee or what criteria it used for selection. He quoted his predecessor,[127] who had told the House that, according to Erskine May,

'the Committee enjoyed full discretion and was under no obligation to consult, to take advice or indicate any criteria of choice'. It followed therefore that the Committee was procedurally free to choose whom it liked on whatever basis it thought applicable subject to the eventual verdict of the House.[128]

However, the lack of an obligation to consult does not prevent members of the Committee from choosing to consult and taking

---

[125] He stated that there were more than 200 applicants for ninety-six vacancies on the government side (HC Deb., 13 July 1992, col. 917).
[126] HC19 (1989–90), para. 14.
[127] HC Deb., 2 Dec. 1987, col. 1042, quoted 13 July 1992 at col. 915.
[128] HC19 (1989–90), para. 306.

advice informally. Indeed, as the Procedure Committee commented: 'It would be idle to expect the Whips to play no part in the process.'[129]

Moreover, the refusal of the Chairman to outline the criteria for selection leads to speculation that one consideration might be whether an applicant could be relied upon not to embarrass the government. The rule applies only to Conservatives. The government has not sought to extend it to committee membership in general. Indeed, it insists it is a party matter. However, with Conservatives having the majority on all the committees and the chairmanship of ten out of sixteen committees,[130] its effect is significant, not least because it signals that there is no alternative career for back-benchers to that within the government. This was a point pursued in the House by Frank Field:

If this limitation is operated, it will destroy one of the main reasons given for the select committees in the 1979 Parliament—that they offer an alternative career structure for those not in government and for Conservatives who will never have a chance to hold office.[131]

He further noted that the cumulative effect of the rule would be to 'de-skill . . . select committees',[132] as those government back-benchers with the most experience would be prevented from serving. This would reduce the incentive for a Member to become a specialist, for the opportunity to practise the specialism would be limited and would not help him to establish a long-term career within Parliament. It seems that, if government back-benchers wish for career progression, they are best advised to support government policy and beware of putting their names to select committee reports which are critical of the government, for their only route of advancement remains a ministerial one. Thus a further restriction is imposed on the effectiveness of committees.

The 1990 Report of the Procedure Committee minimalized the restrictions on the Committees, reporting that the relations between select committees and the government was 'generally healthy'.[133] It did not support increasing the powers of select committees or requiring the removal of the Osmotherly Rules. The Committee limited itself to proposing that information about inter-departmental

---

[129] Ibid., para. 178.　　[130] *The Times*, 13 July 1992.
[131] HC Deb., 13 July 1992, col. 919.　　[132] Ibid.
[133] HC19 (1989–90), para. 151.

decision-making and policy options should be revealed and that more time should be made available for debating select committee reports.[134] Such proposals do little to address the fundamental problem caused by the government's control of information. The inherent conflict remains between Parliament's belief in its right to information and the government's insistence on its right to govern without interference. It is a conflict of unequal forces and, despite the higher profile accorded to select committees through televised proceedings, this is a conflict that with party discipline the government is likely to win.

The reform of the select committee system has increased the amount of government information made publicly available; it has also provided a routine departmental accountability, and at times allows a parliamentary input into policy-making. However, in situations where the government considers it politically expedient to withhold information, even if this appears to obstruct a committee's inquiry, then the power of select committees to send for persons, papers, and records is of little consequence.

[134] Ibid., para. 192.

Next Steps Agencies: Management Reform in the Civil Service

11.1. INTRODUCTION

One of the major concerns of governments during the 1980s has been the economic, efficient, and effective delivery of government services. This has focused attention upon the management of the bureaucratic machine. In countries with the Westminster system of government, it has also drawn attention to the departmental structure and the possible inhibitory effect of the convention of individual ministerial responsibility on the development of efficient government.[1]

The traditional departmental model requires ministers to have tight control of their departments. This is achieved through a detailed control of expenditure and by the minimal concession of discretion. The result is a lack of personal responsibility on the part of civil servants, a deficiency which is covered, and indeed encouraged, by individual ministerial responsibility. However, the growth in the size and complexity of departments has meant that a minister cannot effectively exercise the required control, and that, although he is legally and politically responsible, in practical terms accountability 'tends to disappear'.[2]

Inefficient government therefore results in poor public accountability, and, conversely, inadequate public accountability masks government inefficiencies and allows them to continue. Moreover, individual ministerial responsibility, which works to condone the ineffectiveness of management, has also provided both politicians and officials with 'a rationale to thwart reform'.[3]

---

[1] In New Zealand and Australia the debate has been concerned with public accountability as well as efficiency, and reforms have aimed at improving both.

[2] New Zealand Treasury, *Government Management: A Brief to the Incoming Government 1987* (Wellington: New Zealand Treasury, 1987).

[3] P. M. Reagan, 'Protecting Privacy and Controlling Bureaucracies: The Constraints of British Constitutional Principles', *Governance* 311 (1990), 32–48.

This rationale was not, however, sufficient in the 1980s and 1990s to prevent radical reforms in the way in which services are delivered. In Britain the stated concern of the government has been the singular one of making service delivery more efficient. This has been a central factor in the transfer, wherever possible, of the delivery of services to the private sector. However, for a variety of reasons, many functions remain departmental responsibilities. It is upon these that the Efficiency Unit report, *Improving Management in Government: The Next Steps*,[4] concentrated. Its recommendations, which involved far-reaching management reforms, were made with only a passing reference to public accountability. However, the constitutional implications of the changes upon accountability are considerable.

The purpose here is to examine the agency concept, as developed by *The Next Steps*, and the establishment of agencies, and to assess the impact upon accountability and the extent to which agencies may widen the divergence between the theoretical and the actual accountability of ministers.

11.2. THE AGENCY CONCEPT

The central recommendation of the Efficiency Unit in *The Next Steps* was that agencies, or units of management, should be established 'to carry out the executive functions of government'.[5] Each agency would be headed by a Chief Executive and set up under a policy and resources framework devised by the relevant department. Strategy or policy, therefore, would remain with the minister, but the Chief Executive would decide how this strategy or the policy objectives should be implemented. The proposal was accepted by the government, and in 1988 Peter Kemp was appointed as Project Manager to oversee the establishment of Next Steps agencies.[6]

The concept of agencies or 'executive units'[7] to ensure accountable management is not new. In 1968 the Fulton Report

---

[4] Efficiency Unit, *Improving Management in Government: The Next Steps* (*Report to the Prime Minister*) (1988), HMSO (hereafter *The Next Steps*).
[5] Ibid., para. 19.
[6] In July 1992 he was unexpectedly replaced after William Waldegrave became the minister responsible. He was not found another position within the civil service. His successor was Richard Mottram.　　　[7] *The Next Steps*.

recommended setting up 'management units' so that individuals and groups could be held accountable for their performance against set objectives.[8] Fulton's recommendations concerning accountable management were never implemented across the departments, but the ethos that lay behind the establishment of agencies in the late 1980s owed much to the Report.[9]

The Next Steps envisaged a fundamental change in the way in which government delivers services, and also in the structure of the departments, the role of ministers, and the culture of the civil service. The aim is not just to increase efficiency through developing clearly identifiable management units, but 'to establish a quite different way of conducting the business of government'.[10]

Agencies are seen as a means by which most of the detailed management functions can be removed from the centre, leaving only a small core of policy-makers and departmental managers, and as a way of extending existing managerial schemes, such as Financial Management Initiative (FMI). The emphasis is upon management accountability to be achieved through greater delegation, increased responsibility, and operational independence.

The recommendation by the Efficiency Unit was unaccompanied by any detailed plan. Little guidance was given as to the form or structure agencies should take. This lack of detail was deliberate, for the Unit considered that a flexible approach was required, a view shared by the Project Manager, Peter Kemp, who confirmed that there was no 'hard and fast pattern for what an agency might be'.[11] There is, therefore, considerable variation between agencies. The emphasis has been on fitting the individual agency to the task in hand, rather than attempting to mould the task to fit

---

[8] Fulton wrote:

Accountable management means holding individuals and units responsible for performance measured as objectively as possible. Its achievement depends upon identifying or establishing accountable units within government departments— units where outputs can be measured against costs or other criteria, and where individuals can be held personally responsible for their role. (*Report of the Committee on the Civil Service* (Chairman, Lord Fulton), vol. i (1968), Cmnd. 3638, HMSO, para. 150.)

[9] Fulton considered whether parts of the civil service should be 'hived off' from the central government machine and entrusted to autonomous public boards or corporations which would be 'wholly responsible in their own fields within the powers delegated to them' (ibid., para. 188). [10] *The Next Steps*, para. 44.
[11] *Treasury and Civil Service Committee: The Civil Service Management Reforms: The Next Steps, Minutes of Evidence* (1988–9), HC494–i, HMSO, Q14.

uncomfortably into a preconceived structure. There has, therefore, been a move away from 'generalised solutions', which were considered by the Efficiency Unit to have been 'the bane of previous attempts at reform and have led to the structural rigidities that are now part of the problem'.[12]

11.3. AGENCIES AS DEPARTMENTAL UNITS OF GOVERNMENT

The Next Steps envisaged that agencies would range from internal units of management to non-departmental units and that their staff might not necessarily be civil servants. However, the suggestion that agencies might be outside the traditional departmental arrangements was dismissed by the Prime Minister, Mrs Thatcher, who stated that these management units would be 'clearly designated within the departments'. Moreover, she added: 'These agencies will generally be within the civil service, and their staff will continue to be civil servants.'[13]

'Civil service' here would seem to be used interchangeably with 'departmental', although the phrase 'within the civil service' has little meaning, as the civil service has no legal or political responsibility for units of government. The Prime Minister's statement, concerning the location of agencies, was not, however, categorical. An opening was left with the use of 'generally', the inference being that there might be occasions when an agency outside the department could be more appropriate. The TCSC sought clarification on this possibility, but the responses it received were all hedged with qualifications. Agencies would 'primarily' or 'by and large' be part of a government department, or at least those established 'initially' would be so.[14]

Mr Luce, then the Minister for the Civil Service, found it difficult to envisage circumstances where an agency would be established outside the department, and suggested privatization to be the natural option. Mr Kemp, however, considered it possible

---

[12] *The Next Steps*, para. 43.   [13] HC Deb., 18 Feb. 1988, col. 1149.
[14] HC494–i (1988–9), Peter Kemp, Memorandum from the Project Manager, para. 16; *Treasury and Civil Service Committee: The Civil Service Management Reforms: The Next Steps, Annexes, Minutes of Evidence and Appendices* (1988–9), HC494–II, HMSO, Richard Luce, Q316.

that new non-departmental public bodies could be established on agency lines,[15] and his reading of the situation would appear to be the correct one, for on 2 April 1990 Mr Luce announced that agency principles would be applied to all new executive non-departmental public bodies and progressively extended to selected existing ones.[16] The application of 'agency principles' means that such bodies will retain their position outside departments and that responsibility will be delegated

to the maximum extent practicable . . . within an agreed framework which unambiguously sets out the relationship between each body and its sponsoring Department. The approach is designed to improve managerial responsibility for performance and the delivery of results, and improve service to the public and to enhance accountability.[17]

A contradiction that is apparent in evidence given to the TCSC concerned the relationship between the establishment of agencies and privatization. Mr Luce stated that there was no connection. An executive function was either privatized or an agency was established to manage it.[18] But Sir Peter Middleton, Permanent Secretary to the Treasury, suggested that agencies might be a step to privatization.[19] Subsequently, the Prime Minister indicated a half-way house. Agencies were not a 'step' to privatization but they do not preclude it. 'I cannot rule out . . . that after a period of years agencies, like other Government activities, may be suitable for privatisation.'[20]

The 'period of years' has in practice been short. A White Paper, *Competing for Quality*, was produced in November 1991. This stated that, wherever suitable, public-sector work would be put out to contract. This includes work undertaken by agencies.

---

[15] HC494–i (1988–9), Q51.

[16] On 25 July 1990 Mr John Major announced that the Inland Revenue Valuation Office was to be established as an agency and the rest of the Inland Revenue was to be reorganized on Next Steps lines. This suggests that departments, or parts of departments, which are not considered suitable for full agency status can nevertheless still have the discipline of a framework document and a clear separation of responsibilities.

[17] *Eighth Report from the Treasury and Civil Service Committee: Progress on the Next Steps Initiative* (1989–90), HC481, HMSO, Memorandum from the Project Manager, p. 3 n.   [18] HC494–II (1988–9), Q316.

[19] Ibid., Q342.

[20] *The Government's Response to the Report from the Treasury and Civil Service Committee on the Civil Service Committee on the Civil Service Management Reforms: The Next Steps* (1988), Cmnd. 524, HMSO, p. 7.

Moreover, a year later plans were published for the privatization of some of the first agencies, including Companies House, the Driver Vehicle Licencing Agency, and the Vehicle Inspectorate.

11.4. THE POLICY AND RESOURCES FRAMEWORK

The key to the concept of agencies is the policy and resources framework. Much emphasis has been placed on the need for this document to be clear and unambiguous. 'These units . . . need to be given a well defined framework in which to operate, which sets out the policy, the budget, specific targets and the results to be achieved.'[21]

It is this framework, and its translation into a guiding document, that distinguishes the Next Steps agencies from units of government already in existence which otherwise share some of their characteristics.[22] The importance of the framework, and the fundamental difference it makes, was stressed by one of the first Chief Executives to be appointed. He considered the framework document to be 'a very important document simply because it exists. . . . It has brought together a lot of things that existed before . . . [and now] management have a clearer understanding of what our terms of reference are.'[23]

The requirement is for an open relationship between an agency and its parent department, which is given written form in a published framework document and made available to all interested parties. The government has given assurances that this will 'normally' be the case,[24] although qualifying its intention to publish by the familiar exclusions of 'national interest',[25] 'commercial confidence', and 'national security'.[26] Such restrictions may be needed on rare occasions. However, they should never be used as a screen behind which information can be hidden. To prevent this possibility the TCSC required that 'the onus should be upon the

---

[21] *The Next Steps*, para. 20.
[22] e.g. the Inland Revenue (now run on agency lines), which had some separation of operation and policy and an 'arm's-length approach' prescribed by law.
[23] *Treasury and Civil Service Committee: Developments in the Next Steps Programme, Minutes of Evidence* (1988–9), HC348–ii, HMSO, Q101.
[24] HC494–i (1988–9), Peter Kemp, Q16.
[25] HC494–II (1988–9), Richard Luce, Q314.
[26] HC494–i (1988–9), Q17.

Secretary of State to give reasons if he or she decides not to publish the agreement, or publish only part of it'.[27]

By implication, these reasons should be more than a blanket statement citing 'national security' or 'commercial confidentiality' as the grounds for non-publication. However, previous experience suggests that explanations are unlikely. They are not in the tradition of British government; but then, neither are accountable agencies. It may, of course, be pessimistic to believe that government would use such restrictions, still less use them improperly. Seventy-seven agencies had been established by January 1993 and all the framework documents had been published.[28]

The framework documents are the terms of reference for the new agencies and also provide a 'pragmatic test' for those areas of government suitable for agency status. Peter Kemp reported to the TCSC:

we are seeing a sort of pragmatic test emerging, and the question really is: can you write a framework document which says quite clearly what the Agency has to do and says quite clearly on the other side what the Minister or his Permanent Secretary can look after.[29]

It is the clear division of responsibility that is so important. Indeed, the TCSC in its report stated:

Each framework agreement, which sets out what is in the authority of the Chief Executive, should be regarded as a contract. . . . If this principle is not adopted there is a danger that informal contacts of the kind which characterised relations between departments and Nationalised Industries would make it very difficult to establish the precise responsibility for decisions.[30]

It is to be presumed that by 'contract' the Committee did not mean a legally enforceable agreement with redress to the courts if either the minister or the Chief Executive breaches the terms of the framework document. Rather, the Committee had in mind a formal, but non-legal, agreement which could be monitored to ensure

---

[27] *Treasury and Civil Service Committee: The Civil Service Management Reforms: The Next Steps* (1988–9), HC494–I, HMSO, para. 42.

[28] *Independent*, 23 July 1992.

[29] *Treasury and Civil Service Committee: Developments in the Next Steps Programme, Minutes of Evidence* (1988–9), HC348–i, HMSO, Q8.

[30] HC494–II (1988–9), para. 38.

that both sides keep within their areas of decision-making and are therefore clearly accountable for those decisions.

The 'quasi-contractual' relationship between the minister and Chief Executive was again explained by the TCSC when it examined the progress of the Next Steps programme.[31] The Committee also acknowledged the importance and the impact of the framework agreements.

What has emerged clearly is the vital function of the Agreement in making the relationship between the Chief Executive and the rest of Government transparent. This aim is achieved by stating clearly who is responsible for doing what, and setting out ways in which the performance of the agency will be measured.[32]

The framework documents to date have stated clearly the delegated powers and the division of responsibilities. For instance, in one of the first framework documents to be published (that of Companies House) these responsibilities are listed to indicate functions that were delegated on the inception of the agency, functions which were to be delegated by 1 April 1989, and further functions to be delegated, or considered for delegation, after this date.[33]

The documents also detail the performance indicators against which the agencies will be measured and the controls and safeguards that are operated by the parent department over the agency. These include approvals of Corporate and Business Plans and performance targets, control, and monitoring of finance, staffing, and pay matters, and the production of accounts and reports by the agency so that performance can be evaluated.

Within the framework documents there is provision for the formal review of the framework. This review is important to prevent informal practices developing to compensate for any shortcomings in the framework. It is likely that there will need to be changes in the early years of an agency's existence, and it may therefore be sensible to see the framework document as 'an evolutionary tool capable of modification in the light of experience'.[34] It is, however,

---

[31] HC481 (1990), para. 15vii.   [32] Ibid., para. 14vii.
[33] Companies House Executive Agency, *Policy and Resources Framework* (Oct. 1988), DTI, Annexes A–C.
[34] HC348–ii (1988–9), Memorandum from the Vehicle Inspectorate Executive Agency, p. 24, D.6.

crucial that any modification is carried out openly and that necessary adjustments are made throughout the framework document so that accountability is clear.

11.5. ACCOUNTABILITY

Each framework also contains the line of accountability of the Chief Executive to the parent department; that is to whom he reports (usually a deputy secretary) and the structure that exists within the department to advise the minister on agency performance.[35] There is also a specific section which outlines the general responsibilities of the minister and the Chief Executive, and which stipulates accountability to Parliament. The Companies House framework states:

> Companies House is a Departmental body. DTI Ministers answer to Parliament on both the policy governing its work generally and on its day-to-day operation. . . . DTI Ministers will continue to determine the policy framework within which the Agency operates, but they will not normally become involved in the day-to-day management of Companies.[36]

Thus the minister will be answerable to Parliament for the day-to-day operation of the agency, although normally having no direct part in it. This is, of course, a different arrangement from that in the nationalized industries, where the minister has an indirect responsibility for operational matters. He, therefore, is required to exercise only informatory or reporting responsibility, whereby he reports to Parliament what he has been told by the chairman. The difference serves as a reminder that agencies, despite their delegated responsibilities, are still departmental units of management.

The Vehicle Inspectorate's framework document follows the same form of accountability to Parliament. However, it is more definite

---

[35] e.g. the Chief Executive of the Vehicle Inspectorate reports to a Deputy Secretary in the Department of Transport. The Deputy Secretary is supported by a departmental group which advises the Transport Ministers on the agency's Corporate and Business Plans and which also monitors the agency's performance. In Companies House, however, the Chief Executive, although accounting to the Head of the Companies Division within the Department of Trade, also sits on the Steering Board, which supports him and which advises the Minister on the agency's Corporate Plan and on the efficiency and general performance of the agency.

[36] Companies House Executive Agency, *Policy and Resources Framework*, p. 6, 2.1.

about the exclusion of the minister from agency operations, stating: 'Ministers and the Department will not, however, be involved in day to day management of the Inspectorate.'[37]

This is an unequivocal commitment to the Chief Executive's freedom to manage. Moreover, the document makes clear that 'any special extra activities' that ministers may require, in addition to those already approved in the Corporate and Business Plans, should be clearly noted in the annual accounts and, if necessary, the cost should be borne by the department.[38]

The Chief Executive is personally responsible to the minister for all the powers delegated to him within the framework document. These delegations are likely to increase as the loosening of central control continues. Most important for agencies, however, is the extent of financial delegation, hence the amendment to the Trading Fund Act 1973 to enable more agencies to be given Trading Fund status and thus greater financial autonomy.[39]

There have also been agreements with the unions concerning more flexible pay and personnel arrangements. These enable agencies with the necessary delegated power to introduce their own schemes, subject to normal procedures of consultation and Treasury approval (still a very significant limitation).[40] Moreover, all new pay arrangements for agency staff are linked to performance targets and objectives, and from April 1991 the mandatory rules and requirements which operate at the centre and concern matters such as pay and allowances were modified.[41] Agencies have also been given varying degrees of responsibility for the recruitment of their own lower level staff.[42]

---

[37] Vehicle Inspectorate Executive Agency, *Policy and Resources Framework* (1988), DTI, p. 2, B1. [38] Ibid.

[39] As of March 1992, seven agencies operated as Trading Funds. Many more intend to acquire this status, which gives the advantage of greater end-of-year flexibility, although exposing the agency's ability to make a financial return on the investment made in the agency (Price Waterhouse, *Executive Agencies* (4th edn., Mar. 1992)).

[40] By Mar. 1992 nine agencies were operating group incentive schemes so that all their staff would be rewarded if the agency exceeded its target (Price Waterhouse, *Executive Agencies* (4th edn., Mar. 1992)).

[41] e.g. this has enabled Wilton Park Executive Agency, which organizes conferences for the Foreign and Commonwealth Office, to make its own arrangements regarding special allowances for staff working at weekends (Price Waterhouse, *Executive Agencies* (5th edn., Mar. 1992)).

[42] e.g. the Central Statistical Office is able to recruit up to Grade 5; the Social Security Agency (Northern Ireland) is responsible for recruitment and career

Such developments increase the potential autonomy of agencies, an autonomy which is seen as increasing incrementally as individual Chief Executives gain the confidence of the Treasury.[43] However, it is important that, as delegations are conceded, they are clearly stated in the relevant framework document so that the responsibilities of the Chief Executive and those of the department are unequivocal.

11.6. THE CHIEF EXECUTIVE

The Next Steps recommended that the agency head, or Chief Executive, should be given personal responsibility for achievement within the established framework and be left free to manage without departmental interference. Indeed, Peter Kemp suggested, a Chief Executive might resist any such interference, even to the extent of saying 'No, Minister!'

the Chief Executive will start increasingly feeling that he is in charge of the operation, and while he accepts that he is still only a servant of the Minister and the Minister can give him orders, he will point to his framework document and say 'Hey, I know you can give me orders, but it's not quite right there. I want to do it this way. . . .' [These] are tensions between, if you like, the customer who wants the thing done and the contractor who has been entrusted with doing it.[44]

The 'contractor' would not, however, appear to be in a strong position if his territory is invaded either by departmental civil servants or by the minister, for the line of responsibility seems to distance the Chief Executive from the minister and may make access difficult. Peter Kemp insisted that it was not the intention 'to put any fudge between the Chief Executive and the Minister'. Indeed, he stated that the agency head should 'exercise his . . . right of direct access to the Minister'.[45]

This right is assumed rather than guaranteed. It is not written into framework agreements, perhaps a strange omission when the

---

management of the majority of the staff; the Passport Agency can recruit up to and including SEO (Price Waterhouse, *Executive Agencies* (5th edn., Mar. 1992)).

[43] P. Hartnack, Chief Executive of the Patent Office, 'Whitehall Unbound', *Analysis*, Radio 4, 31 May 1990, 20.00 hrs.

[44] HC348–i (1988–9), Q32.   [45] Ibid.

emphasis is on clarity and unambiguity. However, during the review of the progress of Next Steps, Peter Kemp emphasized that the Chief Executive was more directly responsible to the minister than to the departmental hierarchy: 'We are moving from a hierarchical system to a system in which the Minister and Chief Executive are in a quasi-contractual position . . . the Minister has specifically delegated some of his powers to the individual to carry them out on his behalf.'[46]

This may be an example of the 'shifting' position of agencies. The minister in any case has the final say. This in itself can create ambiguity unless the situations in which he can overrule the Chief Executive are clearly stated within the framework document. *The Next Steps* anticipated this problem, recommending that the framework 'must also specify how politically sensitive issues are to be dealt with and the extent of the delegated authority of management'.[47]

The Efficiency Unit did not offer any suggestions as to the specification or indeed as to what might constitute 'politically sensitive issues'. There could be formal procedures for intervention by ministers, and likewise for the referral by Chief Executives of matters upwards for consideration, although there is no guarantee that such procedures would be followed. The tendency could well be that, as with the nationalized industries, the informal, and therefore unrecorded, approach would be preferred by ministers. The existence of a procedural mechanism might, however, give some protection from interference.

These safeguards have not been built into the framework documents. Instead there is a reliance upon the ethos behind the agencies. This presumes a willingness to delegate and, having delegated, to allow as much freedom as possible to the Chief Executive:

once the policy objectives and budgets within the framework are set, the management of the agency should have as much independence as possible in deciding how these objectives are met. . . . The presumption must be that, providing management is operating within the strategic direction set by Ministers, it must be left as free as possible to manage within that framework.[48]

---

[46] HC481 (1990–1), Q170.   [47] *The Next Steps*, para. 20.
[48] Ibid., para. 21.

Such sentiments were reinforced by officials from the Department of Employment, who stated: 'We regard the performance agreement as a formal contract to which both sides have signed up. If either side wants to change it then you re-open the negotiations and that stops the day-to-day intervention . . . it is intended to anyway.'[49]

It may also require resistance on behalf of Chief Executives to interference and an opportunity for them to complain, if necessary in public. Indeed, the TCSC stated:

It is vital that Departments should have to justify interference rather than Chief Executives justify their independence, and that the Chief Executive can complain—if necessary in public—when he or she feels that interference from the Department is unwarranted.[50]

Recruitment from outside the Civil Service

The decision to upgrade the Chief Executive has important implications for accountability, as has the policy of recruiting agency heads from outside the civil service, where appropriate. Peter Kemp suggested that: 'it will become not just acceptable but almost the practice to seek open competition for some of these jobs'.[51]

Such appointments are on fixed-term contracts and there is 'a relatively high risk and reward pattern for these people'.[52] The desirability of recruitment from outside the civil service was supported by the TCSC, who welcomed 'an injection of talent . . . on a non-political basis'.[53]

The Committee's concern about outside appointments was that they may become political appointments. However, Sir Robin Butler, Head of the Civil Service, was reassuring. 'There are procedures of the Civil Service Commission which protect the public and protect ministers against political jobbery. These will continue.'[54]

Sir Robin presumably meant that ministers would be protected from the accusation of political jobbery, for ministers are unlikely themselves to have political appointments thrust upon them. Indeed, the concern has been the extent to which a minister can

[49] HC481 (1989–90), Q94. [50] Ibid., para. 19viii.
[51] HC494–i (1988–9), Q56. [52] Ibid., Q57.
[53] HC494–I (1988–9), para. 21. [54] HC494–II (1988–9), Q270.

influence an appointment, and even change the rules retrospectively to enable his appointee to remain in office.[55] It is not, therefore, a new departure for non-civil servants to be employed at a senior level within government. Between 1979 and 1985 seventy such appointments, or secondments, were made where internal candidates were unable to supply the expertise required.[56]

Indeed, subsequently the Committee has recommended that 'open competition should be held for the appointment of all agency Chief Executives'. Furthermore, it continued: 'As the decision whether or not to hold an open competition is ultimately a ministerial one, we recommend that the Minister should give an explanation of every case in which it is decided not to hold an open competition for the appointment of a Chief Executive.'[57] The Committee's concern would seem to have changed from one of political appointments to concern about civil service 'cosiness'.

The open advertisement of Chief Executives' appointments means that agency heads may fall into three categories. First, there is the civil servant who is appointed internally, or after open competition on normal terms and conditions. It is likely that his appointment will be a promotion and he will be on a fixed-term contract at the end of which he will probably return to the career stream and another job within the service. His position whilst a Chief Executive is different from other civil servants, most importantly because of his visibility, but also because his appointment is for a specific job and not to a grade. He is, therefore, temporarily outside the civil service hierarchy.[58]

Secondly, there is the civil servant who applies for an openly advertised post which has 'exceptional terms and conditions with perhaps pay substantially greater than he might have got as a civil servant'.[59] He will be expected to resign from the civil service upon his appointment as Chief Executive, because, according to

---

[55] When Michael Heseltine appointed Peter Levine, a leading contractor, as defence procurement adviser at the Ministry of Defence, he violated the rules governing the appointment of civil servants. As a result, these rules were retrospectively changed by the Prime Minister to legitimize the appointment. Since then, however, departments have followed a strict set of guide-lines and seek Commission approval of such appointments.

[56] G. Drewry, and T. Butcher, *The Civil Service Today* (Oxford: Blackwells, 1988).

[57] HC481 (1990–1), para. 28xi. In April 1991 Price Waterhouse reported in their survey of agencies that open competition was now 'the norm' (Price Waterhouse, *Executive Agencies* (2nd edn., Apr. 1991)).

[58] HC481 (1989–90), Q175.   [59] HC348–i (1988–9), Peter Kemp, Q18.

Peter Kemp, 'he should not have both the pay and the security, so to speak: he should not get both the bun and the penny'.[60] He is, therefore, employed as a temporary civil servant and when his contract expires he will be outside the service. However, he will be able to apply to rejoin and can be reinstated at a higher grade than when he left.[61] So, for his temporary exposure to the outside world, a civil servant may be well rewarded in terms of both pay and security. However, he is not allowed to enjoy both rewards together.

The third category is the non-civil servant who is appointed as a Chief Executive. He again becomes a temporary civil servant on a fixed-term contract.

The move towards open competition means that, increasingly, Chief Executives can be categorized as temporary civil servants, and many are external appointments.[62] The position of outsiders as Chief Executives could raise some interesting questions about the relationship between the minister and the Chief Executive. For such appointees will not have been steeped in the civil service culture and may not easily accept the contradictory position of being personally responsible but acting only for the minister.[63]

---

[60] Ibid.   [61] Ibid.

[62] By Mar. 1992 nearly three-quarters of all Chief Executives had been appointed after open competition and approaching half the total number of Chief Executives were external appointees—e.g. Head of Defence Research Agency was recruited at a salary of £140,000 p.a. (this is more than the Head of the Civil Service) (Price Waterhouse, *Executive Agencies* (4th and 5th edns., Mar. 1992)).

[63] Appointments are also being made by agencies of outside specialists in areas such as finance, IT, and marketing. (Price Waterhouse, *Executive Agencies* (3rd edn., Apr. 1991)).

12

Next Steps Agencies:
The Problems of Accountability

Next Steps agencies are intended to increase the efficiency of government in the delivery of services. However, there is confusion and uncertainty as to whether they will improve accountability, and even concern that accountability may be the casualty of the drive for efficient government. There are two aspects to the accountability of a department: internal accountability, which involves the arrangements for accounting between the minister and his officials, and external accountability, which is concerned with the accountability of the department to Parliament and the public.

12.1. INTERNAL ACCOUNTABILITY

The internal accountability of the Next Steps agencies is achieved through an extension of existing practices. The Chief Executive is responsible through the departmental hierarchy to the minister of the parent department. His responsibilities, the ways in which he is required to account—for instance, through quarterly reports and performance targets—and the line of accountability are all stated in the framework document, thus ensuring a more formal and specific accountability than has existed before.

Moreover, personal responsibility means that the Chief Executive is measured on his success or otherwise. In the short term, this affects his monetary reward.[1] In the long term, career success may

---

[1] e.g. Chief Executive of the Benefits Agency is on a performance related bonus of 12.5%. Chief Executive of the Employment Agency is on a 10% bonus. To earn it in 1990/1 he had to find 275,000 jobs for the long-term unemployed and place half a million job-seekers in the inner cities (Peter Hennessy, *Analysis*, Radio Four, 31 May 1990).

depend on a successful spell as a Chief Executive, and the promotion prospects for a failed Chief Executive are unlikely to be bright. Indeed, Sir Robin Butler indicated that a Chief Executive who spent over budget should be replaced.[2]

Where agencies are established, therefore, internal accountability looks to be more meaningful than before. Paradoxically, while agency managers have more freedom to manage, ministers also have improved control. The tightened procedures and system of controls provide a mechanism for ministers to be better informed and better able to check errant officials. The Next Steps programme would, therefore, seem likely to produce a civil service that, at least in the agencies if not in the departments, is more accountable to ministers. The important question is whether improved internal accountability will result in improved external, or public, accountability.

12.2. EXTERNAL ACCOUNTABILITY

External accountability has a number of aspects. There is financial accountability to the Treasury and by the Accounting Officer to the PAC, but most facets of accountability come under the responsibility of the minister to Parliament. The minister is therefore accountable on the Floor of the House (his province alone) and before select committees (where his officials may appear on his behalf). He is also accountable to individual Members of Parliament, who act on behalf of their constituents, and to the clients and consumers themselves. He may delegate the responsibility for answering queries or complaints, but he does not, and according to the doctrine of ministerial responsibility cannot, delegate accountability.

Arrangements for Accountability to Parliament are Unchanged

The Next Steps was generally confused and confusing on accountability to Parliament, suggesting ill-defined changes which sometimes seemed to be within the existing framework of accountability, and at other times seemed to require a fundamental

---

[2] Ibid.

change to the framework itself. Suggestions that it may be necessary to change 'the arrangement for formal accountability' sat uneasily with the contention that 'It is axiomatic that Ministers should remain fully and clearly accountable for policy. For agencies which are government departments, or part of departments, ultimate accountability for operations must also rest with Ministers.'[3]

These inconsistencies reflected perhaps 'the liberal dilution'[4] of the original *Next Steps* Report, which advocated a change, by law if necessary, of the convention of individual ministerial responsibility, such that ministers would no longer be responsible for everything done in their names. According to Peter Hennessy: 'The Cabinet didn't buy the original Next Steps argument from Andrew Jackson and his colleagues, that old style ministerial accountability to Parliament should go.'[5]

This was made clear by the Prime Minister, Mrs Thatcher, when she announced the government's acceptance of the main recommendations of *The Next Steps*. She stated that there would be no change in the arrangements for formal accountability to Parliament. This was seen by some as contradictory to the acceptance of agencies, for the very essence of the agency concept is the personal responsibility of the Chief Executive for his delegated powers, the effectiveness of which is in danger of being lost if this is only reflected in internal accountability. The TCSC pursued the issue of accountability with the Minister for the Civil Service and with officials, all of whom repeated the sentiments expressed by the Prime Minister.

Peter Kemp, the Project Manager, reiterated the Prime Minister's comments: 'The Prime Minister said in the House on 18th February—quite clearly—that there would be no change in arrangements for accountability and Ministers will have to continue to account for the work of their departments.'[6]

Sir Robin Ibbs likewise stated that there would be no change, nor, he added, was there need for any. 'I would say the formal arrangements of accountability are unaffected and there is no question of change being required.'[7]

Mr Luce, Minister for the Civil Service, was adamant that 'the

---

[3] *The Next Steps*, Annex A, para. 3.   [4] Hennessy, *Whitehall*, 620.
[5] Hennessy, *Analysis*.   [6] HC494-i (1988–9), Q36.
[7] HC494–II (1988–9), Q114.

basic principles of ministerial accountability to Parliament'[8] must be preserved. However, behind this firm support for the Prime Minister's line, there were again contradictions and confusions with indications that, within the traditional structure, or the formal arrangements, there would be change.

Peter Kemp stated that, although the principle of ministerial accountability would remain, 'the mechanics may change'.[9] Moreover, he suggested that the traditional relationship between ministers and the civil service may also alter. He did not expand upon this point, but any alteration in these relations would be likely to affect the convention of ministerial responsibility itself and produce a radical change to the traditional structure.

Sir Robin Ibbs too indicated that there could be times when the practice of accountability might change.

> For example, when it is plain that a particular civil servant is himself clearly responsible within the framework for operational issues it may well be better to focus an initial question, write a letter to that man asking him about the individual case than it would be to go through the minister.[10]

This was one of the 'changes in operation' also picked up by Sir Robin Butler, who commented: 'I think that the structure of accountability remains; its operation will be changed . . .'[11]

A Direct Approach to the Chief Executive

This change in the operation of accountability is most obvious in the handling of individual complaints. Such complaints, which are usually concerned with operational matters, have traditionally been directed through a Member of Parliament to the minister. However, in some areas of government, such as the Inland Revenue, it is the practice for Members of Parliament to refer cases concerning operational matters to local managers, although Members retain the right to involve the minister if the reply received is unsatisfactory. This enables 'the system itself [to be given] a chance to answer complaints and problems in the first place'.[12]

The Next Steps saw this practice being adopted by agencies, so

---

[8] Ibid., Q301.   [9] HC494–i (1988–9), Q36.
[10] HC494–II (1988–9), Q114.   [11] Ibid., Q277.
[12] Ibid., Sir Peter Middleton, Q376.

that Members could contact the local manager or the Chief Executive, whichever was most appropriate, and the idea has gained force as the agency concept has been developed. In the first memorandum from the Project Team to the TCSC it was merely a suggestion: 'Members of Parliament may wish to approach agencies direct about enquiries concerning operational matters . . .'[13]

However, subsequently, it has become policy to encourage Members of Parliament to approach the Chief Executives in the first instance when operational matters are concerned. This policy is expressed in the framework document of the Vehicle Inspectorate:

> In order to ensure that letters from Members of Parliament are dealt with as quickly and effectively as possible, the Secretary of State has invited them to address correspondence concerning the Inspectorate's handling of constituents' cases to the Chief Executive. If a letter about such a case is received in the Department it will generally be referred to the Inspectorate to reply direct.[14]

Members of Parliament are therefore 'invited' to write to the Chief Executive, an invitation that seems to have been accepted in relation to complaints or queries concerning the Vehicle Inspectorate. Moreover, Members are also writing directly to the lower levels in the organization, that is to the fifty-three districts that comprise the Inspectorate, where their constituents' problems originated.[15]

This trend towards the decentralization of what might be called routine or grievance accountability seems likely to continue, with the Department of Employment notifying Members of Parliament that communications concerning the operations of the Employment Agency are best addressed locally or to the Chief Executive, although the *Framework Document* states that 'The Secretary of State will continue to answer questions from Members of Parliament on matters concerning the Agency.'[16]

The establishment of agencies to manage most of the services government delivers would seem, therefore, to provide an opportunity for developing a formal structure for such accountability,

---

[13] HC494–i (1988–9), Peter Kemp, Memorandum from the Project Manager, para. 15.
[14] Vehicle Inspectorate Executive Agency, *Policy and Resources Framework*, 4.7.
[15] HC348–ii (1988–9), Q117.
[16] Employment Agency, *Framework Document* (1990), para. 4.3.

which would operate on five levels. First, if the agency is dispersed into regional offices, an individual complains at a local level. Secondly, if this is unsuccessful, his Member of Parliament takes up the matter locally on behalf of the constituent. Thirdly, in the case of continued failure or a more serious matter, the Member takes the issue to the Chief Executive. Fourthly, if the Chief Executive is unable or unwilling to resolve the issue, the Member of Parliament writes to the Minister, and, fifthly, the ultimate sanction, he raises the matter on the Floor of the House.

This would result in a pyramid of accountability, with most issues being resolved locally, some being passed to the Chief Executive (either because of a failure in resolution below or because of the centralized nature of the agency), and only the occasional operational issue reaching the minister.

Clearly there are advantages in Members of Parliament dealing directly with agencies on appropriate matters, providing there is an adequate and speedy procedure for processing such questions. However, there is a danger that ministers will abstract themselves completely from operational affairs, or at least will do so when it suits them, and that the political sanction—questioning the minister on the Floor of the House—will be lost. The importance of this sanction is not only its political effect on the minister, but also the check it provides on officials.

The saving virtue of Ministerial Responsibility is that officials live in some fear that a mistake or a failure to redress a grievance might involve their minister in a political row—the consequence of which will rebound painfully back to the official concerned, and perhaps harm his career. An arm's length relationship between ministers and agency removes this sanction and must make the official less responsive to the aggrieved consumer.[17]

However, the personal responsibility of civil servants for their agencies would seem to provide an alternative motivation to ensure responsiveness to aggrieved customers. In any case, a Member can still insist upon a ministerial reply if he is dissatisfied with that given by the Chief Executive. This was a point made by the Chief Executive of the Employment Agency: 'it is of course free for any

---

[17] HC494-II (1988-9), Memorandum from Mr William Plowden and Professor Gavin Drewry, p. 26, para. 9.

Member, if he is subsequently dissatisfied with the reply that I have given, to table a question to a Minister saying specifically he wants the Minister to answer.'[18]

The redirection to Chief Executives of questions, relating to the operation of agencies, has the potential for improving effectiveness and efficiency. It would be preferable, however, if clear procedures were laid down for complaints or grievances. Moreover, where individual grievances are concerned, a system of tribunals would seem to be essential, so that the aggrieved customer has a means of appeal other than to the minister.

One of the initial problems presented by ministers redirecting agency questions to Chief Executives was that the answers were not published in Hansard in the same way as ministerial replies, because they did not originate from the minister. Replies could, at the request of the Member of Parliament, be placed in the Commons Library, but they were not freely available outside the House. Yet, as the TCSC suggested, answers on operational matters might have implications wider than the individual case. As a result, the TCSC asked the government to consider an 'appropriate mechanism' whereby replies of Chief Executives which arose from questions to ministers should be published.

If an acceptable convention is not established, there is a danger that, despite the wholly laudable intention of making those responsible for carrying out the service fully accountable to Parliament, much information currently available to Parliament and the public will no longer be readily available.[19]

The government initially gave assurances that all answers by Chief Executives would automatically go into both the Commons Library and the Public Information Office in the House of Commons. However, this did not provide the public access required. Some agencies failed to supply the Public Information Office with copies of answers, and the Commons Library took a decision, on administrative grounds, only to provide copies of answers that

---

[18] HC481 (1990), Q104. (Note that there is some concern that the right of MPs to insist on a ministerial response may in practice be difficult to claim. Gerald Kaufman MP has reported on his lack of success in extracting a ministerial reply on agency matters concerning his constituents; even correspondence marked for the attention of the minister is redirected to the Chief Executive (*Guardian*, 7 Dec. 1992).) [19] HC481 (1990), para. 70xx.

were reasonably short.[20] In any case, answers recorded in this way did not receive the same coverage that Hansard provides.

Subsequently, the House of Commons Administration Committee recommended that answers from Chief Executives should be published in Hansard:

the Committee resolved that, from the first sitting day after the summer recess, letters sent to Members from agency chief executives in response to parliamentary questions should be printed among the written answers in the daily Official Record, beneath a standard form of reply given by the Minister with responsibility.[21]

The inclusion of the letters of Chief Executives under a standard form of reply given by the responsible minister would seem to remove the objection that Hansard is concerned only with ministerial answers. It also reinforces the direct responsibility of ministers for agencies. This responsibility may at first be effectively exercised by redirecting queries to those best equipped to answer them. However, subsequent queries concerning agency replies may require explanatory responsibility by the minister either to the individual Member or even on the floor of the House.

Chief Executives as Accounting Officers

The position and status of the Chief Executive of an agency is particularly important for accountability, and this has been an issue over which the government has yielded to pressure from the TCSC. The recommendation of *The Next Steps* that the agency head should be given personal responsibility for achievement within the established framework was unaccompanied by the status necessary for him to be summoned by the PAC. Accountability to the PAC for the finances of a department lies with the Accounting Officer, usually the Permanent Secretary, and the Efficiency Unit proposed that he should retain responsibility for those parts of the department that had become agencies, at the same time suggesting: 'In due course formal accountability, before the Public Accounts Committee for example, might develop so that for significant agencies the Permanent Secretary would normally be accompanied by the head of the agency.'[22]

---

[20] A. Davies and J. Willman, *What Next?* (London: Institute for Public Policy Research, 1991). [21] HC Deb., Written Answers, 16 July 1992, col. 941. [22] *The Next Steps*, para. 22.

However, the TCSC believed this to be unsatisfactory: 'If the Chief Executive of an agency is to be given responsibility for the efficient and effective use of the resources provided for within the policy framework, he or she should be held accountable, as the Accounting Officer for the agency.'[23]

The government accepted the Committee's contention, and announced that a Chief Executive would be either an Accounting Officer (AO) or an Agency Accounting Officer (AAO), depending on the vote structure.[24] Both titles mean that the Chief Executive is 'directly answerable to Parliament for the economy, efficiency and effectiveness with which the Agency has used its resources in discharging the functions given to it in the framework document'.[25]

As a further clarification of the Chief Executive's accountability, in May 1989 the Treasury issued guidance on 'the delineation of responsibilities of departmental Accounting Officers and Agency Accounting Officers'.[26] This specified that the AAO is responsible for the agency's use of resources in carrying out its functions and that the responsibilities of the departmental AO include the allocation of these resources to the agency, the contents of the framework document, and the setting of performance targets for the agency. An AAO will usually appear alongside the departmental AO, and agencies with AOs at their head, such as HMSO, will usually be represented by that official alone before the PAC.

The division between departments and agencies for financial responsibilities gives important clarification, which is assisted by an equally clear delineation in the framework document so that there can be no confusion as to the functions for which the Chief Executive is responsible.[27] However, in addition, targets and resources need to be clearly specified and agreed between departments and agencies, for imposed targets could result in the Chief Executive refusing to accept responsibility for a shortfall on the basis that the departmental targets were unrealistic or the resources allocated were inadequate. Targets therefore should be 'specifically spelt out in the public forum' and need to be 'an agreement between . . . [agencies] and the Secretary of State'.[28]

---

[23] HC494–I (1988–9), para. 44.
[24] HC Deb., 10 Nov. 1988, cols. 249–50W.
[25] HC348–i (1988–9), Memorandum from the Project Manager, p. 1.c.
[26] Comptroller and Auditor General, *Report on the Next Steps Initiative* (1989), HC236, HMSO, 410, para. 54.
[27] HMSO Executive Agency, *Framework Document* (1988), HMSO, p. 11, 4.16.
[28] M. Fogden, Chief Executive Employment Agency, in Hennessy, *Analysis*.

Besides aiding financial accountability, AO status would also seem to give the Chief Executive some safeguard from departmental interference within the affairs of the agency. He, like the departmental AO, can presumably express in writing to the minister any disagreement concerning proposals for spending which he believes he will be unable to justify before the PAC. In this instance his responsibility for the efficiency and legality of agency spending overrides his conventional responsibility to the minister.[29]

Indeed, it may be that any intervention that he considers affects the efficient or effective operation of the agency may be brought to the attention of the PAC. Again, however, it is important that the framework is clear. It should state in specific terms the circumstances under which a minister can intervene or overrule the Chief Executive, or ask him to provide additional services not included in the agency plans.[30]

As long as framework documents provide clear definitions of responsibilities, then the PAC should be able to assess the efficiency of an agency and apportion responsibility if its performance is inadequate. The PAC is provided with ammunition by the Comptroller and Auditor General (CAG), who has statutory responsibility to report to Parliament on the economy, efficiency, and effectiveness of government departments, including agencies.[31] Of course, whether this assessment carries the weight necessary to produce changes is another matter. Professor Drewry describes the PAC as having 'an enviable reputation as the one select committee before which even the most exalted permanent secretary can be made to tremble. . . . The Committee's reports can have seismic effects throughout Whitehall.'[32]

However, Clive Ponting, when discussing the personal responsibility of the permanent secretary for the financial affairs of the department, commented: 'there is no real comeback on him

[29] This is a rare procedure, but e.g. in 1975 Peter Carey, 2nd Permanent Secretary in the DTI, submitted an accounting officer's minute relating to Tony Benn's decision to provide funds for the Kirkby Workers' Co-operative (T. Benn, *Against the Tide, Diaries, 1973–76* (London: Hutchinson, 1989), 294, 296–7).

[30] e.g. as in the Vehicle Inspectorate Executive Agency, *Policy and Resources Framework*, which states that such 'special extra activities' shall be 'taken into account in the setting of any relevant statutory fee and shall be referred to in a note appended to the Inspectorate's Accounts'. If the cost cannot be recovered in this way, then 'the Department shall provide reimbursement of reasonable costs incurred by the Inspectorate' (p. 2, B1).   [31] National Audit Act 1983.

[32] Drewry and Butcher, *The Civil Service Today,* 207.

whatever the shortcomings of a department's financial procedures and practices.'[33]

Indeed, according to Ponting, his accountability is 'unsustainable' and one of the 'myths' of British government. However, Ponting ascribes this failing in accountability to the size of modern departments, and it will not therefore be applicable to agencies, whose establishment in part was to remove this problem of size and the problems of locating accountability and blame.

The CAG sees the accounting arrangements of agencies to the PAC as safeguarding 'the principle of accountability to Parliament for funds'.[34] This also expresses its limitation, for accountability to the PAC is financial accountability. The CAG has the remit to examine the effectiveness of programmes in meeting the objectives of government policies, but there is no regular evaluation;[35] and besides, there are wider evaluations of effectiveness that may need to be made. Such evaluations may be in terms of 'the transfer of the voters' preferences into outcomes',[36] or the effectiveness of the delivery of services in improving people's life chances, both of which place the emphasis on the electorate as clients rather than on ministers.

It is the departmental select committees that deal with these wider issues, and there has been uncertainty about the accountability of Chief Executives to these committees. An AO's obligation is to account personally to Parliament through the PAC for his financial responsibilities and to ensure that business is conducted ethically and legally. However, any other accountability is by courtesy of the minister, and thus may be subject to the restrictions imposed by the convention of ministerial responsibility.

Accountability to Departmental Select Committees

The Next Steps had in mind some amendment to the accounting arrangements to accommodate agencies, particularly, it would seem, in relation to select committees. Its intentions, however, were never quite clear. The Report stated: 'We believe it is possible for Parliament, through Ministers, to regard managers as directly responsible

[33] C. Ponting, *Whitehall: Changing the Old Guard* (London: Unwin, 1989), 22.   [34] HC236 (1989), para. 52.
[35] Drewry and Butcher, *The Civil Service Today*, 209.
[36] New Zealand Treasury, *Government Management*.

for operational matters . . .'[37] It added: 'There is nothing new in the suggestion that Ministers should not be held answerable for any day-to-day decisions involving the public services.'[38]

There are indeed many cases where ministers are either distanced, or distance themselves, from day-to-day operational accountability: for example, areas of government which concern decisions involving individual tax or social security cases; quasi-judicial functions, such as immigration appeals; regulatory functions, such as the Office of Fair Trading; some management and executive functions in, for instance, Customs and Excise, and, of course, the nationalized industries. Some of these instances, such as the nationalized industries, involve a clear statutory division of responsibilities, while others are internal departmental arrangements, arising from convention rather than law. This is the case relating to particular aspects of individual tax arrangements: 'there is a very clear constitutional convention that civil servants do not tell Treasury Ministers details of the tax affairs of individual taxpayers.'[39]

Such a convention is in addition to the statutory duty of a tax officer, which is 'not to disclose information otherwise than for the purpose of . . . [his or her] duties'.[40] It provides the individual with greater protection than that offered by law, for it may well be part of a tax officer's duties to give ministers such information if they demand it. It is a conventional rather than a legal operational responsibility that *The Next Steps* had in mind for Chief Executives. The Report suggested:

What is needed is the establishment of a convention that heads of executive agencies would have delegated authority from their Ministers for operations of the agencies within the framework of policy directions and resource allocations prescribed by Ministers. Heads of agencies would be accountable to Ministers for the operations of their agencies, but could be called—as indeed they can now—to give evidence to Select Committees as to the manner in which their delegated authority has been used and their functions discharged within that authority.[41]

This convention of delegation of which *The Next Steps* spoke is puzzling, in terms of both the delegated power it outlines and the relationship of civil servants before select committees. Ministers

---

[37] *The Next Steps*, para. 23.   [38] Ibid., Annex A, para. 4.
[39] HC260 (1989–90), Q27.   [40] Ibid.   [41] *The Next Steps*, Annex A.

delegate all the time. Indeed, there is a presumption that Parliament intends this delegation, for it would be impossible for a minister personally to carry out all the actions for which he is granted power. Nor is delegation in this sense a convention. Officials derive their authority from 'a general rule of law'.[42]

The action of the officials is legally the act of the minister, and of course the constitutional responsibility to Parliament is also borne by the minister, a fact recognized by the courts:

> The duties imposed upon ministers and the powers given to ministers are normally exercised under the authority of the ministers by responsible officials of the department . . . constitutionally, the decision of such an official is, of course, the decision of the minister. The minister is responsible. It is he who must answer before Parliament for anything that his officials have done under his authority . . .[43]

Only when an official is empowered by law to act in his own name, rather than in that of his minister, as for instance when power is given to inspectors to decide certain planning appeals, is the situation different, and a specific delegation by statutory instrument is required.[44]

However, this is not the situation with Chief Executives. Even when answering correspondence from the public and from Members of Parliament in their own names, they do so by virtue of authority delegated from ministers, and these delegated authorities are exercised on the ministers' behalf. Thus Chief Executives are always acting on behalf of their ministers, regardless of how much delegated authority they are given, and this of course is the problem before select committees, for they speak not for themselves but for their ministers.

The Report from the CAG indicated the position of Chief Executives regarding select committees: 'Ministers will . . . regard the Chief Executive as normally being best placed to answer on their behalf before Select Committees in relation to the operation of agencies.'[45]

This is an outline of the traditional position as laid down by the Osmotherly Rules.[46] Ministers recognize the right of select

---

[42] Sir W. Wade, *Administrative Law* (6th edn., Oxford: Clarendon Press, 1988), 359.   [43] *Carltona Ltd.* v. *Commissioners of Works* [1943] 2 All ER.
[44] Town and Country Planning Act 1971, Schedule 9.
[45] HC236 (1989), para. 52.   [46] See Ch. 10.

committees to call named civil servants, while reserving their ultimate right to decide who should appear and answer on their behalf. This is hardly a tenable position for a Chief Executive with personal responsibility for the operational concerns of his agency. He should be in a position to appear before a committee when required. Moreover, he should be able to answer on his own behalf for his own responsibilities.

Since the CAG's report, Sir Robin Butler has clarified the situation, regarding the appearance before select committees of named civil servants.[47] He has stated that there is a duty for an official to appear before a select committee when summoned. His comments were welcomed by the TCSC, which recognized their significance in relation to agency Chief Executives. 'Given our concern that Chief Executives of Next Steps agencies should be accountable to select committees in the same way as other civil servants, we assume that ministers will also accept the right of committees to summon them.'[48]

The expressed wish that Chief Executives should be accountable in 'the same way as other civil servants' would seem to be less than required, given their considerable delegated power and personal responsibility, for such accountability is still on behalf of the minister and therefore can be limited by him. However, Sir Robin Butler has been adamant that the Osmotherly Rules apply to Chief Executives as to all civil servants and that these Rules will not be revised to accommodate any requirement for greater freedom for Chief Executives to answer for their responsibilities rather than on behalf of the minister. He has insisted that nothing has changed in terms of formal accountability. '[Because] accountability is still through ministers to select committees and Parliament generally, I do not think they [the Rules] do need revision on that account.'[49]

This, of course, means that effective questioning may produce ineffective answers because of the limitations imposed, and the protection given, by the Rules. It means that, despite the Chief Executive's responsibility for operational concerns, he speaks only on behalf of, and in accordance with the instructions given by, his minister.

The TCSC believed this to be unsatisfactory and proposed an

---

[47] See Ch. 10.   [48] HC260 (1989–90), para. 22.
[49] HC494–II (1988–9), Q287.

amendment to the accountability of the Chief Executive to select committees, whereby the Chief Executive would be required to explain his decisions and actions, but ultimate accountability would remain with the minister.

We conclude that there must be a modification to the present formal arrangements for accountability. The Chief Executive should give evidence on his own behalf about what he has done as the head of an agency. But if during the course of questioning, a Select Committee is not satisfied with the answers a Chief Executive gives, or finds that the Chief Executive has acted outside his or her area of responsibility, the proper course of action will be to take the matter up with the Minister, who will then be able to go into the matter in depth, remain accountable, and subsequently give an explanation to the committee, which can if appropriate report to the House.[50]

This suggests a widening of the delegated authority given to Chief Executives to include explanatory accountability before select committees. It could be incorporated into the framework document along with the other responsibilities held by the Chief Executive and would not affect the ultimate accountability of ministers for the operation of the agency.

Unlike the nationalized industries, the day-to-day operations of the agency have not been removed from the minister's area of responsibility but delegated. Thus, any dissatisfaction on the part of the select committee with the responses of the Chief Executive can be raised with the minister and he will be responsible for taking whatever amendatory action may be necessary and for providing a full explanation. Moreover, because the minister retains ultimate responsibility, he cannot insist that operational matters are not his concern. There is not, therefore, the same danger of an accountability gap, where the Chief Executive fails to answer adequately but the minister disclaims responsibility.

However, ministers are not prepared for Chief Executives to appear before select committees on their behalf without having some control over what they say. Thus the proposal made by the TCSC was not accepted by the government and the Osmotherly Rules remain unchanged. The government responded to the TCSC:

Chief Executives' authority is delegated to them by Ministers who are and will remain accountable to Parliament as a whole (and its Select

---

[50] HC494–I (1988–9), para. 45.

Committees). The Government therefore believes that the general rule must continue to be that civil servants who give evidence to Select Committees do so on behalf of their Ministers. In practice, where a Committee's interest is confined to the day-to-day operations of an Agency, Ministers will normally regard the Chief Executive as being the person best placed to answer on their behalf. The Chief Executive will be able to give an account to the Committee of how the policies and tasks set out in the framework document have been carried out.[51]

This seems remarkably like a delegation of explanatory accountability for the responsibilities of the Chief Executive. However, it is only a 'practical' arrangement, and thus the sanctity of the doctrine of ministerial responsibility is preserved, and so is the ability of government to frustrate a committee's questioning of civil servants. Despite this, reporting in July 1990, the TCSC stated: 'We are satisfied that Chief Executives are accountable to select committees of the House.' It added: 'we would expect that Chief Executives would always appear as a matter of course before select committees when invited to do so.'[52]

The main question is, however, the extent to which ministers will restrict the evidence they give.

The Separation of Operation and Policy

The concept of agencies is generally seen as requiring a separation of policy—a matter for ministers and departmental officials—and operation. This, of course, presupposes that such a separation can reasonably be made. Moreover, the advantage of such a division would seem to lie with those who make the separation. In some areas it may be possible to make an uncontroversial separation, at least most of the time. Individual complaints by constituents to Members of Parliament are usually concerned with operational matters, or, if not, then the policy issue is clear. However, even then there may be problems of accountability if the categorization into policy and operational, or executive, functions persists, particularly if it is linked with the belief that operational concerns never contain elements of policy. The imprecision produced by an attempted division on this basis was recognized by Peter Kemp: 'I think that it is over-simple and a misrepresentation to say that there

---

[51] Cmnd. 524 (1988), p. 9.   [52] HC 481 (1990–1), para. 65xviii.

is executive work here and there is policy work there. All policy work has an element of execution and all executive work has an element of policy.'[53]

At the highest level within the department there may be a possible, perhaps even necessary, distinction to be made between policy and execution. However, the edges are always blurred, and too frequently so is accountability. The establishment of agencies provides an opportunity to move away from the artifical division. Peter Kemp commented: 'I think people can get over-involved in the question of trying to distinguish policy from execution.'[54]

This is certainly not a distinction that the Project Team wishes to make. Its concern is that a Chief Executive is responsible for the decisions he makes.[55] These responsibilities are laid down in the framework, and will, by the nature of the work of the agency, be mainly executive tasks. However, policy decisions will need to be taken as to how these tasks are performed and these decisions will be for the Chief Executive to make, unless the framework provides otherwise. Indeed, as delegation to agencies increases, it is likely that so too will the policy decisions of this type that are expected from the Chief Executive.

Such a view of accountability is clearly an important move away from the stultifying and at times obstructive division between operations and policy. The essential ingredient is a strong, clear and detailed framework document to prevent the fudging of accountability by either Chief Executives or ministers trying to evade questions by imposing an artifical policy–operations divide. Particularly to be avoided is the imprecise accountability that has existed within the nationalized industries, where many of the arrangements between ministers and chairmen have been informal and undocumented, and the lines between policy and operation have been impossible to draw.

Formality, openness, and clarity thus seem to be the qualities necessary to achieve a true definition of accountability. It is essential that responsibilities can be clearly distinguished. Peter Kemp stated:

It could indeed be and indeed is part of the purpose of Next Steps to try and distinguish just whose fault it is. If, in fact, the shortcoming is such

---

[53] HC494–i (1988–9), Q8.   [54] HC348–i (1988–9), Q21.
[55] Ibid., Q22.

that it was the fault of the lack of resources or legislation which was not within the power of the Chief Executive, the transparency of the system should enable this to be seen. If on the other hand it was simply bad management on the part of the Chief Executive then that should be seen too and the man should be held to account accordingly.[56]

This 'transparency' is an important new dimension and would aid accountability considerably. However, Peter Kemp's examples of ministerial 'fault' or Chief Executive 'fault' are extremes. The system needs to be transparent enough to prevent a blurring of responsibilities in less obvious areas.

The characteristics required may not be easy to sustain, even if originally they are present. There is no guarantee that informality will not develop behind a formal façade. Chief Executives are, after all, still part of the department with a role in long-term policy-making. Again, for purposes of clarity and hence accountability, this role needs to be formally recognized. It should not be 'informal and private, or, as in the case of the nationalised industries, ambiguous'.[57]

Such a policy role is recognized and detailed in the Vehicle Inspectorate framework:

the Inspectorate will be expected to provide any necessary information and advice to policy divisions to assist in policy formation at no additional cost, provided that the costs of provision are small and can be absorbed within existing resources. Where the provision of such information would require a significant resource input on the part of the Inspectorate, the Inspectorate may negotiate with the relevant division an appropriate charge.[58]

The framework does not suggest what might happen if negotiations are unsatisfactory. Perhaps the Chief Executive will be justified in withholding his advice, or the policy division will turn to outsiders who offer advice on more competitive terms. Either scenario would be an interesting development in minister–civil servant relations.

The responsibility of Chief Executives to provide advice on policy is an internal responsibility to the minister and any advice given

[56] HC481 (1990–1), Q31.
[57] HC494–II (1988–9), Memorandum from Leonard Tivey, Appendix 1, p. 84, para. 12.
[58] Vehicle Inspectorate Executive Agency, *Policy and Resources Framework*, Annex 2.5.

is covered by the Osmotherly Rules. The problem posed by a Chief Executive's having such internal policy functions is that it encourages again the divide between policy and operation, and may result in the government ignoring the framework responsibilities and allowing the Chief Executive to answer only on operational matters. Policy decisions, whether inside or outside the framework, may be treated as confidential. Such concern is reinforced by the government's refusal to amend the Osmotherly Rules. This suggests that a Chief Executive's external accountability may not be for all his responsibilities as determined by the framework, but for the 'operational' functions of the agency, with the government deciding what is operational.

Ministerial Interference

There is a further difficulty with any attempt to separate policy and operation and that is the tendency of the government to portray operational or executive functions as being non-political. However, as William Plowden suggested: 'There is always a risk that things that appear to be only of operational executive significance in fact turn out to have a concealed policy content to them.'[59]

This is different from Kemp's point that Chief Executives will inevitably make policy decisions about operations. Here the suggestion is that a minister's policy hides behind an apparent operational decision for which the Chief Executive will be held responsible. This is a concern of the Council of Civil Service Unions, which believes a Chief Executive will be vulnerable generally when things go wrong, even when the fault is the minister's, or has been brought about by ministerial interference.[60]

Even a comprehensive framework, which clearly states the responsibilities of the Chief Executive, will not necessarily protect an agency from ministerial interference. Yet such interference may affect the Chief Executive's ability to manage efficiently, and hence the agency's performance for which he is held accountable.

Ministerial intervention within an agency's territory may pose the most difficult problem for accountability. *The Next Steps* suggested that legislation might be necessary in some instances, 'to

[59] HC494–II (1988–9), Q150.
[60] HC494–II (1988–9), Memorandum from Association of First Division of Civil Servants, para. 10 and Q180.

establish a framework within which the agency can operate with sufficient independence on behalf of the Secretary of State'.[61]

Such legislation would suggest a half-way house between the operational independence of the nationalized industries and the departments, perhaps similar to the limited independence in certain operational areas of the Inland Revenue, which is guaranteed by statute. However, this recommendation was not accepted by the government. Instead, the goodwill and discipline of ministers will be relied upon to ensure a hands-off approach, which in any case can be abandoned if the minister considers that there is 'a wider Government and Parliamentary interest that he has to take into account'.[62]

This is, of course, a subjective judgement by the minister, and, in those areas of government which arouse political interest, it could be frequently exercised. It is not, after all, just an institutional interest with which the minister is concerned, but his own career interest. A minister is unlikely to remain detached as long as ministries are seen as stepping-stones to political advancement.[63] Indeed, the political capital that can be made out of operational successes and the political disasters which may be associated with policy failures make it difficult, and perhaps politically fatal, for a minister not to interfere.

Non-intervention seems likely in areas which are uncontroversial and non-political, such as HMSO, the Meteorological Office, and the Royal Mint. But such agencies are 'hardly in the mainstream of government activity'.[64] However, agencies such as the Employment Agency and the Benefits Agency will be seen as political areas and, as long as there is an equation between a strong ministerial profile and political success, ministers are likely to see their purposes served by intervention rather than detachment.

This could produce a clash of interests between the minister and the Chief Executive, and it may be that the Chief Executive will resist any interference which is likely to affect the performance of the agency on which his salary, and probably his future career, depend. The Chief Executive of the Employment Agency indicated

[61] *The Next Steps*, para. 29.

[62] HC494–II (1988–9), Richard Luce, Q302.

[63] R. Rose, *Ministers and Ministries: A Functional Analysis* (Oxford: Clarendon Press, 1987), 24.

[64] HC494–II (1988–9), Memorandum from Sir Frank Cooper, Appendix 6.

his views about any attempt by the minister to interfere: 'one needs . . . to remind ministers that their practices have to change in the same way that our practices have to change. I mean we're now in the open, out there expected to deliver the stuff, we need to be left alone to get on with it.'[65]

Certainly, if the Chief Executive believes that his minister's interference has financial implications, then, as AO, he will be entitled, even obliged, to record his protest. Moreover, it is possible that hard-pressed Chief Executives may come to view 'financial implications' as being anything that impinges on the efficiency of the agency.

The position of the Chief Executive requires a much higher public profile than that to which departmental civil servants have generally been used. The head of an agency is 'no longer a faceless civil servant'.[66] This public recognition brings substantial accountability of a type more usually associated with politicians than with civil servants, as indicated by the comments of the Chief Executive of the Vehicle Inspectorate: 'People from the press will ring me up to say that I made a public commitment at the time we changed to an executive agency and ask me what progress are you making?'[67]

This change from anonymity to recognition and personal accountability may make it more likely that a Chief Executive will contest a change in policy which he believes makes it impossible for him to fulfil the targets that have been set, or will ask for a revision of the targets in the light of external changes beyond his control. Thus the head of the Employment Agency suggested that he might ask for his performance targets, relating to the placement of the long-term unemployed and to inner-city employment, to be revised if there were a significant downturn in the economy.[68]

However, a civil servant who is appointed as Chief Executive is in a somewhat ambiguous position. He is required to meet performance targets and to provide an efficient and effective service to the customer. He is assessed upon this performance, and indeed his salary is related to it. Moreover, his future success within the service may be related to his proven ability as a manager. All these factors suggest that he should stand firm against departmental interference within his agency.

---

[65] M. Fogden, Chief Executive Employment Agency, in Hennessy, *Analysis*.
[66] HC348–ii (1988–9), Oliver, Chief Executive Vehicle Inspectorate, Q118.
[67] Ibid.   [68] Hennessy, *Analysis*.

Yet the ethos of the civil service militates against such positive action. After all, if the Chief Executive wishes to return to the career mainstream at the end of his contract, he is unlikely to consider it wise to cross his minister, far less the permanent secretary. He may instead choose to get by with 'good old-fashioned fudging and mudging' between the agency and the department.[69] Moreover, his loyalties may go deep: 'There's this umbilical cord, this nexus by which we try to prop each other up and defend each other against policy mistakes.'[70]

The way in which conflicts are resolved probably depends upon the individual Chief Executives. The evidence suggests that the Chief Executives appointed so far are the forerunners of change within the civil service, a change that eventually will result in the 'umbilical cord' being cut. However, until departmental civil servants, seen by Peter Kemp as the 'losers' in the reform, accept such change, Chief Executives may have a struggle on their hands.[71]

Chief Executives appointed from outside the civil service may not face the same conflict. Their interests are likely to be served by producing the best results possible in terms of effectiveness and efficiency. If ministerial interference threatens these results, there are not the traditional loyalties and discipline to prevent open disagreement with the minister. Nor is there necessarily the aversion to public exposure that such a disagreement might bring. The appointment of Chief Executives from outside the civil service may therefore give the system a further jolt.

Clearly the Next Step agencies raise problems of accountability, some of which are similar to those of the nationalized industries. They mainly centre on the extent to which Chief Executives will be free to exercise their delegated responsibilities without ministerial interference, and how far public accountability for these responsibilities will be restricted.

---

[69] G. Mather, Institute of Economic Affairs, in Hennessy, *Analysis*.

[70] Ibid.

[71] Hennessy, *Analysis*. This problem was subsequently confirmed by a survey conducted by Price Waterhouse. The twenty-two Chief Executives interviewed, top civil servants, and the Next Step Team all expressed concern at the degree of contact that still existed between the departments and agencies. 'Virtually all those questioned reported weekly contact with departmental officials, and two or three of them said there was daily contact. Twenty five per cent had weekly contact with ministers' (Price Waterhouse, *Executive Agencies* (3rd edn., Apr. 1991)).

12.3. THE ROLE OF SELECT COMMITTEES: SCRUTINIZING

The accountability of agencies can only be meaningful if they are adequately scrutinized and their effectiveness, as well as their efficiency, is examined. This was made clear by the CAG, who, whilst recognizing that financial accountability to Parliament would be of major significance, pointed out that financial results cannot be the only measure of performance in the public sector.[72]

However, the drive for efficiency may result in a tendency to present evidence as if stating a financial case. Peter Kemp commented: 'I think the agencies will produce reports and accounts rather similar to the way in which responsible organizations, public or private, will produce reports and accounts, and these will be of benefit to Parliament, as shareholders.'[73]

This is an echo of comments made by Sir Peter Parker when he was Chairman of British Rail. He suggested that a select committee hearing was 'in a sense . . . a form of annual meeting with the shareholders' representatives'.[74]

This is a misleading analogy, for the shareholders' concern is usually only with the financial return upon their investment, not with company policy. Indeed, commercial confidence means that policy issues are seldom discussed unless there is a financial crisis. However, the accountability of the nationalized industries to Parliament involves more than the scrutiny of a financial statement. It provides select committees with the right, indeed the duty, to examine all aspects of the workings of these public bodies. This includes 'the right to probe widely and deeply'.[75]

This right will apply to agencies as well. Within the boundaries of the framework, the select committees will be concerned with all decisions made by the Chief Executive, not just the way in which he spends public money.

The financial scrutiny required to assess efficiency will be conducted internally by the parent department and the Treasury, and externally by the National Audit Office, under the CAG and PAC. This may be relatively simple, providing the targets are clear and the means of assessment are laid down within the framework

---

[72] HC494–II (1988–9), Memorandum from the CAG, Appendix 10.
[73] HC494–i (1988–9), Q41.
[74] HC494–II (1988–9), Memorandum from Professor Likierman, Appendix 20.
[75] Ibid.

document. It is the scrutiny of the agency's effectiveness—how good it is at delivering the service—that may at times be more difficult. It is part of the remit of the CAG to examine the effectiveness of government programmes. However, the regular evaluation of effectiveness lacks the emphasis given to efficiency and value for money studies.[76] Effectiveness, particularly in a wider sense, is therefore mainly left for departmental select committees to scrutinize, a scrutiny that increases in difficulty as the network of agencies develops and encompasses more sensitive and political programmes.

Doubts have been expressed as to the suitability, indeed ability, of the departmental select committees to provide scrutiny of the type required. *The Next Steps* noted that select committees tend 'to concentrate on impropriety or incompetence, and making political points, rather than on demanding evidence of steadily improving efficiency and effectiveness'.[77] This was refuted by the TCSC, which stated: 'Certainly impropriety and incompetence are matters of legitimate concern for the House of Commons, but Parliament has also been increasingly successful in demanding evidence of efficiency and effectiveness.'[78]

Yet there may be an understandable tendency to focus on the more glamorous and newsworthy areas of policy and political controversy, rather than on the mundane and perhaps tedious monitoring of policy implementation. Indeed, this has shown itself with the monitoring of the nationalized industries.

Committees have varied in their effectiveness, but Professor Likierman commented:

Oral evidence sessions themselves have not always been wholly satisfactory. Many Committee Members have found the degree of detail required in preparation for these sessions, as well as the sessions themselves, to be too technical and not of sufficient political interest. Nor do many members have the financial or managerial background to feel confident in following up some of the technical aspects of the questions.[79]

This may be equally applicable to the monitoring of agencies, where financial and management understanding may at times be necessary to ask the right questions.

---

[76] Drewry and Butcher, 209.   [77] *The Next Steps*, para. 9.
[78] HC494-I (1988–9), para. 40.
[79] HC494-II (1988–9), Memorandum from Professor Likierman, Appendix 20.

However, in other aspects select committees should be better placed to scrutinize agencies than they have been to monitor the nationalized industries. First, the select committee system is well established now, whereas with the nationalized industries parliamentary control was imposed upon the already established departmental control system with all its informalities and ambiguities.[80] Secondly, the select committees will have the advantage of the framework documents, which promise to set out in clear terms the responsibilities of the minister and the Chief Executive. Such documents must, however, be scrutinized, and select committee members may not always possess the will to do this. 'Committees may prefer not to review the operational framework. They may feel they have other things to do . . .'[81]

The framework document lists the reports and accounts that the Chief Executive has to produce and on which he is assessed. These presumably will be made available to select committees, if not automatically then at least on request. The document will not, however, alert the committee to internal reports which may be relevant to any assessment of effectiveness. Nor will it necessarily alleviate the complaint made by the TCSC that it is often hampered in its task of collecting evidence concerning effectiveness by 'the lack of the right kind of information and the obscure way in which the information made available is presented'.[82]

The requirement, therefore, is for all relevant reports to be made available to select committees and for them to be in a form which is 'user friendly'. Only then will committee members be in a position to monitor the effectiveness of agencies and ensure that the Chief Executive is accountable for the running of the agency.

12.4. NEXT STEPS AGENCIES AND THE NEED TO REVISE INDIVIDUAL MINISTERIAL RESPONSIBILITY

The Next Steps and the subsequent establishment of agencies has raised again the issue of accountability in the British system of government. Claims that the delivery of government services by executive agencies will improve accountability have been countered

---

[80] HC494–II (1989–9), Memorandum from Leonard Tivey, p. 84, para. 4.
[81] HC494–II (1988–9), Professor Drewry, Q162.
[82] HC494–II (1988–9), para. 41.

by claims that such a development will result in accountability becoming more imprecise, elusive, and even evasive.

In an 'optimistic' perspective (that is, with more and better accountability) there would be increased accountability at all levels and to all interested parties. Agency heads would account both to ministers and to select committees for their responsibilities within the framework agreement, and the production of detailed reports by the agencies would ensure that the committees were better informed and so better able to scrutinize the performance of the agency within the framework agreement. Ministers would retain responsibility for policy and answer before select committees for this. Moreover, they would also answer questions on the Floor of the House for both policy and operations, although complaints concerning agency matters would generally be directed at the Chief Executive or local managers, where they would be dealt with efficiently and effectively.

A more 'pessimistic' analysis, however, would suggest that, whilst internal accountability, that is the accountability of the agency to the minister, may be more effective, external accountability would be weaker. The minister, although retaining overall responsibility, would in practice be accountable only for policy, and this would not be counterbalanced by full operational accountability from the agency head through select committees to Parliament. He would adopt the conventional attitude that his responsibility to Parliament could only be through, and on behalf of, his minister. Furthermore, there would be a fudging of lines of responsibility, with an inability to separate policy from operation, or a masking of policy within operations. This analysis also indicates a weakness within the system of scrutiny. If agency reports are produced as financial statements demonstrating efficiency against their set targets, few select committee members will have the expertise or the interest to scrutinize them. Even if reports are produced as management documents, most Members of Parliament lack the management skills required to ask the right questions, and lack the time to cultivate such skills. Besides, Members are more interested in policy than in management. Parliament may, therefore, be unable to take advantage of any increased opportunities to scrutinize the internal workings of government.

The establishment of the first agencies would seem to diminish some of the fears. Their responsibilities are clearly defined in the framework documents, and targets have been set and made public. Moreover, Chief Executives talk openly about their accountability and the need for vigilance to prevent departmental interference.[83] However, there does need to be a distinction made between internal and external accountability.

In terms of internal accountability the responsibility of the Chief Executive for his delegated powers as detailed in the framework document is a significant progression in personal accountability along the route already travelled by the Management Information System for Ministers (MINIS) and FMI. However, this meaningful managerial accountability of the Chief Executive seems to conflict with the external political accountability of the minister to Parliament, at least in the way in which the convention of ministerial responsibility is understood at present. The political accountability of the minister for the operation of the agency, as well as the policies associated with it, would seem to encourage interference by the minister rather than the hands-off approach required. Indeed, it may be that 'individual responsibility for management in any area may therefore be possible only in reverse proportion to the level of interest in that area shown by Parliament'.[84]

This need not necessarily blur accountability. However, it does raise questions about the suitability for agency status of the more politically sensitive government services. Agencies such as Benefits and Employment would seem likely to be subject to a degree of political attention that could be detrimental to managerial independence. Alternatively, they may become 'de-politicized', with the emphasis being on the efficiency of the service delivery rather than what is actually being delivered; that is, on the output rather than the outcome.

There have been changes made in exernal accountability, the most significant of which is that Chief Executives now have AO or AAO status. However, this only ensures the personal accountability of the Chief Executive for the financial affairs of the agency

---

[83] One agency chief told Price Waterhouse that 'the enthusiasm of the centre for departmental policies and consistency requires constant vigilance if Next Steps is to be realised in practice' (Price Waterhouse, *Executive Agencies* (3rd edn., Apr. 1991)). However, a year later Price Waterhouse reported that 'working out relations with the parent department' appeared 'significantly less dominant in the lives of chief executives' (Price Waterhouse, *Executive Agencies* (5th edn., Mar. 1992)).

[84] *Third Report from the Treasury and Civil Service Committee: Efficiency and Effectiveness in the Civil Service* (1982), HC236, HMSO.

to the PAC. There is no further accountability to departmental select committees that derives from AO status, nor indeed from the position of Chief Executive.

The Next Steps Project Manager, Peter Kemp, expressed the accountability of the Chief Executive as being for the decisions he makes when exercising the powers delegated to him in the framework document. This would certainly provide for the greatest clarity of accountability, removing the artificial division between 'policy' and 'operations', a division which has proved so obstructive where accountability is concerned. However, it may remain an aspiration, for the government has refused to contemplate a revision of the Osmotherly Rules, which contain the policy–operational divide.

This may lead to the conclusion that, while the government is concerned with the efficient and effective delivery of services, it is not concerned with effective accountability. Certainly, there has been no attempt to devise a strategy for accountability. The emphasis has been on preserving the convention of individual responsibility, despite the fact that aspects of the convention may already be changing and that the establishment of agencies is likely to accelerate this change. Chief Executives will not be anonymous civil servants, but named and known managers with acknowledged responsibilities. Moreover, both Members of Parliament and members of the public are encouraged to write to them about these responsibilities. In addition, the whole ethos of the agency concept is founded on the personal accountability of the Chief Executive, and upon his taking responsibility for his actions. This does not in itself provide for improved public accountability, but it may affect the traditional relationship between ministers and civil servants and make inappropriate the requirement that Chief Executives give evidence to select committees only on behalf of the minister.

More than ever, therefore, it becomes a façade for a minister to assume sole explanatory accountability for the management affairs of a government unit. This does not mean, however, that he should no longer have ultimate responsibility. Indeed, this is imperative to avoid the situation of the minister disclaiming responsibility for matters which have not been resolved satisfactorily by the Chief Executive. The requirement is for the minister to delegate managerial and operational powers to a Chief Executive along with accountability for the use of those powers. This in practice is the situation with regard to answering correspondence. It should also apply to answering questions before select committees.

Delegating such responsibility would not enable ministers to escape from their overall responsibility to the House. The political sanction of raising an issue on the Floor of the House would remain, and ministers would still be accountable to select committees both for policy and for any inadequacies in the performance of a Chief Executive before a committee.

The establishment of agencies to deliver most of the services of government offers the ideal opportunity to strengthen the convention of ministerial responsibility by giving it a clear and realistic structure. Instead, the accountability it represents looks uncertain and confused. There is, on the one hand, recognition of the individual responsibility of the Chief Executive and, on the other, insistence that he only operates and speaks on behalf of his minister. This refusal of government to develop a logical system of operational accountability for agencies does nothing to counter suggestions that the convention of individual ministerial responsibility is being used as a means of retaining control over information, while at the same time enabling ministers to distance themselves from mistakes made in the agency.

All the evidence suggests that constitutional change is not on the agenda as far as ministers are concerned. However, there are indications that some civil servants are prepared to accept, indeed would welcome, an amendment to the arrangements for public accountability. The Council of Civil Service Unions, whilst acknowledging that ministerial responsibility plays a 'crucial part' in democratic control, has stated: 'We as civil servants, though our members would be the ones perhaps in the forefront of any criticism, do believe we should be held accountable for the service we provide . . .'[85]

This sentiment, indeed such confidence, needs to be extended upwards (as far as the Cabinet Secretary and Head of the Civil Service) and outwards, so that the modernization of accountability can take place along with the modernization of the civil service. The evidence suggests that those who have taken Chief Executive

---

[85] *Treasury and Civil Service Committee: Developments in the Next Steps Programme, Minutes of Evidence* (1988–9), HC348–iv, HMSO, Q222.

appointments, and their managerial staff, are prepared, even eager, to move away from the protection offered by ministerial responsibility, although this may not be the case with departmental civil servants. However, the establishment of agencies is now well under way, with just over half the civil service affected by mid-1992. The programme is expected to be complete by the end of 1993, when three out of four civil servants will work in executive agencies.

Such a reform needs a corresponding change in accountability if it is to gain full political acceptance. Ultimately it would seem to require the establishment of a system of administrative law procedures to process individual grievances. This would relieve the anxiety that ministers may disclaim responsibility for agency affairs, thereby leaving the citizen without redress in a dispute with the Chief Executive. The Citizen's Charter, whilst important in the focus it places on the consumer or client, is not a substitute for formal grievance procedures. However, as a first step, it would be appropriate to see an amendment to the convention of individual ministerial responsibility which would ensure the full accountability of the executive agencies to select committees.

PART FOUR

Conclusion

13

Comparative Perspectives on Accountability and Constitutional Reform

13.1. INTRODUCTION

Part Three examined the reform of the select committee system and the changes within the civil service, both of which have an impact upon the operation of ministerial responsibility. A significant feature of these reforms, which were conceived and executed independently of each other, is that they have been undertaken in isolation from wider concerns about public accountability.

Indeed, whilst the reform of the select committee system at least engendered debate about the possible implications for ministerial accountability, the changes in the structure and operation of the civil service have not been related to any consideration of the constitution. The rationale behind the establishment of Next Steps agencies has been the government's requirement that the delivery of public services should be made more efficient, where possible by transferring functions to the private sector and elsewhere by introducing private-sector methods of management to the public sector. Public accountability has not been on the agenda for reform or even discussion. There has been no overall perspective on, or theory of, accountability nor any attempt to co-ordinate management reforms and constitutional requirements.

It is not just the government which has been constitutionally complacent or indifferent with regard to the establishment of executive agencies. Parliament too has shown little constitutional concern. Discussions relating to the implications of Next Steps agencies have been confined mainly to the subcommittee of the TCSC, which has monitored their development. The debate has not extended outwards, either geographically to the Floor of the House, or in content to include wider issues of public accountability. The approach in Britain contrasts with that in both Australia and New Zealand, where there have been similar concerns about improving the efficiency of the public service, but these have been coupled with concerns about accountability. Particularly important has been the need to strengthen the accountability of senior public servants and their responsiveness to the political executive.[1]

Both countries have also endeavoured to fit accountability into the wider perspective of their constitutional arrangements. In New Zealand this has resulted in a radical reform of government departments, the direct accountability of departmental heads to Parliament, and more open government. In Australia the reform of the public service has been within the context of extensive constitutional reform which has aimed at producing a coherent system of public accountability. The reforms undertaken in both countries have had their critics. In New Zealand the most frequent criticism has been that far-reaching reforms were imposed upon a reluctant public service and may be damaging to the public-service ethos.[2] In Australia critics note the increased expenditure involved in making government more open and accountable, at times to the detriment of efficiency.[3] Nevertheless the approaches taken offer valuable perspectives on the relationship between public accountability and efficiency. They suggest ways in which both can be improved within the Westminster system of government and the confines of ministerial responsibility, and highlight the lack of constitutional thinking underlying the British reforms.

13.2. THE NEW ZEALAND MODEL

In New Zealand, as in Britain, the concern has been to increase the efficiency and effectiveness of the public (civil) service. The method chosen has similarly been to provide managers with a greater freedom to manage within strengthened structures of accountability. However, while in Britain *The Next Steps* viewed accountability as mainly a managerial device to provide efficiency, the New Zealand debate has addressed accountability as a consti-

[1] R. J. Gregory, 'The Attitudes of Senior Public Servants in Australia and New Zealand: Administrative Reform and Technocratic Consequences?', *Governance*, 4/3 (1991), 296.   [2] Ibid.
[3] See Ch. 14 for a discussion of the criticisms.

tutional issue. In particular there has been concern to strengthen the accountability of senior civil servants to the political process. Efficiency and public accountability have therefore been seen as interdependent.

The Report from the New Zealand Treasury, which triggered the reforms, stated:

The starting point in considering the way in which the conduct of government may be most effectively administered is . . . our unwritten constitution. . . . The extent to which that constitution enables the preference of the electorate to be transformed into action, and the strength of accountability of the Government and Parliament for that action, will be a determining factor in shaping the nature of administration.[4]

This approach to reform has therefore produced a co-ordination of efficiency and constitutional accountability which is in sharp contrast to the piecemeal changes in accountability that the Next Steps efficiency reforms have produced.

Departmental Restructuring

The reforms themselves have been much more radical, involving a fundamental restructuring of departments and the public service.[5] Within departments there has been a separation into advice and administration units or agencies, and managers have been given the increased discretion and personal responsibility associated with the Next Steps agencies. The difference between New Zealand and British reforms lies in the application of the agency concept to policy advice as well as to operations. Operational or administrative agencies do not, therefore, report to policy departments, as in Britain, for policy advice is itself an agency of the core department. Moreover, operational agencies are not expected to make an input into the policy advice function of the department, as is frequently the case with Next Steps agencies.

---

[4] New Zealand Treasury, *Government Management*, 51.

[5] Unlike the British experience, privatization has not featured on the political agenda. There has, however, been a separation of commercial and non-commercial activities, with nine areas being designated 'commercial' and established under the *State Owned Enterprises Act 1986* as State Owned Enterprises. The Act ensures accountability to Parliament through two ministers who are designated 'shareholders'.

Chief Executives

This restructuring of departments has had a fundamental effect upon the role of the permanent secretary and his relationship with the minister. His responsibilities have been given legal definition and all powers delegated to him must be specified in writing.[6] He is no longer a 'permanent' secretary but a chief executive, working to a specific five-year contract agreed with the minister,[7] and, in a radical move of decentralization, he has become the employer of all staff within the department.[8] The performance of the chief executive in all spheres is monitored by the State Sector Commission, which acts for the minister and is assisted by a Cabinet Committee.

The New Zealand reforms employ a different (and perhaps less confusing) division of responsibilities as compared with the Next Steps division. Chief executives and agency heads are monitored strictly on 'outputs'—that is, the service or the goods they deliver. They are not responsible for 'outcomes', which concern the effect of the outputs on the community. These remain the responsibility of the minister, along with the initial policy or strategy choice. This monitoring of outputs extends to the advice agencies, for policy advice is regarded as an output and therefore can be evaluated to ensure that it provides an appropriate range of options. In Britain monitoring is for responsibilities within the framework document, but this can result in a mix of output—outcome responsibilities.

Included in the New Zealand reforms is the legal requirement for chief executives to report to Parliament on the outputs of their departments. Indeed, the funds approved by Parliament are linked to the performance of departments, and departments have to

---

[6] The *State Sector Act No 20*, 1988, s32, lists responsibilities as including the carrying-out of the functions and duties of the department, being responsible for its general conduct, tendering advice, and being responsible for the efficient, effective, and economic management of the department. More recently consultation with other departments has been added (J. Boston, 'The Problems of Policy Coordination: the New Zealand Experience', *Governance*, 5/1 (1992), 94).

[7] The contract is for a maximum of five years and is renewable (s38).

[8] In this capacity he makes decisions about the number and type of staff, appointments, and dismissals, and eventually he will take over negotiations with the unions on pay and conditions of staff, although there will be a degree of co-ordination by the State Sector Commission (the New Zealand equivalent of Civil Service Commission).

provide adequate information and meet certain standards in providing the proof of this performance.[9] This is a far more exacting accountability than that of British departments to the PAC, although the Next Steps agencies may come closer to realizing it. However, they will at best provide only windows of more intense accountability, while departmental accountability remains as before.

The retention by New Zealand ministers of responsibility for the choice of outputs and for outcomes ensures that they are answerable for 'political' matters. However, as the New Zealand CAG reported, at present the mechanism for their accountability falls short of that expected of chief executives. There is certainly no legal requirement for ministers to produce documentation or statements of performance, as there is for departments, and the CAG commented: 'This is a significant omission in what is otherwise a well-structured set of accountability and reporting procedures.'[10]

The New Zealand Select Committee on Finance and Expenditure suggested that Parliament should consider how best to cover these criticisms made by the Comptroller. This in itself indicates a different approach from the British reforms, where the TCSC refers matters concerning improved mechanisms for accountability to the government not Parliament. This supports the overriding assumption of the British Constitution that Parliament is not government; a separation of powers, or division of labour, has been built into a formally fused system. It is also a recognition by the select committee that power is located within the executive, and that Parliament, as an institution, is either unable or unwilling to force change upon ministers.

As with the Next Steps reforms, there is debate as to how the reforms in the public sector in New Zealand will affect ministerial accountability. The inclusion of departmental heads within the reforms would indicate a far more radical change in the relationship between the minister and his civil servants than the change in Britain. The permanent secretary has become in name and function far more like a private sector chief executive with all the power and responsibility that is entailed. His accountability to his minister and to Parliament would seem likely to make visible not

---

[9] *Public Finance Act 1989.*

[10] *Finance and Expenditure Select Committee Report* (1989), 18, referred to in G. Scott, P. Bushnell, and N. Sallee, 'Reform of the Core Public Sector: The New Zealand Experience', *Governance*, 3/2 (1990), 215–30.

just operational aspects of government but also policy-making. Indeed, the system of reporting and monitoring should 'allow the results of political decisions to be seen' along with any political arm-twisting that may have occurred.[11]

Official Information Act 1982

This openness is aided in New Zealand by the Official Information Act 1982, which ensures a greater release of information than in Britain, whilst adhering to the principle of ministerial accountability to Parliament. An interesting feature of the Act is that this adherence is expressed 'for the time being'. This suggests an openness of thinking about the mechanisms of accountability or the possibility of future change, although for the moment New Zealand has limited the accounting mechanisms for the release of information to the political process, excluding the courts.

However, despite the greater potential for transparency (a favourite word in all such reforms), success still depends upon ministers and public servants accepting the new culture and responding to the ethos behind the reforms. As in Britain, ministers will need to resist the temptation to interfere, and chief executives must concentrate on managing their departments.

Increased Ministerial Control

The New Zealand reforms would seem to bring the top public servants under greater ministerial control, for, whilst the new chief executives have greater freedom to manage, ministers have more effective mechanisms for bringing them to account. This should mean that the accountability of ministers to Parliament is in turn enhanced and that it more accurately reflects their actual responsibilities. This point was made in the Treasury Report that advocated the reforms:

An increase in the personal accountability of public servants would recognize an increase in their responsibility; this increase in responsibility has in fact been occurring for a long time with the increasing complexity of administration. . . .

[11] Scott *et al.*, 'Reform of the Core Public Sector', 215.

However, this increasing responsibility of public servants for decision-making, coupled with proposed accountability for these decisions, does not imply a weakening of ministerial accountability. Quite the reverse; since Ministers would have much greater control over the means to ensure that their objectives were met by departmental managers, they could be held to account much more directly than at present for the performance of their departments.[12]

Thus the minister retains overall responsibility for his department but within a structure which provides for, indeed requires, the direct accountability to Parliament of public servants for their responsibilities.

13.3. THE AUSTRALIAN MODEL

In Australia the need for greater efficiency in the provision of services has been tempered by concern to produce an overall improvement in public accountability, first, by improving Parliament's role as scrutineer, and, secondly, by reforming the public service and bringing it under closer ministerial control. The reforms, therefore, have a different focus from those in Britain and New Zealand, where the entire role of government as a provider of services has been under review.

However, many of the reforms reflect those in Britain, and more particularly New Zealand. There has been a similar devolution of managerial responsibilities, the central personnel function has been abolished, and procedures to measure performance and to review programmes have been installed. There has also been a restructuring of departments into 'super-departments', changed procedures for appointing departmental heads with the government of the day being given much more flexibility in their appointment and deployment,[13] the opening of top public service positions to open competition, and the appointment by ministers of non-public service advisers.

Increased Accountability to Parliament

However, the needs of accountability have been particularly served by the establishment of procedures which ensure that Parliament

[12] New Zealand Treasury, *Government Management*, 64.
[13] Gregory, 'The Attitudes of Senior Public Servants in Australia and New Zealand'.

has the necessary information on which to make judgements. The main way in which this information is presented is through 'explanatory notes' for each programme. These are presented together with the annual budget for consideration by Parliament and provide details of the specific objectives for each programme along with financial information and, wherever possible, quantitative information concerning performance. In programmes concerned with policy advice, such quantitative information is unlikely to be available, or indeed relevant, and in such cases a 'qualitative assessment' is included.[14]

The other major accounting document is the annual report to the minister, which is produced by the head of the department or agency. This corresponds more closely to its British counterpart. Internal accountability therefore appears to be similar, but external accountability in Australia would seem to be more extensive and provide better opportunities for Parliament to hold the minister, and through him the relevant public servant, to account.

A Programme of Constitutional Reform

The public-service changes are the latest in an overall reform of the constitution which has developed since the mid-1970s and which has involved public debate and participation. This may explain why departmental reforms have emphasized accountability rather than efficiency, and why safeguarding the rights of the citizen has been a high priority. The concern has been to legitimize the public service by bringing it firmly under ministerial control and by providing the citizen with the means of redress against the decisions and actions of administrators. The resulting reforms have been part of an overall strategy which is kept constantly under review.[15] They are not the outcome of inconsequential tinkering, nor have they evaded the constraints of ministerial responsibility.

The safeguarding of the rights of the citizen has been accomplished through the establishment of an Administrative Appeals Tribunal and an Ombudsman and by passing a Freedom of Information Act. None of these directly aids efficiency, and they may

---

[14] M. Keating, and M. Holmes, 'Australia's Budgetary and Financial Management Reforms', *Government*, 3/2 (1990), 180.

[15] Administrative Review Tribunal established under the *Administrative Appeals Tribunal Act 1975*.

even be detrimental to it. The Australian experience suggests that in a democracy it may be necessary to make a choice (or rather a trade-off) between the priorities of public accountability and government efficiency, for it may not be possible for them to be served equally. There has not as yet been recognition in Britain that such a choice may sometime be required.

The Australian reforms have in part been brought about by the creation of new institutions. These include a Commonwealth Ombudsman and an Administrative Appeals Tribunal (AAT). The Ombudsman, in contrast to his British counterpart, receives complaints directly from the public rather than through Members of Parliament and can initiate his own investigations. The AAT has developed as the central focus for the review of administrative action on its merits and has the power to determine the correct or preferred decision, even if this decision is in conflict with departmental policy. Such an approach clearly has implications for the convention of ministerial responsibility, and this was one of the reasons why such a body was rejected in Britain by the JUSTICE–All Souls Committee (1988), which saw its adoption as 'substitut[ing] for ministerial answerability in Parliament an unaccountable policy-making tribunal'.[16]

Similar criticisms have surfaced in Australia, although it would appear that the tribunal, mindful of the problems, has exercised self-restraint, differentiating between ministerial policy and departmental or administrative policy. It has indicated that ministerial policies will normally be followed unless there is evidence that they are unlawful or produce an unjust decision in a particular case. Moreover, where a policy has been exposed to parliamentary scrutiny, 'cogent reasons' are required before the tribunal will depart from it.[17]

There is, in addition, a political restraint upon the tribunal's powers, for its jurisdiction in any area is conferred by statute and can therefore be denied if it is considered more appropriate for ministers to retain complete accountability. However, the denial of jurisdiction cannot be made without particular reference to Parliament, where two standing Senate Committees are required

---

[16] JUSTICE–All Souls Review of Administrative Law in the United Kingdom, *Administrative Justice: Some Necessary Reforms* (London, 1988).

[17] J. Griffiths, 'Australian Administrative Law: Institutions, Reforms and Impact', *Public Administration*, 63/4 (1985), 445–62.

to report on any proposed legislation affecting the rights and liberties of citizens for which there is no provision for review on its merits.[18] Such an arrangement provides an important check upon the government, the source of most legislation, as well as enhancing the power of Parliament. The central place of Parliament within the constitution is evident in the reforms, which also include a Freedom of Information Act. This provides that the minister is accountable to Parliament rather than to the courts for the exercise of his discretion to withhold information. Parliament thus retains its constitutional right to bring ministers to account for political decisions.

The Australian reforms have also included the reform of judicial review by, amongst other things, simplifying the procedure for obtaining review, codifying the grounds, and requiring that upon request a statement of reasons for a reviewable decision must be given by the administration.[19] This requirement for reasons was supported in Britain by the JUSTICE–All Souls review on administrative law (1988), which proposed a change in the law to give it effect. No such legislation has been forthcoming.[20] The Australian reforms in judicial review and the establishment of both the AAT and the Commonwealth Ombudsman provide additional methods of accountability. They do not detract from the accountability of ministers to Parliament. Rather they supplement accountability, particularly for administrative malpractice and individual administrative mistakes.

The Australian experience is not without its problems, notably its cost both in money and manpower. Further there is always likely to be a divergence of opinion over the powers given to such bodies as the Administrative Appeals Tribunal. However, the establishment of the Tribunal, even if controversial, is important because it is a recognition by the government and Parliament that ministerial responsibility is not by itself an adequate mechanism

---

[18] Ibid.

[19] *The Administrative Decisions (Judicial Review) Act 1977*, which came into force in 1980.

[20] There have been indications that in the absence of legislation the requirement for reasons may be developed by the courts; e.g. In R v. *Civil Service Board ex parte Cunningham* (Indep. 30/5/90), it was held that reasons may be required in 'exceptional circumstances'. In R v. *Secretary of State for Home Department ex parte Doody* (TLR 8/5/92) it was held that the failure to give reasons might in certain circumstances result in the decision being challenged for irrationality.

for accountability in modern government. The minister's political accountability to Parliament and his legal accountability to the courts are not a sufficient check on the exercise of public power or a safeguard against its abuse. The arrangements need to be diverse and move through a spectrum of accountability in which Parliament, the Ombudsman, tribunals, and the courts all play a part.

13.4. THE BRITISH MODEL

In Britain there has been no attempt to take an overall perspective of public accountability, although the reforms of both the select committee system and the civil service have provided ideal opportunities for a wider review. Moreover, too frequently ministerial responsibility seems to be an impediment to the developments that have happened elsewhere. Any changes that threaten to impinge upon the power of government or Parliament through a diminution of the convention of ministerial responsibility seem unlikely to succeed.

Ministerial Responsibility and Freedom of Information

The need to retain the uncompromised accountability of ministers to Parliament has featured consistently in any response by the British government to the passage of a Freedom of Information Act. The Green Paper on Open Government in 1979 stated:

In the Government's judgement further steps designed to achieve greater openness must be fully in accord with our constitutional tradition and practice which has developed in this country. Nothing must be allowed to detract from the basic principle of Ministerial accountability to Parliament . . .[21]

The Australian and New Zealand models indicate that it is possible to increase the openness of government whilst retaining the accountability of ministers to Parliament. Moreover, such openness would seem to be in accord with one of the benefits attributed to Next Steps, making government more 'transparent'. One

[21] *Open Government* (1979), Cmnd. 7520, HMSO, para. 2.

of the most positive aspects of the Next Steps agencies is the greater amount of information that it seems will be made available. However, the material released will only be a small part of the departmental total, most of which will not be consistently open to public scrutiny. The inaccessibility of much of this information, indeed the public ignorance of the existence of some of it, hinders the work of select committees and obstructs the cause of public accountability.

At present, however, the purported aim of transparent government conflicts with the insistence of government that information should remain in the hands of ministers. Inadvertently the government indicated the problem this presents for accountability.

[ministerial responsibility] is the hub around which so much of our administrative and political life revolves. . . . In essence, it means that Ministers have to provide information about the exercise of their responsibilities in order that an account can be rendered to Parliament.[22]

Thus Parliament is dependent upon ministers providing the necessary information so that they can be held accountable. When, as is frequently the case, the provision of information is inadequate, then so too is accountability. There has been a commitment by John Major to more open government, and some previously secret documents have entered the public domain, *Questions of Procedure for Ministers* being an important example. However, without a Freedom of Information Act, the situation remains that the government retains the initiative over the release of information, and the expectation is still that secrecy will prevail.[23]

The Ombudsman and Tribunals as Mechanisms of Accountability

As in New Zealand and Australia, public accountability in Britain is not confined to the political accountability of ministers to Parliament and its select committees. The Parliamentary Commissioner for Administration (or Ombudsman), specialist tribunals, and the courts all provide avenues of accountability. However, the

---

[22] Ibid., para. 11.
[23] The signing by ministers, as a matter of duty, of Public Interest Immunity Certificates in the Matrix Churchill (arms to Iraq) case (Nov. 1992) is indicative of the tendency to secrecy of British government.

effectiveness of these mechanisms may be questioned. The number of cases of maladministration with which the Ombudsman can deal is limited by the procedural requirement that complaints must be referred through Members of Parliament and by the resources made available to the office of the Ombudsman. During the period 1980–8 a total of 803 cases were referred to the Ombudsman but only 20–30 per cent were investigated.[24] The tribunal system too is a long way from providing an integrated and coherent network through which the accountability of administrators can be ensured. This is partly because of the variation and number of tribunals in Britain,[25] but also because of the lack of consistency in the subjects which are referred to tribunals. The Council on Tribunals (1980) reported:

Parliament's selection of subjects to be referred to tribunals . . . does not form a regular pattern. Certain basic guidelines can be detected, but the choice is influenced by the interplay of various factors—the nature of the decisions, accidents of history, departmental preferences and political considerations—rather than by a coherent set of principles.[26]

This absence of 'a coherent set of principles' with regard to tribunals may be seen as a reflection of the overall lack of cohesion concerning the ways in which public accountability can be provided.

The Courts

The extent to which the courts can be seen as reliable vehicles for producing accountability is also debatable. The procedural complexities and the requirements of standing necessary for an individual to be able to bring an action for judicial review have been detrimental to an accessible and effective system. Moreover, this has been compounded by a lack of clarity concerning the areas over which the courts are prepared to exert their jurisdiction. There are many indications that the principle of ministerial accountability to Parliament has inhibited the development of the

[24] Turpin, *British Government and the Constitution.*
[25] De Smith identifies fifty different types of tribunal and some 2,000 tribunals altogether (S. de Smith, and R. Brazier, *Constitutional and Administrative Law* (6th edn., London: Pelican, 1989)).
[26] *Special Report by the Council on Tribunals: The Functions of the Council on Tribunals* (1980), Cmnd. 7805, HMSO.

judicial role, serving to limit the jurisdiction of the courts and in some instances to provide a justification for the lack of judicial intervention.

This has been especially evident in decisions concerning national security, which the judges have consistently asserted is the responsibility of the government and not the courts. Judicial statements imply that the lack of legal accountability is compensated by the minister's answerability to Parliament, or that, because of this political answerability, accountability to the courts is not required. Such attitudes are clearly expressed in cases which concern the issuing by the Home Secretary of deportation orders on the grounds of national security. Thus in 1977, when the Court of Appeal refused to review the controversial decision of the Home Secretary to deport a journalist in the interests of national security, Lord Denning stated: 'He [the Home Secretary] is answerable to Parliament as to the way in which he did it, not to the courts here.'[27]

More recently in two separate cases this doctrine of answerability to Parliament has been restated, and the refusal of the courts to review deportation notices has been confirmed by Lord Justice Mann, who held:

The Home Secretary was accountable to Parliament for his decisions. Although the Home Secretary was subject to the court's jurisdiction, the exercise of the jurisdiction in national security cases was necessarily restricted . . . by the subject matter. National security was the exclusive responsibility of the Executive.[28]

Subsequently, Lord Justice Mann indicated the effect on the role of the courts that the responsibility of ministers to Parliament has in such instances: 'The Home Secretary, who had himself taken the decision, was answerable for those decisions to Parliament. The judicial role was circumscribed.'[29]

A total restriction of the judicial role is exceptional, but the fact that in constitutional theory ministers are accountable to Parliament provides a constitutional justification, even requirement, for judicial restraint. The role of the courts in reviewing government

[27] R v. *Secretary of State for Home Affairs, ex p. Hosenball* [1977] WLR 766.
[28] R v. *Secretary of State for the Home Department, ex p. Chebiak* (Indep. 7/2/91).
[29] R v. *Secretary of State for the Home Department, ex p. B* (Indep. 29/1/91).

actions, where there is political accountability, is thus firmly confined to the lawfulness or otherwise of the decision or action. In
a series of cases during the 1980s the position of judicial review
in a system where there is also accountability to Parliament has
been considered.[30] The leading statement came from the House of
Lords:

> It is not . . . a sufficient answer to say that judicial review of the actions
> of officers or departments of central government is unnecessary because
> they are accountable to Parliament for the way in which they carry out
> their functions. They are accountable to Parliament for what they do as
> regards efficiency and policy, and of that Parliament is the only judge;
> they are responsible to a court of justice for the lawfulness of what they
> do, and of that the court is the only judge.[31]

Such comments by the courts emphasize the traditional view
that the constitution requires these twin aspects of accountability:
Parliament holds ministers to account for 'efficiency and policy'
and the courts hold them to account for 'lawfulness'. It is implied
that accountability is thus complete. Further judicial pronounce-
ments suggest mistakenly that ministers can no more escape their
conventional obligations to Parliament than they can their legal
obligations to the courts. 'This condition [responsibility to Parlia-
ment] is inherent in the constitutional doctrines of parliamentary
government and ministerial responsibility, and Ministers can neither
waive it nor escape it.'[32]

This statement neglects the fact that ministers may escape
accountability to both Parliament and the courts if they plead
national security, public interest, or confidentiality.[33] More im-

---

[30] *Inland Revenue Commissioners* v. *National Federation of Self-Employed and Small Businesses Ltd* [1982] AC 617. The sentiment was similarly stated and sup-
ported in *Preston* v. *IRC* [1985] 2 All ER 327; *Nottingham County Council* v. *SOS for Environment* [1986] l AC 240; *R* v. *Home Secretary, ex p. Brind* [1990] 2 WLR 787; *R* v. *SOS for the Environment, ex parte Hammersmith and Fulham LBC* (T.L.R. 4/9/90).

[31] *Inland Revenue Commissioners* v. *National Federation of Self-Employed and Small Businesses Ltd* [1982] AC 617.

[32] *R* v. *SOS for Foreign and Commonwealth Affairs, ex p. Council of Civil Service Unions* [1984] IRLR 303.

[33] The ability of the government to escape accountability to Parliament when it
claims that national security is at issue was demonstrated by the attitude of the
leader of the Opposition during questioning on the Zircon Affair in the House on
23 Jan. 1987. Neil Kinnock indicated that he would accept a statement from the
government that a serious matter of national security was involved, and would not

portantly, it shows no recognition that there are inherent problems in the accountability of a dominant and multi-functioned
government to a party-dominated Parliament.[34] The evident confidence of the British courts that ministerial responsibility provides
an adequate check upon the powers of ministers is in contrast to
the reservations expressed in the Australian High Court in 1981.
There it was recognized that 'under modern conditions of responsible government Parliament could not always be relied upon to
check excesses of power by the Crown or its Ministers'.[35] By
contrast the courts in Britain seem to ascribe to Parliament not
only sovereignty but wisdom, omniscience, and an almost mystical
virtue.

A Spectrum of Accountability

Parliament alone cannot be expected to ensure accountability for
the wide range of powers exercised by the government and its
agents. Indeed, the same mechanism for accounting is not always
suitable. Ministerial responsibility may be appropriate for political
decision-making (that is, decisions on broad policy), but it is an
inadequate mechanism for the redress of individual grievances
against the administrative machine. The requirement is, therefore,
for diverse means through which accountability can be ensured.
This has become even more necessary as the search for efficient
government has distanced the minister from areas of decision-
making, thus reducing his immediate political accountability. The
need is for a coherent and integrated system of accountability
which moves through the spectrum of Parliament, select committees, the Ombudsman, tribunals, and the courts. Accountability

---

seek further information. See also the Brixton Prison escape (Ch. 8.3), and Parliament's failure to press the minister when he claimed he could give only an edited
version of events because of security considerations.

[34] While the problem of accountability to Parliament has not been recognized,
Lord Justice Purchas has indicated an awareness of the possible consequences on
legislation of executive dominance. In R v. *Secretary of State for Social Services,
ex p. Stitt* (Indep. 6/7/90) he expressed surprise and concern at the unbridled powers given by Parliament to the Secretary of State to issue directions stipulating those
items for which payment could, or could not, be made from the Social Fund. He
speculated that such legislation 'might be an unwelcome feature of a dominating
executive in a basically two-party democracy'.

[35] *Re Toohey, exp Northern Land Council* (1981) 38 ALR 439, Gibbs, CJ,
quoted in Turpin, *British Government and the Constitution*, 59.

should therefore be seen as a whole and have regard to the most suitable institution to ensure accountability in a particular area, the proper relationship between internal (departmental) and external (public) accountability, and the appropriateness of procedures and practices in a particular range of situations.

13.5. CONCLUSION

The approaches taken in Australia and New Zealand to the need for reform have differed fundamentally from the approach taken in Britain. First, in Australia and New Zealand there has been a clear recognition of the relationship between efficiency and accountability, and thus the need to view public (or civil) service reform in conjunction with the operation of the convention of ministerial responsibility. Secondly, there has been the acceptance that the convention needed strengthening, through increasing the effective accountability of senior public servants to ministers, and modification to provide for the direct accountability of departmental heads to Parliament. Thirdly, particularly in Australia, much wider issues of public accountability have been addressed, and, whilst there has been recognition that the political accountability of ministers is fundamental to the system, the convention of ministerial responsibility has not inhibited the development and strengthening of other aspects of public accountability. In Britain, by contrast, there has been no recognition that issues of public accountability need to be addressed, nor even that the convention of ministerial responsibility needs strengthening or modification.

14

Conclusion

The preceding chapters have examined the recent operation of the convention of individual ministerial responsibility and the institutional changes which affect its operation. The purpose of this examination has been to assess, first, the extent to which resignations have been in accordance with the convention; secondly, what effect the reform of the select committee system and the establishment of Next Steps agencies have had—or might have in future—upon the accountability of ministers and the broader structure of public accountability; and, thirdly, whether the changes require a reformulation of individual ministerial responsibility.

14.1. MINISTERIAL RESIGNATIONS: SUPPORT FOR THE CONVENTION OF INDIVIDUAL MINISTERIAL RESPONSIBILITY

During the period 1979–92 there were ten resignations which fell within the categories for which resignation on the grounds of individual ministerial responsibility is required; first, departmental fault in which the minister was involved, or of which he knew or should have known (Carrington in conjunction with Luce and Atkins, and Brittan); secondly, personal fault while acting in a ministerial capacity (Fairbairn, Currie, and Ridley); and, thirdly, personal fault of a private nature (Parkinson, Nicholls, and Mellor).

An analysis of these resignations, and of instances where ministers did not resign, indicates that three conditions need to be fulfilled for resignation to occur. There has to be fault; the fault has to be serious; and the political circumstances must be such that they do not militate against resignation. Thus once the constitutional requirement of fault is present, whether or not there is a resignation depends upon the judgements made about the seriousness of the error and the attendant circumstances. Only when there is a coincidence of the constitutional requirement and political judgements does a resignation occur. However, the fact that resignations are in part a product of political considerations does not devalue their constitutional significance. Neither does the motivation or public explanation or rationale of a resignation affect its constitutional credentials. A resignation is not more 'constitutional' if it is voluntary rather than involuntary (it may in any case be impossible to tell); or if the resignation letter is couched in terms of constitutional obligation.

It may even be possible to see some ministerial retirements and some demotions or dismissals, which are the product of Cabinet reshuffles, as the delayed operation of individual ministerial responsibility. Such cases do not, however, provide the focus for accountability which is the constitutional value of a resignation. Politically, resignations may be temporarily damaging to the government, and of course they inflict damage, which may be permanent, to the political career at Westminister of the minister involved. However, constitutionally, resignations provide an important public demonstration of accountability, giving at least a symbolic illustration of the working of representative and responsible government. This lends legitimacy to the constitutional arrangements and therefore to the political system.

However, resignations may do no more than fulfil the symbolic function. They indicate a recognition by ministers that they are constitutionally accountable for their actions, but there is not always a corresponding recognition that they are also required to give an account or to explain these actions to Parliament (or, if there is this recognition, it may be ignored). Resignations may contain little of substance in the way of explanation. Indeed, Leon Brittan's resignation was an example of accountability avoidance,[1] and Edwina Currie's departure from office was also unaccompanied by adequate explanations.[2] Thus, although the period studied might be considered 'good' in terms of the quantity of resignations on the grounds of individual ministerial responsibility, this was not reflected in terms of the quality of accountability. In fact, the accountability of ministers to Parliament was frequently found

[1] See Ch. 6.2.   [2] See Ch. 4.2.

wanting. Moreover, inadequate explanatory accountability was not confined to resigning ministers. Lord Young failed to provide Parliament with information which, if known at the time, might have resulted in his being required to relinquish office,[3] while Kenneth Baker avoided accounting fully for the Brixton Prison escape, pleading security considerations.[4]

The ability of ministers to evade their responsibilities stems mainly from the dominance of the executive over Parliament, but it is aided by the imprecision or flexibility of the conventional arrangements. Flexibility is traditionally considered a beneficial attribute of the constitution, enabling the constitutional arrangements to adapt to changes within the institutions of government and to the political requirements of the time, thereby avoiding constitutional conflict. However, this view presupposes that more precise arrangements would be unable to adapt to such changes and that the avoidance of conflict is necessarily a virtue. Moreover, it fails to recognize the disadvantages of the lack of definition and the constitutional uncertainty which result.

These disadvantages are apparent in the arrangements for accountability, where the constitutional responsibilities of ministers are expressed in terms of such generality as to lack constitutional authority in specific instances. The minister may ultimately be accountable to Parliament for everything within his area of responsibility, but the extent of this accountability varies, depending upon whether it concerns his department, a departmental agency, a non-departmental public body, or a nationalized industry. Nor do these particular categories carry precise models of accountability. Much depends upon the minister, the issue involved, and the extent to which collective cover and back-bench support is provided.

The ill-defined, or flexible, nature of the arrangements for accountability therefore works to the advantage of ministers, who are able to provide their own definitions, confident that challenges to their position will usually lack both the constitutional authority and the political strength to be effective. Constitutional conflict over the extent to which a minister should be publicly accountable is thus usually avoided—to the advantage of the government and the detriment of constitutional accountability.

The lack of a clear definition of responsibility and accountability

---

[3] See Ch. 8.2.   [4] See Ch. 8.3.

has been evident in the uncertain division between policy and administration. This enabled James Prior, after the Maze Prison escape, to provide his own formulation, in which 'policy' was confined to matters of high policy, and, as a consequence, 'administration' covered everything else. On this basis, he argued that his resignation was not appropriate.[5] Prior's reformulation of individual ministerial responsibility was much criticized in the House of Commons at the time, but subsequently, after the Brixton Prison escape, Kenneth Baker's use of such a formulation seemed to be accepted and his assertion on that basis that responsibility lay with officials and not ministers went unchallenged, at least in Parliament.[6] Parliament's failure to question constitutional adjustments made by a minister demonstrated that constitutional change in Britain may occur not as a result of public debate but by default.

14.2. REFORM OF THE SELECT COMMITTEE SYSTEM

Such parliamentary indifference to constitutional concerns sits uncomfortably with the reform of the select committee system, which was intended to secure more meaningful accountability. However, it may help to explain the failure of the House to address the problems encountered by its select committees.

The reform of the select committee system has been accompanied by governmental restrictions on the information the committees receive and on the appearance of civil servants before the committees. The limits imposed have at times been disputed by select committees, but seldom subjected to a concerted challenge. Committees have avoided confrontation for two reasons. First, they consider that to function effectively they need the co-operation of the government. Moreover, they lack adequate opportunities to bring a conflict before the House, and are aware that, even if they do, the government may apply the whip, turning the issue into one of confidence. Practical considerations therefore suggest that confrontation is not in the interests of the committees. Secondly, the party allegiances of government back-benchers ultimately operate even within the most independently minded select committees and usually act to prevent a conflict which might seriously

---

[5] See Ch. 7.2.   [6] See Ch. 8.3.

embarrass the government. Select committees are therefore constrained by their own members, who identify with the party, to which they owe their positions at Westminster and their places on select committees, rather than with Parliament, which has given them the delegated powers to operate on its behalf.

Thus the committees have allowed their effectiveness to be limited by government restrictions on information. These are imposed on the grounds of confidentiality, which may be applied to background information as well as advice and to non-civil servants as well as officials, or because the conduct (more easily understood as misconduct) and not the actions of officials is at issue. Moreover, whilst the committees have objected to some of these restrictions, most notably those relating to conduct which arose out of the Westland affair, they have not been prepared to provoke a conflict, which, if neither side gave way, could result in a parliamentary, if not constitutional, crisis. The committees have rather settled for reassurances from the government that it has no intention of undermining the work of select committees, and have continued to accept the inadequacies of definition relating to governmental accountability.

Yet, if the select committees are to realize their true potential for improving accountability, they may need to insist on a reduction in the opportunities for accountability avoidance. This is particularly important if they are to be effective in scrutinizing the Next Steps agencies. Just as the agencies are intended to work within strict frameworks of responsibilities, so select committees must be certain that accountability corresponds to these responsibilities.

This means that they must be prepared, if necessary, for conflict with the government should ministers attempt to evade issues or refuse to allow Chief Executives to give a full account of their agency responsibilities. Moreover, as part of the assertion of their authority, they may need to insist on the right to bring disputes with ministers directly and immediately to the attention of the House. However, perhaps of most importance, they need the will and the determination to seize the initiative and ensure that they set the agenda for accountability, rather than allowing the government to impose the boundaries and limitations.

Despite the limitations under which select committees operate, the reform of the select committee system has had a considerable impact upon the workings of government, both by increasing the amount of information made publicly available and by producing within departments, non-departmental public bodies, and nationalized industries the expectation of scrutiny by committees, which in itself acts as an important check upon government.

14.3. THE NEXT STEPS REFORM

The Next Steps agencies have the potential for making accountability clearer in the areas in which they operate. The rigidity of the Policy and Resources Documents, which detail responsibilities and procedures, suggests a welcome and realistic definition of responsibilities for decision-making. However, the concern of the Next Steps programme is with internal or managerial accountability, and there has been little attempt to explore ways of making this compatible with the public accountability that is constitutionally required. It has merely been imposed on top of, or more accurately slid underneath, the existing constitutional arrangements.

Internally, there is a structure of accountability which equates power with responsibility, but externally the prevailing constitutional theory prevents officials being held personally accountable. Thus at the managerial level the Next Steps requires Chief Executives to be personally accountable for their responsibilities as detailed within the Policy and Resources Document, while at the constitutional level ministers retain overall responsibility for the agencies within their departments, and the personal accountability of civil servants is denied. Moreover, although the names of Chief Executives are public knowledge and they give evidence about their responsibilities to select committees, in theory they act only on behalf of their minister, with all the attendant protections and limitations this implies.

However, despite the apparent continuity in constitutional arrangements, internal changes seem certain to affect the practical application of external or public accountability. This has already been demonstrated by the change in arrangements relating to the redirection by the minister of questions from Members of Parliament to Chief Executives. Under these arrangements their answers are published in the daily *Official Report* (Hansard), thus countering criticisms that the delegation of written questions to Chief Executives deprives Members of information previously made available in written answers by the minister. Also of significance has been the granting of AAO status to Chief Executives, which ensures their accountability before the PAC for the financial concerns of the agency.

Moreover, the success of the Next Steps programme depends largely upon civil servants being given an increasing number of delegated powers, and, although these powers are technically exercised only on behalf of the minister, it seems likely that any differences between the way in which internal and external accountability is delivered will become less pronounced. Successful, often high-profile, Chief Executives, many of whom have been recruited from outside the service, will in practice tend to account personally to select committees in the same way as they do to the minister, thereby suggesting a greater openness or transparency of government and improved public accountability.

However, it is necessary to ensure that any benefits in accountability endure, and are not merely in the gift of ministers who can at any time withdraw them by imposing the limitations of ministerial responsibility, through the application of the Osmotherly Rules. Accountability needs therefore to be fitted into a framework which provides constitutional, and not just managerial, authority.

14.4. THE CONSTITUTIONAL IMPLICATIONS FOR ACCOUNTABILITY OF ADMINISTRATIVE REFORMS

The reform of the select committee system and the establishment of Next Steps agencies have effected change through the introduction of new structures. They have also acted to trigger or accentuate other more subtle changes which are likely to affect the operation of British government. These may only be appreciated over the longer term. However, the implications for accountability, as at present operated through the convention of individual ministerial responsibility, may be profound.

Civil Service Accountability

One of the most significant developments during the 1980s and 1990s in relation to accountability has been the trend away from the anonymity of officials towards civil service accountability. The scrutiny by select committees has resulted in a diminution of anonymity as civil servants appear in public (frequently on television) and are addressed by name. The establishment of Next Steps agencies has extended the process with Chief Executives having personal responsibility for the operation of the agency as detailed within the framework document. Indeed, the Next Steps development suggests a fundamental change in accountability; a move away from the overarching ministerial accountability towards a division of accountability between the minister and civil servants. Despite the government's insistence that the convention of individual ministerial responsibility remains unaltered and requires no modification, the responsibilities of officials are clearly stated and accountability for these responsibilities would seem to follow.

The trend towards civil service rather than ministerial accountability for some areas of government has also been apparent within departments, although here it is more contentious because of the lack of a clear division of responsibility. There have been a number of examples where officials have been implicated in departmental mistakes. In the prison escape cases, both Prior and Baker denied their responsibility and blamed civil servants.[7] Officials were also implicated in the leaking of the Solicitor-General's letter in the Westland affair, although culpability is still uncertain.

The 'naming and blaming' of civil servants also extended to the policy misjudgement concerning the rapid rundown of the coal industry, the announcement of which in October 1992 by Michael Heseltine, President of the Board of Trade, was met with political and public hostility. Heseltine took full responsibility for the policy, both in the House and before the Trade and Industry Select Committee, and made no comments that implicated individual officials.[8] However, the senior civil servant in charge of energy policy within the DTI was moved sideways, exchanging jobs with his replacement.[9] The move was said by the department to be necessary in order to have 'a fresh pair of eyes to look at policy'.[10] Such a statement inevitably implicated the deputy secretary concerned in the policy error.

The Times, consistent with its belief that senior civil servants

---

[7] See Chs. 7.2, 8.3. [8] 27 Oct. 1992.
[9] *Guardian*, 28 Oct. 1992. [10] Ibid. and *The Times*, 30 Oct. 1992.

should be publicly accountable,[11] welcomed this apparent location of responsibility within the department. It considered that
'Making senior civil servants responsible when their policies lead
to disaster is not a matter of seeking scapegoats or trying to distract
attention from ministers.'[12]

This position is not entirely satisfactory. Officials may be perceived as scapegoats when any change in their position is publicly
noted yet the evidence against them is unknown, the criteria against
which they are measured is uncertain, and they are unable to
defend themselves. Moreover, the identification of civil servants
with particular policy decisions raises a question of considerable
constitutional significance, for, except in routine departmental
matters, policies do not, or should not, attach to civil servants.
The function of officials is to advise ministers on policy options.
It is the minister who makes the decision and any reduction in his
responsibility for policy choice reduces his role to that of a policy
presenter. This is the logical extension of the line taken by Kenneth
Baker after the Brixton escape, when he implied that he was merely
doing as he had been advised and that responsibility lay with
those who had advised him.[13] In the Heseltine case, the scale and
consequences, for future energy supply and for miners, were significant enough to raise matters of economic strategy and political
sensitivity—clearly matters for the chairman (in this case, the
President) of the Board, not for a line manager. This position is
not only good management practice but essential constitutional
practice in Britain's parliamentary democracy.

The attempts to abdicate responsibility suggest the need for a
clear division of responsibilities and hence accountability. Such a
division would hold officials responsible for providing a range
of appropriate options and advising on the consequences of the
different options. The minister would be responsible for making
and justifying the choice and for its outcome. Such a division in
responsibility would seem an important step in identifying where
accountability is located. However, for accountability to be meaningful, its operation would need to be open to public scrutiny, as
is the case in New Zealand.

The requirement would seem to be for 'visible accountability'[14]

---

[11] *The Times*, 30 Oct. 1992.   [12] Ibid.
[13] See Ch. 8.3.   [14] G. Mather, *The Times*, 30 Oct. 1992.

in areas of policy as well as operations, as suggested by Graham Mather of the Institute of Economic Affairs. He proposes that departments should be restructured to contain policy agencies on Next Steps lines. Such agencies would be responsible for rendering policy advice to the minister, but they could also be responsible for policy detail. This would remove the need for ministers to make an artificial and unhelpful distinction between matters of high policy for which they assume absolute responsibility, and the detail and administration of a policy of which they have little knowledge. The result could be the establishment of agencies such as a Monetary Policy Agency in the Treasury, an Energy Policy Board in the DTI, and a Crime Reduction Bureau in the Home Office.[15] All agencies would need to be 'identifiable, visible and accountable',[16] suggesting an openness of government unfamiliar in Britain and requiring the removal of the trappings of secrecy, such as the Osmotherly Rules. Reform along these lines may also suggest a different role for the permanent secretary, perhaps similar to the New Zealand model, in which he is responsible for his department to the minister and Parliament.[17]

These proposals reflect lines of thought evident in the Fulton Report and in later commentary, although they look to be uncomfortably radical in the context of civil service reform in Britain today and are not on the Next Steps agenda. However, it seems likely that ministers will continue to attempt to push responsibility downwards to their officials, and the muddle over who is, and who should be, responsible will remain until a rational review of the accountability provided by ministerial responsibility is undertaken.

The Trend towards Departmentalism and Managerialism

There has been an identifiable trend in the 1980s and 1990s towards departmentalism and managerialism—that is, the focus on departments as discreet units of government and the use of managerial methods and practices common to the private sector. This is exemplified by the establishment of Next Steps agencies. However, it is possible that the concentration upon departmental structures and management techniques could undermine traditional

---

[15] Suggested by Mather, ibid.   [16] Ibid.   [17] See Ch. 13.

principles associated with the civil, or public, service. There is already evidence from other countries, where similar reforms have been undertaken, of such consequences.

Central to public service reforms has been the introduction of improved mechanisms for the internal accountability of officials to their departmental ministers. In New Zealand there is evidence that this has contributed to the growth in departmentalism at the expense of government co-ordination. The systems of accountability provide little incentive for inter-departmental co-operation because all goals are oriented towards the department.[18] The result is that 'Departments . . . become less concerned with the collective interest of the government and more concerned with the production of outputs desired by their respective portfolio minister(s).'[19]

Thus building structures of accountability within departments would seem to improve vertical responsiveness at the expense of horizontal cross-referencing. This is particularly relevant, although not exclusive, to policy agencies and suggests that effective policy co-ordination between departments is the inevitable casualty of departmentalism. In an effort to address this consequence of management reform in New Zealand, the government has subsequently changed the performance agreement of departmental chief executives to include consultation with other departments.[20]

However, it is not just the structures of accountability that would seem to encourage departmentalism. Research also suggests that officials increasingly see themselves as employed by departments rather than as servants of the government as a whole.[21] Thus allowing departments greater autonomy in the recruitment and promotion of their own staff may erode the ethos acquired through belonging to a wider service with common goals. It may also in the long term result in personal inter-departmental connections being severed because of the lack of common experiences.

The problems associated with departmentalism may be less in Britain because reform has not concerned policy, and departments

---

[18] D. Hunn and H. Lang, 'Review of the Prime Minister's and Cabinet Office' (1989), quoted in Boston, 'The Problems of Policy Co-ordination', 94.

[19] Boston, 'The Problems of Policy Co-ordination'.

[20] Ibid., see also J. Boston, 'Assessing the Performance of Departmental Chief Executives: Perspectives from New Zealand', *Public Administration*, 70/3 (1992), 423–42.   [21] Boston, 'The Problems of Policy Co-ordination'.

have not been given the independence in personnel matters that has been achieved in New Zealand. Nevertheless, it seems possible that the departmental orientation of agencies and the increasing decentralization of personnel functions could have an effect upon the work of officials, and in particular the formal co-ordination and informal consultation known as 'networking'.

Perhaps more serious are the possible long-term consequences of the focus on managerialism evident in all reforms in the public service. There are suggestions that this could produce a conflict with ministerial responsibility and a reduction in the public service ethos. Research in Australia and New Zealand suggests that, particularly in New Zealand, where the reforms have been radical and imposed upon a sceptical bureaucracy, 'conflict may emerge between the aim of inducing stronger compliance with ministerial directions, on the one hand, and on the other, the intention to promote a more managerially-oriented public service'.[22]

Management techniques and procedures may prevent the required responsiveness to political commands and 'a more proactive public service might be developed at the expense of constitutional integrity'.[23] The concern is that civil service adherence to principles of impartiality and the proper functioning of the public service will be weakened, as will the acceptance that the function of the civil service is to carry out the wishes of ministers. The basic premiss that civil servants advise on and implement the policy choices of ministers will be undermined.

The long-term result could be the undermining of the convention of individual ministerial responsibility and the attraction of people to the service who have little interest, understanding, or commitment to 'values that ought to underpin the democratic process'.[24] This possibility is borne out by research in Canada, where the emphasis of reform in the public service has likewise been upon managerialism. In addition, evidence suggests that those working within a managerial-oriented service acquire a different balance of skills and priorities. There is a shift towards managers who have less experience of policy advice work or programme management than previously, and who are therefore less concerned

---

[22] Gregory, 'The Attitudes of Senior Public Servants in Australia and New Zealand', 296.
[23] Ibid.   [24] Ibid.

with the legitimizing and technical roles of the public service than with its management function.[25]

The trend towards managerialism seems likely to continue in Britain as government plans to 'contract out' many of the support services in central government are implemented. The White Paper, *Competing for Quality*,[26] suggests that contracting out should apply not just to services such as cleaning, catering, and maintenance, but also to professional services, such as those provided by lawyers, accountants, and inspectors. Indeed, the government has indicated that it expects to contract out up to a quarter of the work at present done by civil servants, within both agencies and the core departments.[27]

'Government by contract' will need far fewer civil servants to operate it, and those required will be managers, contract negotiators, and supporters of the value-for-money approach. Technicians and perhaps policy advisers are likely to be less in demand, as their services can be 'bought in' and an adherence to the 'public service ethos' may seem out of place in the civil service of the future where so much government is provided by the private sector.

The research in New Zealand, Australia, and Canada, and the trends in Britain, suggest the possibility of significant long-term change in the culture, attitude, and expertise of the public service which may make it incompatible with the traditional form of public accountability, which centres upon the minister. Whether the change is for better or for worse is debatable, but either way it is essential that a realistic and effective system of accountability is in place to cope with it. This reinforces the requirement, already evident through the Next Steps reforms, that modifications be made to the convention of individual ministerial responsibility and the recognition that other means of accountability are also appropriate.

14.5. THE FUTURE OF ACCOUNTABILITY IN BRITAIN

Fundamental reform would seem to be needed if accountability mechanisms are to deal with a more publicly accountable civil

---

[25] B. Carrol, 'Politics and Administration: A Trichotomy?', *Governance*, 3/3 (1990), 236.
[26] Issued Nov. 1991.   [27] *Guardian*, 15 July 1992.

service, which is managerially, rather than constitutionally, oriented. There is no indication that Next Steps agencies will extend further than operational matters and the application of agency methods to non-departmental public bodies. Indeed, it seems that the Next Steps project team will be disbanded as soon as all the proposed agencies are 'up and running', leaving the responsibility of the core departments largely untouched,[28] except by the requirements of contracting out. There would seem to be no plans to reconsider the position of permanent secretaries, their relationship with ministers, and the extent to which they should be publicly accountable for their responsibilities. This contrasts with Australia and New Zealand, where reforms have acted to increase the accountability of departments to Parliament. The explanatory notes required by the Australian Parliament and the reporting mechanisms for the heads of departments to the New Zealand Parliament are part of the enhanced public accountability of both civil servants and ministers, which would be appropriate in Britain. Moreover, there is no reason, except for the lack of political motivation, why such reforms, which are aimed at better accountability, could not be transplanted in similar form into the British system.

Similarly, a Freedom of Information Act would be a useful, if not essential, reform to ensure that the aims of transparent and open government are achieved. The Australian and New Zealand experiences suggest that such an act can coexist with ministerial responsibility. In addition, increased powers and resources for the Ombudsman are necessary to ensure that maladministration does not go unchecked, and there needs to be a coherent tribunal system to deal with citizens' grievances, and a simplified and accessible procedure to provide access to the courts.

A further resource for accountability would be the development of a code of administrative practice. Such a code would be important both for its content and for the administrative culture it would encourage. Civil servants would be given a positive perspective on safeguarding the rights of individuals through good administrative practice. This would be in contrast to the evident purpose of the civil service in-house publication, *The Judge over*

[28] HC481 (1990), Memorandum from the Project Manager, p. 3 (3a).

your Shoulder,[29] which indicates the steps necessary to keep the minister out of the courts, rather than emphasizing the need to protect the individual. Unlike the Citizen's Charter, such a code should penetrate to the heart of the departments.

14.6. THE NEED FOR CONSTITUTIONAL ADJUSTMENTS

Just as important as any programme of reform is the initial assessment of the inadequacies and problems of public accountability. The starting-point for reform in Britain must be the recognition that, while the convention of ministerial responsibility cannot ensure accountability for all the powers exercised by modern government, it should provide effective accountability for policy choices and overall administrative management. Its failure to do so does not necessarily mean that it is an unsuitable mechanism for accountability, but it does indicate that adjustments need to be made if the constitutional requirement of accountable government is to be a reality. Both the reform of the select committee system and the establishment of Next Steps executive agencies have provided the opportunity for adjustments to be made. Indeed, the reforms within the civil service would seem to make such adjustments imperative, particularly when the implications of large-scale 'contracting out' are considered. However, as the previous chapters have demonstrated, the government has insisted that the convention of ministerial responsibility remains unchanged, and Parliament has failed to produce a strong challenge to the government's position.

At the very least three related issues of accountability should be addressed. First, agency civil servants should be given the constitutional authority to account publicly and on their own behalf to select committees for their delegated responsibilities. Secondly, a clear definition of the 'ultimate responsibility' of the minister should be provided. This should include ministerial responsibility for the effective public accountability of those to whom he has delegated responsibility and also for those for whom he is indirectly

---

[29] See D. Oliver, 'Politicians and the Courts', *Parliamentary Affairs*, 41/1 (1988), 13–33.

responsible to Parliament. Such a definition would provide 'ultimate responsibility' with a positive force which, where agencies were concerned, would also strengthen the internal accountability of agency staff to the minister. Indeed, constitutional and management accountability would act to reinforce each other. The third requirement is the strengthening of the powers of select committees to insist upon information and explanation. This would necessitate the removal of the Osmotherly Rules.

Such moves would clarify ministerial responsibility and provide improved mechanisms for accountability, particularly for administrative matters. They would also make it easier in many situations to assess the responsibility of the minister. However, the actual extent of improvement in the accountability of ministers to Parliament would depend upon the determination of Parliament and its select committees to secure it, and the co-operation of ministers and civil servants in its provision.

Political accountability can never be assured. Governments will always seek to hide information which they consider politically damaging or simply embarrassing. Even with a reformed committee system, Parliament's ability, and indeed its desire, to secure accountability is limited. However, accountability can be improved by making certain that the principle and the mechanism for producing it—the convention of individual ministerial responsibility—is able to cope with modern political and administrative conditions, the given situation.

During the 1980s the government frequently proclaimed the importance of accountability and the need for it to be improved. Indeed, much political rhetoric was expended, and policies implemented, in the name of accountability. The community charge (poll tax) was introduced to ensure the accountability of local authorities to the community; trade union reform was undertaken to make union leaders accountable to their members; the overhaul of the health service was in part to provide better accountability by the health authorities and hospitals to their patients; and broadcasters were required to be more accountable to their viewers and listeners. In addition, the programme of returning the nationalized industries to the private sector has been accompanied by the assertion that this will improve accountability, and the opposition from the Bruges group and other politicians to further integration into the European Community has focused partly on the lack of accountability in Brussels. Further, there was serious public and political concern over incidents, such as Westland, Barlow Clowes, Rover, salmonella in eggs, and Matrix Churchill. Despite all the expressions of concern and the assertions of principle, the central constitutional issue of the accountability of ministers has still to be grasped. The reform of government administration will not in itself produce accountable government, for the changes concern the means, and accountability is the end result.[30] Similarly, the reform of the select committee system may be of limited value unless the House of Commons is prepared to use its powers to secure the accountability of ministers and administrators.

The accountability of ministers, which operates through the convention of ministerial responsibility, underpins the British Constitution and the Westminister system of government. It provides the rationale for the institutional structure of government and the basis for political relationships. The strength of the doctrine lies in its theoretical contribution to the democratic process, whereby it provides public accountability. Its weakness lies in the execution of the theory, in the gap between the expectation of accountable government and the reality of a dominant executive able to impose its own limitations upon accountability.

The corruption of ministerial accountability to Parliament, mainly through the operation of party solidarity, challenges Parliament to continue to play its constitutional role in accountable government, or to accept a diminished constitutional position and concede the accountability function to others. Its failure to recognize that accountability needs to be addressed as a major constitutional issue in which it should lead the debate acts to emasculate the central doctrine of the British Constitution, confirming that individual ministerial responsibility frequently provides a façade behind which the government can hide, safe in the knowledge that Parliament lacks the constitutional integrity to offer a sustained and effective challenge.

[30] See Sir K. Stowe, 'Good Piano Won't Play Bad Music: Administrative Reform and Good Governance', *Public Administration*, 70/3 (1992), 387–94.

BIBLIOGRAPHY

BOOKS AND ARTICLES

ALDERMAN, R. K., 'The Prime Minister and the Appointment of Ministers', *Parliamentary Affairs*, 29/2 (1976), 101–34.

AMERY, L., *Thoughts on the Constitution* (Oxford: Oxford University Press, 1947).

ANSON, Sir W., *Law and Custom of the Constitution* (Oxford: Clarendon Press, 1909).

AUCOIN, P., 'Administrative Reforms in Public Management', *Governance*, 3/2 (1990), 194–208.

AUSTIN, R., 'Freedom of Information: The Constitutional Impact' in J. Jowell, and D. Oliver (eds.), *The Changing Constitution* (2nd edn., Oxford: Clarendon Press, 1989), 409–51.

BAGEHOT, W., *The English Constitution* (Introduction by R. H. S. Crossman) (London: Fontana, 1963).

BALDWIN, G. R., and VELJANOVSKI, C. G., 'Regulation by Cost-Benefit Analysis', *Public Administration*, 62/1 (1984), 51–69.

BALDWIN, R., and McCRUDDEN, C., *Regulation and Public Law* (London: Weidenfeld & Nicolson, 1987).

BALDWIN, R., 'The Ibbs Report', *The Modern Law Review*, 53 (1990), 321–37.

BARKER, A. (ed.), *Quangos in Britain* (London: Macmillan Press, 1982).

—— 'Government Bodies and Mutual Accountability', in A. Barker (ed.), *Quangos in Britain* (London: Macmillan Press, 1982).

BEER, S. H., *Modern British Politics* (3rd edn., London: Faber & Faber, 1982).

BENN, T., *Against the Tide, Diaries, 1973–76* (London: Hutchinson, 1989).

BENNETT, P., and PULLINGER, S., *Making the Commons Work* (London: Institute of Public Policy Research, 1992).

BIRCH, A. H., *Representative and Responsible Government* (London: Unwin Hyman, 1964).

BIRKENSHAW, P., *Freedom of Information* (London: Weidenfeld & Nicolson, 1988).

—— *Grievances, Remedies and the State* (London: Sweet & Maxwell, 1985).

BORRIE, Sir G., 'The Regulation of Public and Private Power', *Public Law* (1989), 552–67.

BOSTON, J., 'Transforming New Zealand's Public Sector: Labour's Quest for Improved Efficiency and Accountability', *Public Administration*, 65 (1987), 423–42.

—— 'The Problems of Policy Coordination: The New Zealand Experience', *Governance*, 5/1 (1992), 90–111.

—— 'Assessing the Performance of Departmental Chief Executives: Perspectives from New Zealand', *Public Administration*, 70 (1992), 405–28.

BOYLE, Lord, 'Address to the Royal Institute of Public Administration', *Public Administration*, 58 (1980), 1–12.

BRAZIER, R., *Constitutional Practice* (Oxford: Oxford University Press, 1988).

—— *Constitutional Texts* (Oxford: Clarendon Press, 1990).

BRUCE-GARDYNE, J., *Ministers and Mandarins* (London: Sidgwick & Jackson, 1986).

BUTLER, D., and BUTLER, G., *British Political Facts 1900–1985* (London: Macmillan Press, 1986).

—— and HALSAY, A. H. (eds.), *Policy and Politics: Essays in Honour of Norman Chester* (London: Macmillan, 1978).

BUTLER, Sir R., *New Challenges or Familiar Prescriptions: The Radcliffe–Maud Memorial Lecture* (Royal Institute of Public Administration, 1990).

CARR, Sir C., *Concerning English Administrative Law* (Oxford: Oxford University Press, 1941).

CARRINGTON, Lord, *Reflect on Things Past: The Memoirs of Lord Carrington* (London: Collins, 1989).

CARROL, B., 'Politics and Administration: A Trichotomy?', *Governance*, 3/3 (1990).

CHAPMAN, R. A., and HUNT, M. (eds.), *Open Government* (London: Croom Helm, 1987).

COLE, J., *The Thatcher Years: A Decade of Revolution in British Politics* (London: BBC Books, 1987).

COSGRAVE, P., *Carrington: A Life and a Policy* (London: J. M. Dent, 1985).

CRAIG, Sir J., *A History of Red Tape* (London: MacDonald & Evans, 1955).

CRAIG, P. P., *Administrative Law* (London: Sweet & Maxwell, 1983; 2nd edn., 1989).

DAVIES, A., and WILLIAMS, J., *What Next?* (London: Institute for Public Policy Research, 1991).

DEARLOVE, J., 'Bringing the Constitution Back in: Political Science and the State', *Political Studies*, 37 (1989), 521–39.

DELL, E., *Collective Responsibility; Fact, Fiction or Facade? Policy and*

Practice: The Experience of Government (Royal Institute of Public Administration, 1980).

DE SMITH, S., and BRAZIER, R., *Constitutional and Administrative Law* (6th edn., London: Pelican, 1989).

DICEY, A. V., *Introduction to the Study of the Law of the Constitution* (10th edn., London: Macmillan, 1959).

DOHERTY, M., 'Prime Ministerial Power and Ministerial Responsibility in the Thatcher Era', *Parliamentary Affairs*, 41/1 (1988), 49–67.

DREWRY, G. (ed.), *The New Select Committees* (Oxford: Clarendon Press, 1985; 2nd edn., 1989).

—— 'Forward from FMI: The Next Steps', *Public Law* (1988), 505–15.

—— 'Next Steps: The Pace Falters', *Public Law* (1990), 522–9.

—— and BUTCHER, T., *The Civil Service Today* (Oxford: Blackwells, 1988).

DRUCKER, H. (ed.), *Developments in British Politics* 2 (London: Macmillan, 1988).

DUNLEAVY, P., *et al.*, 'Prime Ministers and the Commons: Patterns of Behaviour', *Public Administration*, 68 (1990), 123–40.

ELLIS, D., 'Collective Ministerial Responsibility and Collective Solidarity', *Public Law* (1980), 367–96.

FINER, S. E., 'The Individual Responsibility of Ministers', *Public Administration*, 34 (1956), 377–96.

FOLEY, M., *The Silence of Constitutions* (London: Routledge, 1989).

FOREMAN-PECK, J., 'The Privatisation of Industry in Historical Perspective', in A. Gamble and C. Wells (eds.), *Thatcher's Law* (Cardiff: GPC Books, 1989), 130–48.

FRANKLIN, M., 'Whatever Happened to the English Constitution?', *Talking Politics*, 2/2 (1989–90), 59–65.

FRY, G. K., 'Thoughts on the Present State of the Convention of Ministerial Responsibility', *Parliamentary Affairs*, 23 (1969), 10–20.

—— 'The Sachsenhausen Concentration Camp Case and the Convention of Individual Ministerial Responsibility', *Public Law* (1970), 336–57.

—— *The Changing Civil Service* (London: Allen & Unwin, 1985).

GAMBLE, A., and WELLS, C., 'Privatisation, Thatcherism and the British State', in A. Gamble (ed.), *Thatcher's Law* (Cardiff: GPC Books 1989), 1–20.

GRAHAM, C., and PROSSER, T. (eds.), *Waiving the Rules: The Constitution under Thatcher* (Open University Press, 1988).

GRAY, A., and JENKINS, W. I., 'Public Administration and Government in 1987', *Parliamentary Affairs*, 41/3 (1988), 321–39.

GREENLEAF, W. H., *A Much Governed Nation* (London: Methuen, 1987).

GREENWOOD, J., and WILSON, D., *Public Administration in Britain Today* (London: Unwin Hyman, 1989).

GREGORY, R. J., 'The Attitudes of Senior Public Servants in Australia and New Zealand: Administrative Reform and Technocratic Consequences?', *Governance*, 4/3 (1991), 296–314.

—— and DREWRY, G., 'Barlow Clowes and the Ombudsman', *Public Law* (1991), 192–214, 408–42.

GRIFFITH, J. A. G., 'Crichel Down: The Most Famous Farm in British Constitutional History', *Contemporary Record*, (1987), 35–40.

GRIFFITHS, J., 'Australian Administrative Law: Institutions, Reforms and Impact', *Public Administration*, 63/4 (1985), 445–62.

HAGUE, D. C., 'The Ditchley Conference: A British View', in B. Smith and D. C. Hague (eds.), *The Dilemma of Accountability in Modern Government: Independence versus Control* (London: Macmillan, 1971).

HAILSHAM, Lord, *The Dilemma Of Democracy* (London: Collins, 1978).

HANHAM, H. J., *The Nineteenth Century Constitution: Documents and Commentary* (Cambridge: Cambridge University Press, 1969).

HANSON, A. H. (ed.), *A Book of Readings* (London: Allen and Unwin, 1963).

HARDEN, I., 'A Constitution for Quangos?', *Public Law* (1987), 27–35.

—— and LEWIS, N., 'Privatisation, De-Regulation and Constitutionality: Some Anglo-American Comparisons', *Northern Ireland Quarterly*, 34 (1983).

—— *The Noble Lie: The British Constitution and the Rule of Law* (London: Hutchinson, 1986).

HARLOW, C. (ed.), *Public Law and Politics* (London: Sweet and Maxwell, 1986).

HARRIS, K., *THATCHER* (London: Weidenfeld and Nicolson, 1988).

HAYEK, F. A., *The Constitution of Liberty* (London: Routledge & Kegan Paul, 1960).

HEALD, D., 'Will the Privatisation of Public Enterprises Solve the Problem of Control?', *Public Administration*, 63/1 (1985), 6–21.

HENNESSY, P., 'Helicopter Crashes into Cabinet: Prime Minister and Constitution Hurt', *Journal of Law and Society*, 13/3 (1986), 423–32.

—— *Cabinet* (Oxford: Blackwells, 1986).

—— *Whitehall* (London: Fontana Press, 1990).

HERMAN, V., and ALT, J. E. (eds.), *Cabinet Studies* (London: Macmillan, 1975).

HOLDSWORTH, Sir W., *History of English Law* (6th edn., London: Methuen, 1938).

HOLME, R., and ELLIOT, M. (eds.), *1688–1988 Time for a New Constitution* (London: Macmillan Press, 1988).

HOOD PHILLIPS, O., *Constitutional and Administrative Law* (7th edn., London: Sweet and Maxwell, 1987).

HOWELL, D., 'Public Accountability: Trends and Parliamentary Implications', in B. L. R. Smith and D. C. Hague (eds.), *The Dilemma of Account-ability in Modern Government: Independence versus Control* (London: Macmillan, 1971).

INGHAM, B., *Kill the Messenger* (London: Harper Collins, 1991).

JENKINS, P., *Mrs Thatcher's Revolution: The Ending of the Socialist Era* (London: Jonathan Cape, 1987).

JENKINS, R., *A Life at the Centre* (London: Macmillan, 1991).

JENNINGS, Sir I., *The Queen's Government* (London: Pelican, 1954).

—— *The Law and the Constitution* (5th edn., Cambridge: Cambridge University Press, 1959).

—— *Cabinet Government* (3rd edn., Cambridge: Cambridge University Press, 1961).

JOHNSON, N., *In Search of the Constitution* (London: Methuen, 1977).

—— 'Accountability, Control and Complexity: Moving beyond Minis-terial Responsibility', in A. Barker (ed.), *Quangos in Britain* (London: Macmillan, 1982).

JORDAN, G., 'Individual Ministerial Responsibility: Absolute or Obsolete?' in D. McCrone (ed.), *Scottish Yearbook* (Edinburgh: Unit for Study of Government of Scotland, 1983).

JOWELL, J., and OLIVER, D. (eds.), *The Changing Constitution* Clarendon Press, (1985; 2nd edn., 1989).

JUDGE, D., *Ministerial Responsibility: Life in the Strawman yet?* (Strath-clyde Papers in Government and Politics, 37; Glasgow: Unit for the Study of the Government of Scotland, 1984).

JUSTICE–ALL SOULS REVIEW OF ADMINISTRATIVE LAW IN THE UNITED KINGDOM, *Administrative Justice: Some Necessary Reforms* (London, 1988).

KAY, J., MAYER, C., and THOMPSON, D. (eds.), *Privatisation and Regula-tion; the UK Experience* (Oxford: Clarendon Press, 1986).

KAVANAGH, D., *British Politics; Continuities and Change* (Oxford: Oxford University Press, 1985).

KEATING, M., and HOLMES, M., 'Australia's Budgetary and Financial Management Reforms', *Governance*, 3/2 (1990), 180–9.

KEAYS, S., *A Question of Judgement* (London: Quintessential Press, 1985).

KEIR, D. L., *The Constitutional History of Modern Britain* (9th edn., London: A. C. Black, 1969).

KEMP, P., 'Next Steps for the British Civil Service', *Governance*, 3/2 (1990), 190–6.

LANGFORD, P., *A Polite and Commercial People: England 1727–1783* (Oxford: Oxford University Press, 1989).

LAWSON, D., 'Saying the Unsayable about the Germans: An Interview with Nicholas Ridley', *Spectator*, 14 July 1990.

LE GRAND, J., and ROBINSON, R., *Privatisation and the Welfare State* (London: Allen & Unwin, 1984).

LE MAY, G. H. L., *The Victorian Constitution* (London, 1979).

LEWIS, N., 'Who Controls Quangos and the Nationalized Industries?', in J. Jowell and D. Oliver (eds.), *The Changing Constitution* (Oxford: Clarendon Press, 1985), 198–229.

—— 'Regulating Non-Government Bodies: Privatization, Accountability and the Public-Private Divide', in J. Jowell and D. Oliver (eds.), *The Changing Constitution* (2nd edn., Oxford: Clarendon Press, 1989), 219–47.

LIKIERMAN, A., 'Management Information for Ministers: The MINIS system in the Department of the Environment', *Public Administration*, 60 (1982), 127–42.

LINKLATER, M., and LEIGH, D., *Not with Honour* (London: Sphere Books, 1986).

LOW, S., *The Governance of England* (London: T. Fisher Unwin, 1904; rev. edn., 1914).

LOW, Sir T., 'The Select Committee on Nationalized Industries', in A. H. Hanson (ed.), *A Book of Readings* (London: Allen and Unwin, 1963).

LOWELL, A. L., *The Government of England* (New York: Macmillan, 1919).

MACAUSLAN, P., and MCELDOWNEY, J., *Law, Legitimacy and the Constitution* (London: Sweet and Maxwell, 1985).

MACKENZIE, K., *The English Parliament* (London: Pelican, 1950).

MACKENZIE, W. J., and GROVE, J. W., *Central Administration in Britain* (London: Longmans, 1957).

MACKINTOSH, J., *The British Cabinet* (London: Stevens, 1962).

MADGWICK, P. J., 'Resignations', in V. Herman and J. Alt (eds.), *Cabinet Studies* (London: Macmillan, 1975), 77–102.

MAITLAND, F. W., *The Constitutional History of England* (Cambridge: Cambridge University Press, 1908).

MARSHALL, G., 'Police Accountability Revisited', in D. Butler and A. H. Halsey (eds.), *Policy and Politics: Essays in Honour of Norman Chester* (London: Macmillan, 1978).

—— *Constitutional Conventions* (Oxford: Clarendon Press, 1986).

—— 'Cabinet Government and the Westland Affair', *Public Law* (1986), 184–92.

—— 'Civil Servants and their Ministers: Frank Stacey Memorial Lecture 1987', *Public Policy and Administration*, 3/2 (1988).

—— (ed.), *Ministerial Responsibility* (Oxford: Oxford University Press, 1989).

—— 'Parliamentary Accountability', *Parliamentary Affairs*, 44/4 (1991), 460–9.

—— and MOODIE, G., *Some Problems of the Constitution* (London: Hutchinson, 1959).

MASCERENHAS, R. C., 'Reform of the Public Service in Australia and New Zealand', *Governance*, 3/1 (1990), 76–90.

MAY, E., *Treatise on the Law: Privileges, Proceedings and Usage of Parliament* (London: Butterworths, 4th edn., 1857; 19th edn., 1946; 20th edn., 1983; 21st edn., 1989).

MILLIGAN, F., 'The Limits of Ministerial Action', in A. H. Hanson (ed.), *A Book of Readings* (London: Allen & Unwin, 1963).

MUNRO, C., *Studies in Constitutional Law* (London: Butterworths, 1987).

NEW ZEALAND TREASURY, *Government Management: A Brief to the Incoming Government 1987* (Wellington: New Zealand Treasury, 1987).

NICOLSON, I. F., *The Mystery of Crichel Down* (Oxford: Oxford University Press, 1986).

NORMANTON, E. L., 'Public Accountability and Audit: A Reconnaissance', in B. L. R. Smith and D. C. Hague (eds.), *The Dilemma of Accountability in Modern Government: Independence versus Control* (London: Macmillan, 1971).

NORTON, P., 'Government Defeats in the House of Commons, Myth and Reality', *Public Law* (1978), 360–78.

—— *The Constitution in Flux* (Oxford: Martin Robertson, 1982).

—— 'The Glorious Revolution of 1688: Its Continuing Relevance', *Parliamentary Affairs*, 42/2 (1989), 135–47.

OLIVER, D., 'Politicians and the Courts', *Parliamentary Affairs*, 41/1 (1988), 13–33.

—— and AUSTIN, R., 'Political and Constitutional Aspects of the Westland Affair', *Parliamentary Affairs* 40 (1987), 20–41.

PAGE, B., 'Ministerial Resignation and Individual Ministerial Responsibility in Australia 1976–89', *Journal of Commonwealth and Comparative Politics* (Nov. 1990).

PARRIS, H., *Constitutional Bureaucracy* (London: Allen & Unwin, 1969).

PARTINGTON, M., 'The Reform of Public Law in Britain: Theoretical Problems and Practical Considerations' in P. McAuslan and J. McEldowney (eds.), *Law, Legitimacy and the Constitution* (London: Sweet and Maxwell, 1985).

POOLE, K. P., 'The Powers of Select Committees of the House of Commons to Send for Persons, Papers and Records', *Parliamentary Affairs*, 32 (1979), 268–78.

PONTING, C., *Whitehall: Tragedy and Farce* (London: Sphere Books, 1986).

—— *Whitehall: Changing the Old Guard* (London: Unwin, 1989).

PRICE WATERHOUSE, *Executive Agencies* (2nd and 3rd edns., 1991; 4th and 5th edns., 1992).

PRIOR, J., *A Balance of Power* (London: Hamish Hamilton, 1986).

PROSSER, T., *Nationalized Industries and Public Control: Legal, Constitutional and Political Issues* (Oxford: Blackwell, 1986).

PYPER, R., 'The F.O. Resignations: Individual Ministerial Responsibility Revived?', in L. Robins (ed.), *Updating British Politics* (London: Politics Association, 1984).

PYPER, R., 'Sarah Tisdall, Ian Willmore and the Civil Servants' "Right to Leak"', *Political Quarterly*, 56 (1985), 47–57.

REAGAN, P. M., 'Protecting Privacy and Controlling Bureaucracies: the Constraints of British Constitutional Principles', *Governance*, 3/1 (1990), 32–48.

REDLICH, J., and ILBERT, C., *Procedure of the House of Commons*, ii (London: Archibald Constable, 1908).

RIDDELL, P., *The Thatcher Government* (Oxford: Blackwell, 1985).

RIDLEY, F. F., 'The British Civil Service and Politics: Principles in Question and Traditions in Flux', *Parliamentary Affairs*, 36 (1983), 28–48.

—— 'There is no British Constitution: A Dangerous Case of the Emperor's Clothes', *Parliamentary Affairs*, 41 (1988), 340–61.

ROBINSON, A., and SANDFORD, C., *Tax and Policy Making in the United Kingdom* (London: Heineman Educational Books, 1983).

—— SHEPHERD, R., RIDLEY, F. F., and JONES, G. W., 'Symposium on Ministerial Responsibility', *Public Administration*, 65/1 (1987), 61–91.

ROSE, R., *Ministers and Ministries: A Functional Analysis* (Oxford: Clarendon Press, 1987).

—— *Steering the Ship of State: One Tiller but Two Pairs of Hands* (Studies in Public Policy, 154; Glasgow: Centre for the Study of Public Policy, University of Strathclyde, 1986).

—— *Giving Directions to Civil Servants* (Studies in Public Policy, 156; Glasgow: Centre for the Study of Public Policy, University of Strathclyde, 1986).

—— *A House Divided: Political Administration in Britain Today* (Studies in Public Policy, 158; Glasgow: Centre for the Study of Public Policy, University of Strathclyde, 1986).

—— *Politics in England: Change and Persistence* (5th edn., London: Macmillan, 1989).

SCARMAN, Lord, 'Public Administration in a Time of Change', *Public Administration*, 63/1 (1985), 1–5.

SCOTT, G., BUSHNELL, P., and SALLEE, N., 'Reform of the Core Public Sector: The New Zealand Experience', *Governance*, 3/2 (1990), 215–30.

SHELL, D., 'The British Constitution in 1987', *Parliamentary Affairs*, 41 (1988), 305–20.

SMITH, B. L. R., and HAGUE, D. C. (eds.), *The Dilemma of Accountability in Modern Government; Independence versus Control* (London: Macmillan, 1971).

STEEL, D., *Government and the New Hybriads in Privatizing Public Enterprises* (Royal Institute of Public Administration, 1984).

STOWE, Sir K., 'Good Piano Won't Play Bad Music: Administrative Reform and Good Governance', *Public Administration*, 70/3 (1992), 387–94.

THEAKSTON, K., *Junior Ministers in British Government* (Oxford: Blackwells, 1987).

THORNTON, P., *The Civil Liberties of the Zircon Affair* (London: National Council for Civil Liberties, 1987).

TURPIN, C., *British Government and the Constitution* (London: Weidenfeld and Nicolson, 1985; 2nd edn., 1990).

—— 'Ministerial Responsibility; Myth or Reality?', in J. Jowell and D. Oliver (eds.), *The Changing Constitution* (London: Weidenfeld and Nicolson, 1985; 2nd edn., 1989), 53–86.

VELJANOVSKI, C., *Selling the State* (London: Weidenfeld & Nicolson, 1987).

VILE, M. J. C., *Constitutionalism and the Separation of Powers* (Oxford: Oxford University Press, 1967).

WADE, Sir W., *Administrative Law* (6th edn., Oxford: Clarendon Press, 1988).

—— *Constitutional Fundamentals* (London: Stevens & Sons, 1989).

WASS, Sir D., 'The Public Service in Modern Society', *Public Administration*, 61 (1983), 7–20.

—— *Government and the Governed* (London: Routledge & Kegan Paul, 1984).

WHEARE, K. C., *Modern Constitutions* (Oxford: Oxford University Press, 1966).

WHITEHEAD, C., 'Reshaping the Nationalized Industries', *Policy Journals* (1988).

WHITELAW, W., *The Whitelaw Memoirs* (London: Autum Press, 1989).

WILDING, R., 'A Triangular Affair: Quangos, Ministers and MPs', in A. Barker (ed.), *Quangos in Britain* (London: Macmillan, 1982).

WILENSKI, P., 'Administrative Reform, General Principles and the Australian Experience', *Public Administration*, 64 (1986), 257–75.

WILLETTS, D., 'Prime Minister's Policy Unit', *Public Administration*, 65 (1987), 443–54.

YOUNG, H., *One of Us* (London: Macmillan, 1989).

—— and SLOMAN, A., *The Thatcher Phenomenia* (London: BBC Publications, 1986).

ZELLICK, T., 'Government Beyond the Law', *Public Law* (1986), 177–84.

OFFICIAL PUBLICATIONS (IN CHRONOLOGICAL ORDER)

Report from the Select Committee on Official Salaries (1850), HC611, HMSO.

Report from the Machinery of Government Committee (Chairman, Lord Haldane) (1918), Cmnd 9230, HMSO.

Report from the Select Committee on Nationalized Industries (1952), HC332–I, HMSO.

Report from the Public Inquiry into the Disposal of Land at Crichel Down (1954), Cmnd 9176, HMSO.

Report from the Committee of Privileges (1967–8), HC34, HMSO.

Report from the Select Committee on the Parliamentary Commissioner for Administration (1967–8), HC238, HMSO.

Report from the Select Committee on the Parliamentary Commissioner for Administration (1967–8), HC350, HMSO.

Report from the Select Committee on Nationalized Industries (1967–8), HC371, HMSO.

Report of the Committee on the Civil Service, (Chairman, Lord Fulton), vol. i (1968), Cmnd 3638, HMSO.

Report of the Tribunal of Inquiry on the Vehicle and General Insurance Company (1971–2), HC133, HMSO.

Report from the Committee of Privileges (1975–6), HC22, HMSO.

Report from the Committee of Privileges (1976–7), HC417, HMSO.

Memorandum of Guidance for Officials Appearing before Select Committees (1976), Gen 76/78, Civil Service Department.

NEDO, *A Study of UK Nationalized Industries* (1976), HMSO.

Report from the Expenditure Committee (1977), HC535, HMSO.

First Report from the Select Committee on Procedure, vol. i (1977–8), HC588–I, HMSO.

Fifth Report from the Select Committee on Nationalized Industries (1977–8), HC238, HMSO.

The Nationalized Industries (1978), Cmnd 7131, HMSO.

Open Government (1979), Cmnd 7520, HMSO.

First Report of the Select Committee for Home Affairs (1979–80), HC434, HMSO.

Third Report from the Defence Committee: The D Notice System (1979–80), HC773, HMSO.

First Special Report from the Select Committee for Education, Science and Arts (1979–80), HC606, HMSO.

Third Report from the Foreign Affairs Committee (1979–80), HC553, HMSO.

Second Report from the Treasury and Civil Service Committee (1979–80), HC584, HMSO.

The Role of the Comptroller and Auditor General (1980), Cmnd 7845, HMSO.

Special Report by the Council on Tribunals: The Functions of the Council on Tribunals (1980), Cmnd 7805, HMSO.

Report on Non-Departmental Public Bodies (by Sir Leo Pliatzky) (1980), Cmnd 7797, HMSO.

Memorandum of Guidance for Officials Appearing before Select Committees (1980), Gen 80/30, Civil Service Department.

Report from the Committee of Public Accounts; The Role of the Comptroller and Auditor General, vol. 1 (1980–1), HC115, HMSO.

Education, Science and Arts Select Committee: Minutes of Evidence (1981–2), HC24, HMSO.

Report of the Select Committee on Welsh Affairs: Water in Wales (1981–2), HC299, HMSO.

Third Report from the Treasury and Civil Service Committee: Efficiency and Effectiveness in the Civil Service (1982), HC236, HMSO.

Report from the Liaison Committee (1982–3), HC92, HMSO.

Report from the Committee of Privileges (1982–3), HC336, HMSO.

Report by a Committee of Privy Councillors: The Falkland Island Review (Chairman, Lord Franks) (1983), Cmnd 8787, HMSO.

Fourth Report from the Select Committee on the Parliamentary Commissioner for Administration (1983–4), HC619, HMSO.

Report on Security Arrangements at the Maze Prison (Chairman, Sir Peter Hennessy) (1984), HC203, HMSO.

Financing and Administration of Land Drainage, Flood Prevention and Coast Protection in England and Wales (1985), Cmnd 9563, HMSO.

Observations by the Government on the Role of the Parliamentary Commissioner for Administration (1985), Cmnd 9563, HMSO.

Eighteenth Report from the Committee of Public Accounts (1985) HC249, HMSO.

Second Report from the Trade and Industry Committee: The Tin Crisis (1985–6), HC305–I, HMSO.

Seventh Report from the Treasury and Civil Service Committee: Civil Servants and Ministers: Duties and Responsibilities (1985–6), HC92–I, HMSO.

Government's Response to the Seventh Report from the Treasury and Civil Service Committee: Civil Servants and Ministers: Duties and Responsibilities (1985–6), Cmnd 9841, HMSO.

Third Report from the Defence Committee: The Defence Implications of the Future of Westland plc (1985–6), HC518, HMSO.

The Defence Implications of the Future of Westland plc: Minutes of Evidence and Appendices (1985–6), HC169, HMSO.

The Fourth Report from the Defence Committee: Westland plc: The Government's Decision-Making (1985–6), HC519, HMSO.

Building Businesses not Barriers (1986), Cmnd 9794, HMSO.

Privatization of the Water Authorities in England and Wales (1986), Cmnd 9734, HMSO.

The Government's Response to the Fourth Report from the Defence Committtee on 'Westland plc: The Defence Implications of the Future of Westland plc: The Government's Decision-Making' (1986), Cmnd 9916, HMSO.

First Report from the Liaison Committee (1986–7), HC100, HMSO.

First Report from the Treasury and Civil Service Committee (1986–7), HC62, HMSO.

Government's Response to the First Report from the Treasury and Civil Service Committee (HC62), and to the First Report from the Liaison Committee (HC100) (1986–7), Cmnd 78, HMSO.

First Report from the Trade and Industry Committee (a supplementary report) (1986–7), HC71, HMSO.

Efficiency Unit, *Improving Management in Government: The Next Steps (Report to the Prime Minister)* (1988), HMSO.

HMSO Executive Agency, *Framework Document* (1988), HMSO.

Companies House Executive Agency, *Policy and Resources Framework* (1988), DTI.

Vehicle Inspectorate Executive Agency, *Policy and Resources Framework* (1988), Vehicle Inspectorate Executive Agency.

Treasury and Civil Service Committee: The Civil Service Management Reforms: The Next Steps, Report and Minutes of Evidence (1988–9), HC494–I, HC494–II, HC494–i, HC494–ii, HMSO.

The Government's Response to the Report from the Treasury and Civil Service Committee on the Civil Service Management Reforms: The Next Steps (1988), Cmnd 524, HMSO.

First Report from the Defence Committee (1988–9), HC68, HMSO.

Treasury and Civil Service Committee: Developments in the Next Steps Programme, Minutes of Evidence (1988–9), HC348–i, HC348–ii, HC348–iii, HC348–iv, HMSO.

First Report from the Agriculture Committee: Salmonella in Eggs (1988–9), HC108–I, HC108–II, HMSO.

Report from the Comptroller and Auditor General, on the Next Steps Initiative (1989), HC236, HMSO.

Report from the Parliamentary Commissioner for Administration: The Barlow Clowes Affair (1989), HC76, HMSO.

Report from the Comptroller and Auditor General: Department of Trade and Industry: Sale of Rover Group plc to British Aerospace plc (1989), HC9, HMSO.

Fifth Report from the Treasury and Civil Service Committee: The Civil Service Pay and Conditions of Service Code (1989–90), HC260, HMSO.

Second Report from the Select Committee on Procedure: The Workings of the Select Committee System (1989–90), HC19, HMSO.

Report of a Review by Her Majesty's Chief Inspector of Prisons for England and Wales of Suicides and Self-Harm in Prison Service Establishments in England and Wales (Stephen Tumim, Chief Inspector of Prisons) (1990), Cmnd 1393, HMSO.

Employment Agency, *Framework Document* (1990), Employment Agency.

Eighth Report from the Treasury and Civil Service Committee: Progress on the Next Steps Initiative (1989–90), HC481, HMSO.

First Report from the Trade and Industry Committee: Sale of Rover Group to British Aerospace (1990–1), HC34, HMSO.

INDEX